Also by Greg Dunn

The Unknown Soldier Reloads

Take Me Out To The Ball Game

The Chain
(a play in one act)

May songs again be sung of men
Who never sought to hide
Whose bearing knew no reticence
Nor blench or balk of stride

– Anonymous
Missouri, U.S. 1867

Locked in Brockton

Greg Dunn

©2024 Greg Dunn. All rights reserved.
ISBN 979-8-878-25554-7

To Austin J. Dunn and Armond C. Colombo

NOTE TO THE READER:

Although this collection of vignettes concerns some of my life's most influential principals, it should not be construed as a History, nor a Biography; and it would be preposterous to pass it off as Fiction, for disclaiming as "entirely coincidental" any resemblance between persons and events contained herein to those of the real world would be patently disingenuous. I prefer instead to classify these vignettes, collectively and on each's own merit, as Impression: of the sort obtained walking one's dog on a summer evening past the big house on the corner, registering beyond the spacious lawn and hedges, and idle porch swing, assorted brief exposures glimpsed through screen doors and first floor windows, some abustle and well lit, others hushed and still, bedimmed by long-drawn shades.

To be sure, the opinions expressed here are those of a child in the world connecting dots. Events and personal interactions are exactly as I remember them. If you find that your name appears in these pages, I beg your indulgence and pardon, and I hope you draw the intended conclusion which is that, for what it's worth, you're alright in my book.

– GD
April, 2024
Brockton, MA

BOSTON, MASSACHUSETTS
(Codman Square, Dorchester)
Early 1970s

From very early on as kids, my brother Joe and I realized that we were the luckiest family in the world. For one thing, our beloved grandmother also happened to be our beloved landlord, occupying the floor above us in her two-family house. Not only that, but our schoolyard fence and our backyard fence were the exact same fence! Sometimes at recess my mother would bring the twins outside so they could watch us running around playing dodgeball and tag with our classmates. That tall chainlink barrier, with its forbidding pointy prongs across the top, deterred even the most daring climbers. It was rare that a heaved or kicked ball ever made it over into our yard, but Emily A. Fifield fifth-graders (in Joe's case) and especially third-graders (in mine) were a determined bunch, so when the inevitable did periodically occur, our young little brothers, Rich and Steve, were only too happy to mind the kickball for us until one of the players was dispatched to fetch it.

Living as luckily close to school as we did, it made zero sense to me and Joe when we were informed that in the near future we would be required to go to a school other than the Fifield. It made less than zero sense to my parents.

"Guys," Dad said. "Me and Ma have been thinking about it. We're going to have to move somewhere else pretty soon."

"What?" "Huh?"

"Everybody moves some time. It's okay. Won't be far away."

"Where," Joe thought to ask.

"Maybe to Kingston."

In all my years I'd never heard of such a place. Geographically speaking, I knew for certain that a.) My parents were born and raised in Dorchester, and b.) That was all I knew.

Joe's the man, though. He said, "Out of Dorchester?"

"Or maybe Brockton."

"Why?" "How come?"

"Where Rocky Marciano's from."

Marciano was a name I recognized from evenings in our parlor when my father would relax in his chair listening to radio rebroadcasts of classic boxing matches and I'd sit on the rug, nestled back against his legs, imagining what guys called Dick Tiger and Mickey "The Toy Bulldog" Walker must look like in real life. I knew their names like I knew my Fifield classmates. Dad's favorites were Sugar Ray Robinson and the undefeated heavyweight champion Marciano, hence they were my favorites too.

"How come though?"

"They're trying to tell everybody where they can and can't go to school." Dad mentioned as an aside to my mother, "It's going to screw a whole generation of kids out there, watch. White, black, doesn't matter. it's going to go south right off the bat."

"We already go to the Fifield!"

"They want to send you guys across town, to a different school."

"Who does," Joe asked. "The politicians?"

It sounded like he was trying out a new vocabulary word again, but Dad knew what he meant.

"No – every candidate for mayor's against it. Even Hicks. This comes straight from the judges." Extending his aside: "What do they think, nobody's going to fight it? Who's kidding who?" My father was starting to fume, "That's not how it works…"

"Hey, don't take it out on me."

I remember looking out our back door across the schoolyard's mildly sloping blacktop where the Fifield's vast brick walls loomed over an angling cast of shadows.

"Me and Joe have to go to different schools now? Across the town?"

Dad laughed and playfully pushed me down on the couch. "It wouldn't be till next year," he said. "Or the year after."

'Oh!' I thought. 'Why didn't you say so?' I was immediately put at my ease. 'Sheesh…'

The near abstract idea of *years* meant as little to my young mind as the concept of adulthood. I understood the dictionary definition of the word alright, but in real terms it was a thing I couldn't imagine myself ever having to actually come to grips with.

"But we'll be long gone and hard to find by then, right Rosie?"

"You got that right."

The ready assurance in my mother's voice could cool the caverns of hell. Suddenly everything was all better.

"We're moving in July," said Dad. "As soon as the Fifield lets out for the summer." My father must have read my mind and the questions written all over my face. He reiterated one of our family mantras, "Dunns go where Dunns say." Then he paraphrased his own axiom. "And more important, Dunns go *when* Dunns say."

Later, I walked in on Joe standing before the toilet with his pajamas partway down. He scooched over, making room for me: "Bow and arrow?" I joined in to make of our mutual micturitions a reasonably perpendicular cross stream.

"I don't want to move anyplace."

Joe said, "Me either."

"Why *not* the Fifield?"

"I know," he agreed. Then, finishing up, "Make sure you flush it."

"Don't want to live in no Broxton…"

"Brockton," Joe explained on his way out. "Rocky Marciano." As a final order of business he flipped the bathroom lightswitch off.

"Come on!"

—

As young parents attending to the concerns of raising a family, with daily strains and emergencies great and small, my father and mother were not the type given to equivocations of any sort – nevermind pipe dreams or flights of fancy. If they said we were moving away, we were moving away. However, the vexation of confused little-boy minds was hardly lost on them. They made it a point of reassuring us that our future would include regularly scheduled trips back to visit our old neighborhood. I remember Dad making enthusiastic ceremony, too, of reading me the Brockton Public Schools daily lunch schedule. As much as I had always enjoyed peanut butter and jelly, and the precise triangular origami folds with which my mom secured our lunch bags, and her occasional day-brightening napkin notes, to hear Dad reciting so many fun food choices, with assorted drinks and desserts – all provided *at school* in an enormous *cafeteria!* (for, alas, the Fifield's offerings à la carte were limited to half-pint cartons of white milk delivered to our classroom door in plastic crates and consumed on the spot at our desks) – was to marvel at the legends of Atlantis and El Dorado.

Of course, though, Dad would be true to his word. In the months following our move, and into the next year, I was able to reunite with my pals Jerry Cahill and Marco Rivera on weekends and holidays whenever we came back to visit my grandmother. Gram's old-world upbringing, which holds the Family Home as a thing of highest regard and permanence, had her somewhat dismayed at the prospect of our moving away. In fact, having already completed the voyage of a lifetime in 1921 ("The same year we never saw Caruso again," she often confusingly clarified) when she came by steamship to America as part of the last great wave of post-World War I Italian immigration, Gram hardly ever again saw reason to venture very far beyond the outer limits of greater Boston.

"Ma, was Gram on the Titanic?"

"No, honey, lucky for all of us. Gram was still way over in Italy just being born when the Titanic sank. The same year. The very same month."

"Is she coming to Brockton with us?"

"No."

"But–"

"She's lived in this house a long time. Since I was a little girl. Even before that."

"Before you were born?"

"Yup. And don't forget, Gram's the landlord here, so she has to be around to keep an eye on things."

"So she can't ever move?"

"No, she can. She just doesn't want to, honey. This is her home."

"But who's going to move in now?"

"We don't know yet."

"But... So when she bangs on the pipes–"

"When we move, Gram's not going to bang on the pipes anymore."

"What about when she needs–?"

"Only families bang the pipes."

It wasn't until a full ten years after our relocation to Brockton that Gram was finally coaxed from her cozy 30 Torrey Street home by the most persuasive of forces. The schoolyard had long since degenerated into a nocturnal haunt for local drug addicts, while the neighborhood itself had begun giving way to growing street crime and concomitant municipal neglect. My mother had been in Gram's ear all along anyway, so making a move was probably inevitable, as I guess was her ultimate destination: Brockton, Massachusetts.

BROCKTON, MASSACHUSETTS
(SOUTHFIELD, CAMPELLO)
Subsequent 1970s

Despite our parents' assurances, the change was hardly any less disorienting for us kids. Compared to Dorchester, our new neighborhood felt like something entirely else. If Joe and I had been aware of such terms, we might have referred to Southfield as 'quaint' or 'boondocks.' All we knew was it was an out of the way place in the middle of nowhere, the likes of which we'd only seen in magazines or on TV. One of our neighbors had chickens walking around the back yard. Where were all the cars? Where were the crowds of people? Where was the corner store? Our new street was so seldom traveled that we could actually play entire one-on-one tag football games out front before dinner, with Dad as official quarterback and telephone poles as goal lines, without ever having to pause for a passing vehicle.

Our first day in town, after all that pre-move hullabaloo, I half expected to see Rocky Marciano himself hailing us from the Brockton city limits, or sparring in a parking lot, or signing autographs or something. I had listened to several of his bouts in the parlor with Dad, and even a neophyte such as myself knew how special the distinction "undefeated champion" was. I also knew Marciano to be an Italian, like my mother's whole side of the family (from 'It-lee' as Gram would put it). However, one thing I certainly did not know about the great man was that he was already deceased.

"What...?"

"Two years ago."

"But I thought—"

"The day after Joe's birthday."

I tried to think back, but Dad confused things further by adding, "And only one day before his own birthday."

As we started to settle in and get down to the business of making our new home our own, one of the minor but wholly unexpected adjustments I remember encountering with Joe was having to get used to all those new noises peculiar to a quiet suburban bedtime, particularly after having spent our lives falling asleep amid the brash disharmony of Dorchester nights.

In their effort to help ease with the transition, my parents' lofty promises began piling up. Summer would bring fireworks and a Fourth of July celebration at the Brockton Fair, a prospect my brothers mooned over for weeks but which held for me not the slightest allure, for it had been at our local carnival the previous summer where I'd thrown up in the middle of the Scrambler and had taken to my bed, seized by nightmares as twisted as sweaty sheets, miserably suffering what my mother told me was something called Trench Mouth. Most of my parents' attempts worked as intended, soothing our anxieties to some extent, but certain declarations just came across as parental pie-in-the-sky bologna; none more so than Dad's, "Mark my words, guys: Within five years everybody in this town will know our name."

Come on! Even Ma couldn't be buying that one.

Dad reminded us, though, "Remember Butch for a Day?"

My brother Joe and I nodded at one another, remembering indeed. A couple years earlier, Dad had blown our minds by taking us to TV's Bozo the Clown show. Even from the top row of the bleachers, all the vivid colors of Bozo's Big Top dazzled us, and – *Wowee Kazowee!* – there was Bozo himself, the *real* Bozo, right down there! We gawked and cheered and gleefully jostled each other the whole time. Joe and I were going to be on TV! Ma would see us, and the twins and baby Gary, and maybe kids from school too! The mere thought of any such recognition was as jarring to me as it was enjoyable, running counter as it did to the pleasant sense of anonymity that I'd come to know in this enormous world of busy people.

When it came time for the high point in the show – Bozo's selection of a child from the audience to serve as temporary helper, 'Butch for a Day' – Joe bent me double with a brotherly elbow to the rib cage. From the center of the Big Top ring, Bozo quickened a hundred eager hearts by dramatically covering his eyes with one gloved hand and leveling his other pointer finger blindly at the crowd. As a rousing drum roll played, he spun himself slowly around once, then once again. When Bozo came to a stop, he was pointing to some lucky kid in the section down to our right. Then suddenly [Note to Reader: *There is not one syllable of exaggeration here.*] Bozo said, "No no!" and reversed direction by a quarter turn until his pointing finger was trained on me and Joe! "The young man in the glasses," Bozo specified. "Yes, you!" (For the record, Dad has steadfastly denied responsibility for this miraculous turn of events, claiming never to have even met Bozo the Clown or Frank Avruch or any of the show's producers, much less conspired to orchestrate such an elaborate backstage fix.)

The rest of the show was a blur. I don't remember a damn thing. All I know now is that Joe and I delighted in playing at home with the wagonfull of gifts Bozo had given me – until one morning when I found my red Butch-for-a-Day top hat filled with water in the bathtub. Although Ma and Dad's alibi seemed suspiciously convenient (Asleep all night in bed together, huh? Please.), and Joe certainly had ample opportunity and motive (He'd been jealous of my relationship with Bozo from the start!), my evidence against them was, in fairness, circumstantial; so, that infamous day would ultimately mark the first major unsolved case in our young family's mystery-filled history.

In spite of this, and one or two other such youthful transgressions along the way, Joe would go on to serve as my example and mentor and lifelong lookout. Elder by one year, and wiser by considerably more, he paved the way for me everywhere. I remember spending many a morning riding bikes together that first summer, exploring Southfield's boundaries. We'd take turns walking Gary – and later Julie, the youngest of our six-sibling brood – around the huge block. We made friends with other neighborhood kids, and eventually were included, basically as mascots, in street games of the older guys who lived one road behind us; Joe on one team, me on the other. They got a kick out of our ability to catch the occasional check-down passes they sent our way, although Dad had long since

coached us on using both hands, looking the ball in, and making tricky over-the-shoulder receptions.
—

While the name of Marciano loomed over our new hometown like the sky itself (its importance reaffirmed daily with the solemnity of lore by neighbors and teachers alike, by my parents' friends visiting our home, by K-Mart cashiers and Christo's waitstaff, by our new classmates at the Edward B. Gilmore School), and although it was rumored that Rocky's own brother Peter, proprietor of a sporting goods store a couple towns away, still lived in Brockton, it soon became clear that the preeminent name and driving force behind the city's continuing reputation as a superlative sports town belonged to the Colombo family.

Armond Colombo, the high school's fiery head coach, was widely credited with breathing new life into Brockton's moribund varsity football program and reestablishing the Boxers as a statewide powerhouse, returning them to the glory of decades past. By just his second year in charge, Coach Colombo had brought to an end a woeful string of losing seasons, guiding the 1970 team to Brockton's first undefeated campaign since the Eisenhower administration. Thus began the carving out of his rightful place amid the legendary visages of E. Marion Roberts (1920s-30s), Frank Saba (40s), and Chet Millett (50s) on the Mount Rushmore of BHS football coaches. With next year's Boxers squad shaping up to be perhaps Colombo's finest yet, the local sports pages were abuzz, as was the talk around town: If things kept going to plan, we could be witnessing the birth of a football dynasty.

"Brockton has the best team around," Dad explained.

"Can they beat Hyde Park?"

I had accompanied my father to White Stadium many times to watch his brother Kevin play. One of the few truly gifted athletes I have ever known, uncle Kevin was the yardstick by which Dunn family sportsmen would be gauged for years to come, having even eclipsed our uncle Jimmy's unbelievable accomplishments.

(According to oft-repeated family legend, Jimmy had publicly predicted scoring two touchdowns in Hyde Park's forthcoming game against rival Brighton, and had then been lauded in the *Globe* for doing so after ripping off scoring runs of 55 yards and 66 yards. Uncle Jimmy's personality was always a little on the large side, so I had no problem picturing him sounding off somewhere and then backing up his braggadocio on the field come game day. Also, this story had been independently corroborated to the last detail on separate occasions, not only by Dad but also two of his older brothers, and by uncle Kevin too, and even by my mother. Only brother Joe, ever the sage, wise beyond his years, would object to their testimonials, querying when we were alone, "They make it sound like uncle Jim was going around making Namath guarantees, at a press conference or something. It was the fucking Boston District League, regular season! Who the hell was he making these predictions to?" Joe had a point, especially when the unanimously reported *coup de grâce* of this particular tale was "Then, next morning in the *Globe* Sports, the caption was: Dunn Dood It!")*

Old scrapbook pictures of uncles Jimmy and Kevin, each bearing the same slender builds and erect strides of their shared DNA, still exist as vividly as ever in my memory. Both are captured breaking away from plainly dispirited defenders, en route to long touchdown runs; both fleet halfbacks in Hyde Park blue-and-white; both wearing jersey number 43.

"Brockton would stick Hyde Park up their ass."

Dad as always had a way with words so that even from a young age when I couldn't really make sense of the imagery as stated, I was still able to understand exactly what he meant.

*[Fact Checker Alert: see *Boston Globe, 04 Oct 1962, p.56*]
—

From what I could gather from bits and pieces picked up at home and around town, the Colombo scuttlebut pyramided downward something like this: From the redoubtable and unapologetically family-first Armond at the apex; to his wife Betty, who just so happened to be the little sister of – you guessed it – *Rocky Marciano*; to their brood of six children (like us Dunns), five boys and a girl (like us Dunns). Three of their sons played for the football team, with the eldest Peter at quarterback, and twins (not unlike us Dunns!) Danny and Donny on defense. Next in the pecking order were young Beth, then Chuck, then Tommy.

Our *Brockton Enterprise* paperboy, a sharp entrepreneurial older kid from around the corner who had as his lucrative delivery domain the entirety of burgeoning Southfield, would regale us with dreadful accounts of what to expect in the dark, and what to do, step by step, once we were inevitably shanghaied by our own bodies and pubescent girls into the Forbidden Zone, never to return. He also reported on the necessity for "guardians" at the high school, what with recent racial tensions and all.

"It's dangerous. Girls need guardians just to get back and forth to class safe."

"Guardians?"

"Guys to walk with them in case there's fights or something."

"Who gets to be guardians?"

"Football players. Wrestlers. Donny Colombo's one. Ken MacAfee. Coots, too, he's one."

"Donny's the oldest one?"

"Donny and Danny are the twins. But he's an animal."

"Oh– you know them?"

"I don't know them, but I know who they are. I see them at school every day."

"Oh."

"They're all guardians, though. I know that."

As a naive youngster, I took it on faith that paperboy Mike was being straight with us and I never have followed up with anyone on the question of guardianship in the halls of Brockton High during the early seventies. It could very well have been an overblown racial rumor, or just more Colombo-related hyperbole, or it could have been completely accurate (*but* if Mike's guardian explanation was anywhere near as bizarrely wrongheaded as his assertions concerning

21

methods of birth control and foreplay turned out to be, then, well...). Either way, though – factual or myth: this anecdote demonstrates in some small way the level to which Colombo goings-on permeated the daily routine of life in our city. Their news was shared at local dinner tables like family gossip, spread and debated at the Y and the downtown bus stop and every neighborhood tavern because, as Brockton's de facto First Family, their business was our business.
—

It was Woody Allen who said, "If 80% of life is showing up, the other 80% is luck." Of course he was right. In life, Timing (aka Luck) is paramount, with Talent and Hard Work battling it out for a distant second place. This is true in youth sports too, but to a greater degree. Something as arbitrary as the moment in someone else's lifetime that you happened to have been conceived can come to be the difference between your being continually relegated to the back of the pack or enjoying as your birthright a calendar year's head start in every race you run. When it happens to be in your favor you go along with it. That's human nature. However, when it works against you, don't expect to get over it anytime soon, and please don't expect anybody else to give it a second thought. After all, they're dealing with their own private difficulties and disappointments.

For evidence of this you don't have to look far. In my case I could see it anytime I wanted in my own childhood bedroom by simply glancing over at the bed across from mine. Brother Joe was born barely one year before I was (375 days, to be exact). Yet, when we started our new school year at the futuristic Edward B. Gilmore School (which boasted, among other amenities, a gigantic cafeteria where we were served different tasty lunches everyday *for free* by merely presenting our colorful lunch card (gone was the need to carry milk money every day); an entire baseball field on the school grounds for recess with an outfield fence and everything; restrooms on the same floor as the classrooms (so we never again would have to request permission to literally "go to the basement" whenever nature called during class)), Joe was entering school as an eleven-year-old sixth-grader whereas I was aged ten but starting two full grades behind him in fourth.

Although the genesis of this incongruity could be traced to our days in Dorchester where that school system's deadline for first-grade enrollment was September 1st, by which date students were required to be six years of age, the discrepancy had never really occurred to me before.

Anyway, it turns out it was all Joe's fault: According to Saint Margaret's Hospital records, the birth of master Austin Joseph Dunn, Jr., occurred on the 30th day of August, in the year of our Lord 1960, thereby ensuring that he would ever after be one of the absolute youngest students in his grade, and if not youngest of all, then at the very least the second youngest by a single day.

I, on the other hand, had the good sense to postpone my own debut until the 9th of September the following year, landing comfortably on the sunny side of Boston's enrollment deadline. In so doing, I had unwittingly hoisted the first banner in what would become a lifelong and still ongoing feud with deadlines. (It also marked the first of many oh-so-sweet examples of procrastination paying off for Yours Truly.) The short-term result of this crapshoot was that I would benefit by having the fourth, fifth, and sixth grades in which to acclimate to the new Gilmore School, whereas after spending just one year there Joe would find himself on his own at yet another strange school next fall as an incoming seventh-grader at South Junior High.

Permanently installed as one of my grade's very oldest students, I got to enjoy an extra year of social maturity, along with the obvious advantage over my classmates of a whole year's physical development (which in those formative years cannot be overestimated), reaping the benefits of this crucial edge for the rest of the Seventies, again and again: Pure dumb luck, but hey – I'll take it. Meanwhile, Joe was trying to negotiate the business of real-world growing up as one of his grade's perpetual underdogs.

—

Our first year in Brockton passed far less miserably than I had imagined it would. The Dunns all made friends with the other families on Deanna Road, parents and kids alike. Coincidentally, within three houses from ours, there were two fathers who worked on the Boston Fire Department, just like Dad. One of my old kindergarten classmates from the Fifield, Gerard McGunnigal, now actually lived in Southfield too.

Our street had plenty of boys so, with Joe and myself as captains, street hockey games could take place without any particular day's teams being too lopsided one way or the other. Also, our neighbors the Sullivans, McCoys and Thompsons all had at least one daughter just about our age, so it wouldn't be long before the beguiling began.

One evening toward the end of that first school year, Joe and I were on our front lawn playing catch with Dad, seeing how many times in a row we could field one-hoppers cleanly.

"Keep your eye on it," Dad coached. "Both hands, it's not going to hurt you. That's the way." Joe and I loved this game like you love a rivalry. No formal score was ever discussed or kept but if I had to ballpark it, I'd say at that point it was somewhere around two-hundred-something to two- hundred-something-and-one.

"Nice throw, AJ!" No matter how hard we whipped it back to Dad, he caught it, and he never even had a glove. "Did you guys hear Little League tryouts are on Saturday?"

I had heard nothing of the kind. "No."

"Kids at school haven't been talking about it?"

Joe said, "Wayne told me they're having tryouts for the Downey league."

"Right, Saturday at the Downey."

"But we go to Gilmore."

"For school, people who live in Southfield go to the Gilmore, but for Little League we go to the Downey."

Logic such as this must have been behind that screwy gerrymandering fiasco that drove us out of Dorchester. "Rich and Steve too?"

"When they're old enough, sure," Dad said. "But for now just you and Joe."

I didn't like the sound of this one bit. Joe apparently had no problem with it. "Downey has a nice field," he said, punching the palm of his baseball glove a couple times, signaling Dad with a nod to resume the game.

"What's wrong, Gregga? You want to play for the Little League, don't you?"

Just the thought of it was giving me a bad feeling. "I don't know."

"Sure. Little League's fun. Why do you think we always go for batting practice, and play catch? So you guys can try out. Then you'll get picked by one of the teams, like the Tigers, or the Braves. I heard they give you real nice uniforms here too. It might even be for the Red Sox, you never know. Right, Joe?"

"Yup," Joe responded, nodding, feeding his glove a steady diet of knuckle sandwiches.

It required some convincing for me to overcome my hesitancy at entering an unknown environment; not so, Joe. Like most everything else in his life, he took it right in stride. At tryouts, he made two stellar throws to the plate on deep fly balls, along with a nice over-the-shoulder catch at the fence. Comparatively, my day as an infielder was undistinguished, limited to fielding some grounders on the parking lot's tar surface and making the throws to "first" before taking my five allotted cuts on the playing field at batting practice. I made fair ball contact on four swings and fouled one back before the man doing the pitching barked, "Next!" He proved harder to hit than my father, mainly because he was lobbing the ball, which I was not accustomed to, and also because no more than a few of his fourteen or fifteen pitches could have possibly been considered strikes, which I was equally unaccustomed to. All Dad threw were strikes. This guy bounced a couple in the dirt, threw one completely behind me, air mailed another, and for one I just hunched and let it harmlessly nudge against my shoulder. All in all though, my father was right, as usual: Once everything was over with I was glad to have gone through with it.

Dad was right about the uniforms, too. They looked just like the pros' used to look before Major League Baseball decided to switch to double-knits. Unlike the getups handed out to Joe's Dorchester team the year before (flimsy caps and t-shirts), which my brother promptly threw in the trash as soon as he found out we were moving mid-season, we were issued actual uniforms that needed real belts, to be worn proudly and taken care of, flannel jerseys and knicker pants, stretchy stirrup socks, and nice wool caps with the big embroidered Downey *D* on them.

I was kind of disappointed, though, when we found out that Joe (National Bank) and I (King's Department Store) had wound up on different teams.

"Probably for the best," he reasoned after a few games. "You probably wouldn't like it, me playing every game and you sitting on the bench."

"So what? I'll get my chance."

"Probably make you mad."

"I'm just as good as you are. Faster runner too."

"Too bad they don't have running on the bench."

"Shut up... I'm a better hitter, too."

"Then how come you're riding the bench and I play every game?"

"I played last game."

"The sixth inning! And you didn't even get up. I played the whole game."

"You're eleven years old, Joe. I'm just ten."

"So?"

"You're way older, that's a big difference! I'm the only guy who's ten on my whole team."

"No sir."

"Yes sir! Every other player's eleven or twelve. Except me."
"Well it's not my fault you got kept back in kindergarten."
"I didn't get kept back!"
"*Ow!* Cut the shit!"
"Never got kept back… anyplace…"
"Then how come you're one year younger than me, Einstein? But two grades behind me in school?"
"Because of my birthday."
"Sure…"
"Ma even said! And the only reason you get to play every game is because National Bank sucks!"

Joe kept right on logging more field time that first season and breaking more bench balls, but at least King's ended up taking the league championship, thanks in no large part to me. There was actually a write up in the *Enterprise*: King's are Kings. Winning the title earned us the privilege of representing Downey in the annual postseason competition known as the City Series which pits the league champs from each of Brockton's seven wards in a hyphen-strewn two-week-long double-elimination round-robin tournament for citywide bragging rights.

I actually had a surprisingly active, and even more surprisingly effective, City Series. Two of our best players, twelve-year-olds Steve Loud and Doug Crowell, would be unavailable for week one of the tournament due to family vacation conflicts. If King's could manage to survive without them, they would both return to play in week two. Such an outcome was unlikely, though, considering that we drew as our first round opponent the tournament favorite, South Little League champions, Kiwanis; and equally unfortunately our next opponent on the schedule was listed as Security Federal of the East Side Improvement League with their unbeaten behemoth of a pitcher, Dave Nelson.

Despite never having seen them play in person, and certainly in part because of that, the Kiwanis renown was daunting, to say the least. How many undefeated seasons had they had in a row? How many City Series could one team win? (Had they ever lost? Not as far as anyone knew.) How did so many newly arrived star players always happen to end up on Kiwanis? This year's juggernaut was led by twelve-year-old captains Paul Duford, whose five o'clock shadow looked like it required a belt sander to shave, and Mike Bergeron ("He's a six-footer! They showed his birth certificate to the umps, right there on the field. He's legit!"). They were backed up by a talented supporting cast: Bob Johnnson was going to go pro someday, and of course when child prodigy Chuck Colombo became eligible for the draft at ten years old, and it came time for Kiwanis to pick, the kid was somehow available. As usual, the team's success was directly attributed to their shrewd head coach, Dick Williams ("*That* Dick Williams?" "No, but he's just as good. Hard to kill.") ("What's the other Dick Williams doing now?" "No idea.").

Our Kiwanis game would be played at the immaculately maintained Producers Field, the best in the city by far, located adjacent to the Producers Dairy ice cream stand near the high school. In addition to the pleasure of playing on such lush grounds-crew-cut grass and a 100% pebble-free infield, the players on both teams would be treated to a post game ice cream cone, win or lose, courtesy of Producers.

The coaches had told me to come prepared to play since we knew we would be without Steve and Doug. I was slated to start in left field for game one, but having failed to arrive at the park until King's warmups were almost completely over, I was assigned for my tardiness the well deserved penance of "coaching" third base, a position generally reserved for our manager or his assistant. Meanwhile, one of the least athletic players on our team got to jog over that beautiful infield and out to left as part of the home team's starting nine.

Hey, I deserved it, but sitting on the bench sucked so much worse when I should have been in the game, playing. It really *really* sucked when I watched as a two-out high fly ball down the left field line turned from a can of corn into a hot extra base mess. Our guy –

bless him — was doing his best but he never should have been out there, it was my fault. He was camped under it, eight or ten feet from the fence, punching the palm of his mitt as the ball descended and plopped to the ground somewhere behind him, apparently surprising no one in the park as much as our poor left fielder himself.

When it came our turn to bat, I took my place in the third base coach's box and watched Kiwanis warm up. Their uniforms were designed just like ours, light gray with red lettering across the chest, red numbers on back, red piping on the pant legs, red stirrup stockings and caps. Kiwanis uniforms seemed to fit them better, though; through the shoulders and back, and through the thigh; and somehow the arch of their stirrups stretched all the way up to the knee for an undeniably high coolness factor. Our uniforms just sort of hung on us. The coach's box dirt was every bit as pure as the infield's, and it was outlined in the same shocking white lime powder used for the batter's box and foul lines (if in fact shocking white is an actual color).

On the field there, a few feet away, the kid playing third base for Kiwanis was none other than Chuck Colombo, Armond's fourth son and namesake. I had seen my teammates pointing him out earlier. This guy must be pretty good, I thought, to be starting third baseman for Kiwanis in the City Series at just ten years old.

When the home half of the inning got underway proper, all of the Kiwanis infield began chattering like hedge sparrows. I never heard anything like it. Colombo, chomping a cheekful of bubble gum, kept urging his pitcher on with a raspy, "Hayyyy, come on! He's no sticka! He's no sticka! Come on! Hayyyy!" He and I hadn't spoken to each other or made eye contact or anything but from what I saw he struck me as very self-assured, and although I knew absolutely nothing about Chuck Colombo, I felt an immediate kinship with him, I'm not sure why. It could have been our similar ages (it would eventually transpire that he was four days my elder), or our somewhat similar positions on the totem poles of our respective teams — I really don't know.

With the start of the second inning, my sins apparently absolved, I was tapped to replace our unfortunate left fielder. The lush outfield grass – not a dandelion in sight – made me want to tumble through a couple somersaults on my way out to my position. I had never felt, let alone played on, anything like it. The splendor of the whole ballpark was downright weird, and the absolute strangest part of playing on Producers' pristine field was that the batter's box was plumb level with the baselines, perfectly even with home plate, as God intended, instead of several sunken inches lower from overuse and neglect, like Downey's and every other Little League field I'd ever seen.

By game's end I had made a pretty good catch of a line drive and had scored a run in the middle innings. After the catch, as a nice round of applause was dying down, some lady in the crowd shrieked, "That's Greg Dunn!" (presumably in response to another spectator saying "Who the hell's that kid?" or something) which startled me, to say the least. One more protective layer of childhood anonymity was stripped away in that lady's unanticipated endorsement, to the extent that she – whoever she was – has ever since occupied a permanent place in my memory, for sheer shock value, right beside Bozo the Clown himself.

Final score of the game? I'm not sure. It was close (4-2 maybe? 2-1?), but I do remember milling around the ice cream stand afterwards, Kiwanis and King's intermingled, waiting our turn for cones. One of their players scoffed, "Lucky catch."

It was! But, hey – I'll take it. The damn ball was hit so hard (by Paul Duford, that grown man in Little League togs) it nearly spun me around.

No, I don't remember the score, but I certainly do remember standing there among them at the ice cream counter, avoiding the dejection in their eyes, noticing how their uniforms didn't seem to fit so great anymore, drooping now at the shoulders. They didn't look so hot at all when you came right down to it; not like ours.

"Good game," Joe patted me on the back.

"Thanks."

"That was a nice catch. When you go up, get a cone for me. Then go back for another one for you."

"What?"

"Yeah, they won't know."

"Come on…"

"Chocolate," he patted my back again.

There were never any flies on my brother Joe. Needless to say, he was right again.

—

Game two against Security Federal was played at King's home turf on the Joseph H. Downey School grounds. During warmups, our third baseman, twelve-year-old Ralph Abbruzzi, turned to me as he was taking ground balls and said, "Come on, we'll alternate." I was not a hundred percent sure what that word meant, but after he fielded one and threw to first, he stepped aside and nodded me over.

'Aha: Take turns!' (See? I catch on.)

Along with Steve Loud and Doug Crowell, Ralph Abbruzzi rounded out the Big Three of our team. They would have been in the running for top three players in the whole league, and (vacations notwithstanding) we had them all in our infield! Since I was at the very bottom of the King's totem pole, there was seldom occasion for us to converse much but whenever such occasions did arise, these guys were without exception friendly, helpful, and encouraging. As a matter of fact, the example they set was one I would follow throughout my life in athletics. You know something? Three cheers to those three guys. They were brought up right! I'm glad to have known them.

Before the game, Joe teasingly dubbed our matchup with Security Federal "Underdog vs. Overcat."

Fortunately for us, Overcat – in the person of colossal Dave Nelson – had pitched in Security Federal's opening-round game, so he'd be safely off to the side at first base. Instead, we had to deal with a rangy lefthander whose deceptively slow herky-jerky delivery took a little getting used to.

It was a weird game. The lefty hurt his shin on a line drive back to the mound. A lot of walks followed on both sides, a lot of singles; several run-scoring rallies, multiple pitching changes. Barely halfway through the game, the umpires were already conferring over whether to call it because of darkness. In the dugout for the bottom of the fourth, Ralph was whispering to us with a gleam in his eye, "Listen, we have to get this thing over with as fast as we can. They're going to call it. We're winning, but the game's not official until after four innings. We need to go up there and strike out as fast as we can."

"On purpose?"

He looked me in the eyes. I was due up this inning. "Yes!"

Sharp as a tack and hard to kill, Ralph Abbruzzi was right. Had I been older and wiser, seeing the bigger picture, I'm sure I would have gone along with him, but I just couldn't bring myself to do it – not with Dad and Joe standing right there at the fence along the left field line.

Meanwhile, on the pitcher's mound in the growing gloom, Dave Nelson, in for relief, stood firing warm-up fastballs. My vision without glasses wasn't great to begin with, so unless the umps broke out a bunch of bright new baseballs, I was going to have to take their word on this guy's balls and strikes.

Ralph led off, whiffing on one monstrous swing, and then another. Down 0-and-2, it was all he could do not to swipe at the next pitch which sailed wildly high to the backstop. That ball was removed from play as soon as the umpire was able to pry it free of the chain link fencing. Next pitch, strike three. Ralph's frown could have easily been construed as frustration, but actually he was signaling our cheering bench to shut the hell up.

Another King's batter, another Nelson **K**.

"Let's go, Greg. Come on, Greg," our coach, Mr. Dole, clapped with unironical encouragement.

Exhibiting the mockery mastered by pre-teens everywhere, my teammates cheered, "Come on, Greg! Go get him!"

Better believe it, I thought. This might end up being my only at-bat ever against the indomitable Dave Nelson, and I'd be damned if I was going to tank it. When I got to the plate, I looked back toward my father and Joe watching from the fence beyond third base. The surety of one of Dad's crisp half-nods was all I ever needed.

In a whirling three-hurl blur of grunts and startling pops, Nelson struck me out swinging, fair and square, earning from my teammates the most rousing cheers (throughout the entire at bat!) that I would ever receive in my baseball playing life.

The home plate umpire then walked toward the mound and waved his arms over his head, calling an end to the game.

In the dugout, back slaps and congratulations greeted me. I had taken one for the team. Despite very long odds, King's had prevailed over Security Federal – and this with mild mannered me at shortstop, no less.

Afterwards, Joe said, "You played a good game in the field."

"Thanks."

"Made Dad proud, I could tell. Me, too."

"Thanks, Joe."

"And you were safe at first."

"Shit…" I groused. "I was, wasn't I?"

"Dad said too." Joe patted me on the back. "Who knows what they were looking at?"

"Jerks…"

My father asked me at a stop light on the drive home, "Did you strike out on purpose at the end?"

Fiddling with the rawhide laces on my baseball glove, I glumly admitted, "No."

"Good," he tousled my cap askew. "I didn't think so."

By week two of the tournament, King's was the only undefeated team left, and the Loud-Crowell cavalry was on its way! Between us and Kiwanis, we had combined to knock the other good teams out of the tournament, while the also-rans had each combined to knock out one another. It came down to mighty (but certainly not unbeatable, ahem…) Kiwanis vs. King's at Producers for all the marbles. They would have to sweep us two games straight to win it. If we took one of the next two games, the title was ours.

Luckily for Kiwanis, I'd be sitting these games out. Having been relegated to the duties of third base coach again, my contribution would be limited to appraising our opponent's sartorial refinements while trying to tune out Chuck Colombo's incessant yammering. Oh, they were so relieved in the other dugout that I wasn't playing. *So relieved!* I could see it in their beady Kiwanis eyes. If they had ended up having to tangle with that spunky little bench warmer again, shit would've got ugly quick.

Two games later, about which the less said the better, we found ourselves again milling around together, converging at the ice cream counter in the golden glow of declining sunlight, and you had to admit: Those Kiwanis uniforms were looking pretty... damn... sharp.

Toward the end of the following summer, 1973, after having recently had our solid (not great) King's baseball season foreclosed at the hands of Kiwanis in the City Series, I reluctantly began my very first season playing youth football for the south side team, Hercules Wrecking Co. (great name), in the Brockton Midget Football League (shamelessly insensitive name) (What can I say? It was a different time.). Once again, Dad had to coax and cajole me out of our Southfield comfort zone before I would agree to accompany Joe to the Hercules practice field at South Junior High.

Here was another case of the vagaries of ovaries working against my brother while benefiting me to a large degree. The Midget League was for boys aged 11, 12, and 13, on the condition that they were still of age by that devilish September 1st deadline. You're probably getting ahead of me but let me spell it out for all my fellow right-brain geniuses: Although Joe was one year my elder by a pubic hair's breadth (i.e., twelve years old to my eleven) when we showed up for tryouts at the tail end of August, he would turn thirteen on the 30th of the month, thereby ensuring that his first year on the team would also be his last; whereas with my birthday falling on the safe side of September, I would play out 95% of that first season as a 12-year-old; then my second season as a 13-year-old; and my THIRD season at the ripe old age of FOURTEEN! Okay, big deal, right? It was a big deal. Huge advantage.

Anyway, that first evening's "tryouts" were conducted in street clothes and consisted of everybody forming two long lines and going out for passes one by one while the prospective quarterbacks, including my familiar adversary Chuck Colombo, took turns dropping back two steps and throwing to us. It did not take long to realize that dear old Dad's innumerable tag football games on Deanna Road had positioned us well ahead of most of the other kids when it came to such basic skills as redirecting to catch errant passes, properly tucking and protecting the ball once caught, and even just keeping your eye on the ball. We did this for a good forty-five minutes and then one of the coaches blew his whistle.

"Team race!"

The entire group of four dozen kids was spread out in one wide line for a 50-yard dash en masse. Eric Abel and my friend from school, Don Tessier, left everyone else in the dust. I was among those pulled aside for a second heat, which boded well for me I presumed, having finished near the front of the pack. Again Eric and Tess smoked us, but I came in a respectable fourth and the coaches made note of my name.

When Dad picked us up, he said, "How'd you guys make out?"
"Good!"
"When are they handing out equipment?"
"They said next practice!"

When we reconvened two evenings later, the coaches issued equipment and gathered the second- and third-year veterans to form our starting units. With the rest of us, collectively referred to as the second string, they simply assigned positions. Apparently the races and receptions of two nights prior meant jack squat. Tess was informed he would be playing offensive guard, same as Joe. For reasons known only to the fickle Fates, I too was cast to the trenches as a truly offensive center.

When we got home that night, Dad had us try on our full complement of equipment, from helmets to cleats. I loved it. Our pants were a little too large, but the shoulder pads felt terrific.

Dad said, "Ma, take a look at these guys. What do you think?"

"Very nice."

"Let me get a picture."

"Then you guys get changed and come out for dinner."

I wished we had a mirror in our room. As we undressed, I was asking Joe if I had put my knee pads and thigh pads in properly.

"Let me see your pants. Yeah, you got it. Leave them in just like that."

"Look how long these practice jerseys are. Even with the shoulder pads on!"

Dad came in to ask, "You guys know if you're playing offense or defense?"

"Offense. I'm a guard."

"I'm center."

"Really," Dad considered. "Well, those are two important positions."

"Mr. Watson said they're all important."

"And he's right."

"He smokes cigars just like you."

"Here," Dad took the football from the bed. "Let's see how you snap the ball to the quarterback."

"Okay!"

I took a wide stance and bent to hold the ball on the floor with both hands as Dad stood behind me reaching in for the snap.

He let out a surprisingly shrill gender-neutral yelp the moment he felt my hairless testicles resting on the back of his hand. "Jesus! You got nothing on?"

"I thought you knew," I laughed. "I was getting undressed!"

Joe was just shaking his head at me, the way he sometimes did.

36

Chuck Colombo turned out to be an alright guy. As "starting second-string" quarterback to my "starting second-string" center, we struck up a natural working relationship, a dynamic that would morph over the next several years into a very solid and close camaraderie, working and otherwise. One day at practice he said, "Dunn: You played for King's, right?"

"Yeah, yeah, yeah…"

"No, I'm not saying anything."

"Just kidding. Those were good games."

"You're right, they were. And you guys beat us last year."

"Yeah. Once."

"You the guy that made that catch in left?"

"Hah! That 'lucky' catch? Yeah, that was me."

"Well it couldn't have been complete luck. You didn't just close your eyes at the crack of the bat and stick your glove out… like that other guy you had out there."

"That's true," I agreed. "So I hear you're the one responsible for bringing Eric to try out?"

"Yeah, the Abels just moved here to our neighborhood."

"Any more at home like him?"

"Not like him."

"What a runner."

"I should get some kind of trophy. Just for bringing him in."

"Ten percent finder's fee. Something…"

"Right?" Chuck laughed. "So, seriously, do you have to always wear that cup?"

"Yeah," I said, recalling the cupless hilarity of Dad's testicular yelp. "Why?"

"Every time I take a snap, it kills my hand. Look at this."

"Oh, shit. Sorry about that. But, seriously, yeah."

"Jeepers… Going to be a long season, Dunn."

"Well, hey," I joked, "Now you can have calluses on the back of your hand too."

—

For school-aged boys growing up in Brockton at that time, it was understood that autumn Saturdays meant attending the varsity football team's games. The youngest kids, and newcomers, might not yet be in the know, but it was just a matter of time until they were. Once anointed, the weekly pilgrimage to Marciano Stadium was simply assumed as a matter of course.

One such Saturday, toward the end of a Hercules early morning inter-squad scrimmage, Joe and I overheard some of the older guys making plans to meet up later at the game.

"What game?"

"The football game. Today's the first game of the season."

"Patriots?"

"The Patriots suck! We're going to the Brockton game."

Another guy said, "Brockton would kill the Patriots."

We all laughed with blissfully ignorant hometown confidence and pride, and one of the coaches shrugged, "Probably would this year."

At home later, I asked Dad if we could go to the Brockton High game in two weeks.

"Sure you can. How come not next week?"

"They said they don't play next week."

"Who said?"

"Everybody at the practice."

"You sure the game in two weeks is at Brockton?"

"Ahh…"

"We'll find out one way or another, but sure you can. Matter of fact, why don't we drive by the stadium right now? See how it looks."

"Okay!"

"Joe?"

"Yeah, alright."

As we neared the high school entrance and slowed to a pedestrian pace, the atmosphere felt like a carnival. Police with whistles directed vehicle traffic and foot traffic alike. There were pedestrians everywhere. It must have been halftime because a gigantic marching band, festooned in bright bold red, was trumpeting its synchronized support at midfield. Thousands of fans were crowded into the bleachers.

I heard myself drawl, "Wow…"

"That's it right there, guys," my father declared. "Brockton Football." When he uttered the name, Dad did so with the unspoken tribute of word by word capitalization, as would befit an unquestioned worldwide industry leader (e.g., "Major League Baseball") or a hallowed national monument (e.g., "Grant's Tomb"). This was not some lowercase sport being played for fun in the sandlots of some anonymous berg, this was Brockton Football as played in the Marciano Stadium. Brockton Football: not only the pinnacle and quintessence of its kind, but practically a state of mind.

Even worldly brother Joe had to say, "Look at that."

―

Having moved to Southfield in the early summer of 1971, our period of residency in Brockton had only reached its seventeen month by the time two full seasons of Boxer Football had come and gone. While that '71 team was strong, it did not live up to the lofty precedent set by Armond Colombo's undefeated squad of the previous year. However, in his fourth season at the helm, the 1972 team more than upheld the standard of excellence, going undefeated and winning the inaugural Eastern Mass. Division One Super Bowl, thus unequivocally earning the title of Champion (an honor unfortunately withheld from the great '70 team due to its having finished a fraction of a point behind two other undefeated schools in the seasonlong ratings as the result of a controversial strength-of-schedule equation). To cap off the brilliant 1972 campaign, Colombo was even awarded the Paul Revere Bowl by the *Boston Globe* as Eastern Mass. High School Football's Coach of the Year.

The initial firsthand introduction for Joe and myself to the actual Brockton Football experience would come two weeks after that Hercules inter-squad scrimmage when we went to see the highly touted 1973 Boxer contingent in person at Rocky Marciano Stadium. Dad pulled the car over on Forest Ave. to drop us off, giving us four dollar bills apiece along with instructions to have fun, stay in plain sight of each other at all times, and steer clear of trouble. He would be back to pick us up right here on this exact same spot after the game. "That's the box office to get your tickets. We're across the street from the Fairgrounds grandstand there. And right here's the Registry."

From the backseat I did a slow triangulation and nodded although Dad had been addressing Joe in the front.

"Okay guys, have fun. Should be a good game. Weymouth's been strong since before I was in high school. Real strong."

"But they split Weymouth into North and South," Joe reported. "Two separate high schools now."

"Oh, that's it for them then. Won't have a Chinaman's chance against Colombo's team." Joe and I understood what Dad meant. "That's too bad, though. When'd they do that?"

"Last year, I think. Or the year before."

"That's a shame. Weymouth was a power. Better hope they don't do that in Brockton." Dad might have seen my eyebrows clench in the rearview mirror. "But Colombo wouldn't stand for that."

"Brockton's hard to kill, huh Dad?" I had picked up this phrase after hearing it around town and was trying it out.

"You bet your ass."

Joe bought a program from a hawker as we made our way to the massive flight of bleachers on the home side. Seated shoulder to shoulder about halfway up, we had a fine view of the field as the teams went through their pregame warm ups. Weymouth players in maroon and white occupied the fifty yards to our left, throwing passes, fielding punts, jogging short routes. Brockton guys had for themselves the other fifty yards on the scoreboard side. Lying back on the grass, aligned along the yard lines in perfect rows and columns five yards apart, they were spread out across the field from one sideline to the other. On the coach's whistle, they flipped from their backs to their fronts. With military precision they counted off five push ups. On the coach's whistle they flipped in unison to their backs again, from which they carried out five synchronized sit ups. They flipped twice and counted off five seconds of bridging on their helmets. This display went on to include several other simple stretching exercises in between flips.

Ribbing me, Joe said, "Look at Weymouth looking at them. This game's over already."

When the players in Brockton red-and-black broke off into separate half-speed position drills, Joe pointed, "Number 81 is MacAfee. Look how big he is."

"Wow. He's the tight end?" I was just getting the hang of football, but I knew that the big guy on offense catching touchdowns was your tight end.

"How you going to stop him?"

I had no idea. "Tight end?"

"MacAfee plays *split* end."

"What?"

"I know."

"Then who plays tight end?"

Joe referred to his program. "Right there, 86. Burchard."

"That's weird, though. Right?"

"I know. And two of those hash marks are taller than Dad, but did you see when they were all lying down on the field? MacAfee had two of them completely covered up all by himself."

"Really? And he's split end?"

Throughout the game, Joe cited other points of interest. "The quarterback's the oldest Colombo brother. Peter."

"That guy eleven?"

"Yup, talking to his father. And that looks like Chuck down there handing him the water."

"Oh, yeah. It is."

"Second youngest of the brothers. Of the whole family, actually."

Where Joe had gathered all this intelligence was beyond me.

When the teams left the field for halftime, disappearing beneath us under the stands, Joe said, "You want to get some popcorn or something?"

"I don't want to lose our seats."

"Yeah, you're right. Hey, look at those guys."

A pack of smart alecks had snuck through the gate while the teams were exiting, and now they were scampering around at midfield with one of their own footballs playing kill the man with the ball.

"Are they supposed to be able to do that?"

"Don't think so," Joe laughed.

One of the managers chased them off so the marching band could take the field. Everybody cheered as the hellions hot-footed it straight to the endzone, through the goalposts, across the track, over the fence, under the Marciano Stadium sign, to the triangular tract of open grass by the box office where they could resume their rowdy contest unmolested.

Joe and I did eventually venture out for popcorn and, sure enough, we had to find new seats afterwards, higher up and off to the side.

Near the end of the game, Joe said, "Whoops. That's a safety."

"Oh, cause..."

"If you're tackled with the ball in your own end zone, it's a safety. Two points. Pretty uncommon."

"Right."

Afterwards, Dad was waiting for us outside the Registry although the X I'd made in the gutter grit earlier was nowhere in sight. For all I knew, his tire was right on top of it.

"You guys have fun?"

"Yup. At halftime some guys were playing kill the man with the ball on the field. Greg wanted to go down and play with them."

"No I didn't!"

"Yes you did!"

"Did Brockton win?"

Joe laughed, "28-2."

"Weymouth got a safety?"

"Uncommon," I confirmed, "But, yup."

Sometimes when Dad would come home from work you could smell the wood smoke on his uniform from all the way across our front parlor. He would grab himself a beer, sit down in his chair and put his feet up on the hassock. This was quality time, often just the two of us. Ma might be at the dining room table with her coffee, doing her own thing; my brothers or sister might pass through every now and then, but more often than not it was just us. Dad enjoyed regaling me with stories of the colorful characters at Engine 42/Ladder 30 as much as I enjoyed hearing them.

"Thank you, Gregga," he would say as I started unlacing his work boots.

"Any good fires last night?"

"We had three working fires."

"Really?"

"The second one was tough as a bastard..."

With Dad comfortably in his chair, I'd sit on the rug and lean back against his hassock while we watched the news, or sports, or whatever happened to be on. Being situated closest to the TV, and only too glad to be of some use to my father, I naturally assumed the role of channel changer.

In the fall, we hardly ever missed Monday Night Football. I was allowed to stay up to watch until the halftime highlights were over. Dad would spend the first half educating me on the finer aspects of the game, accurately foretelling the exact causes of penalty flags, predicting the next plays to be run, and pointing out whether Dandy Don was yet half in the bag.

Whenever he'd finished a beer, Dad would utter "hut" or "hut hut" and lob his empty bottle over one of my shoulders, or directly over my head depending on the degree of difficulty he was going for. If I got up to go to the fridge or something, he'd hit me with a quick hip pass on the way. Returning from the bathroom I'd pretend I wasn't looking when he launched a timing pattern toward the kitchen doorway to test my sideline skills. Upon each completion, I would deposit the empty in the kitchen trash and then, switching roles to that of loyal beer bearer, I'd set about achieving my greater objective, i.e., the securing of immediate refreshment replacement. My dual roles (receiver/retriever) tied in with one of my father's deceptively simple – seemingly common sense – football wisdoms: When you're thrown a pass, the number one goal is to catch it, which is to say, the point isn't looking cool while you catch it, or making it look harder than it really is, or being some kind of hot dog out there, patting yourself on the back. "Catching the pass every time is the most hot dog thing you can possibly do," my father would remind me. "You do that every time and you'll play in the pros, because you'll be the only person in the history of football ever to do it. But remember: After you catch the ball, the play's not over. *Now you have to score!"*

I would usually record six or seven receptions on a typical night, and would therefore fetch an equal number of fresh replacements for my quarterback until it was time for me to go to bed.

"Goodnight, Dad. I love you."

"Come here, give me a kiss." As often as not he would rough house me when I bent to kiss him, pulling me down into his chair with him. "What are you, too big now to give your dad a hug?"

"No!"

"You'll never be too big for that," he would reiterate before finally letting go of me.

—

Although I couldn't appreciate it at the time, I have since come to realize that Joe's resignation from Hercules partway through the season wasn't so much "quitting the team" as it was a case of shrewdly interpreting the writing on the wall, and doing things on his own terms. After all, Joe Dunn was no offensive lineman. Come on!

I subscribe to the modern school of thought which holds: The surest litmus test for gauging someone's athletic ability is that which takes place on a basketball court. Put Joe up against anybody on the Hercules team in one-on-one hoops, with the possible exception of Manny Silva, and my money's on Joe.

He didn't make a big deal out of leaving the team. He didn't try to enlist me in his silent protest. After a few weeks he just turned in his equipment and never looked back.

For my part, I was enjoying being on the team, and it had not once occurred to me to quit, even after Joe left. After all, I figured I wouldn't be a second stringer forever, and it is only in retrospect that my time spent toiling on the offensive line struck me as being in any way out of the ordinary. I was having fun, and my game was baseball anyway, so who cared?

Hercules Wrecking Co. won the 1973 Brockton Midget Football League championship my first year, not that I had a damn thing to do with it, and not that I remember a damn thing about it other than one vivid snapshot from our very first game of the season. Don Tessier, Chuck and I were standing together on the sideline following the progress of our starting offense on the field when our veteran quarterback went down with an injury. (Broken wrist? Broken ankle? Don't remember.)

"Colombo!" shouted our cigar-chomping head coach, Jack Watson. "Let's go!"

When Chuck ran out onto the field, Tess and I cheered him on with a gushing fraternal pride: One of our own was out there now, about to play first-string! He disappeared into the huddle for a moment, and only when the huddle clapped and broke could we appreciate how truly formidable was Chuck's spur-of-the-moment task. By no means small in stature, he was nonetheless dwarfed by the Herculean first-string offensive line, particularly its hefty starting center, John Sversky. The mismatch was such that when Chuck positioned himself under center to call out a play's signals, he could more accurately have been described as being *below* center. Sversky's commanding posterior was pretty much eye to eye with the "Hercules" lettering of Chuck's game jersey.

You know what? Three cheers for Chuck Colombo. He must have been nervous as hell being flung into the breach like that, but by season's end he had settled into his new leadership role admirably and he obviously had a major hand in the securing of our undefeated championship season.

Later he would kid me, "The best thing about being moved to first-string was kissing that fucking cup of yours goodbye."

—

As for that 1973 Brockton High season, Joe and I would attend several more home games. Armond Colombo's boys capped off another undefeated regular season by thrashing previously unbeaten Revere in the championship game, capturing a second consecutive Division One Super Bowl title.

On the morning of the big game, two of the dads from our street surprised me and Joe by stopping by to see if we wanted to accompany them to Boston College to watch the Boxers play.

"Can we, Ma?"

"Sure you can."

"Let's go!"

Frank Moore from across the street and Bob McCoy from three houses down had sons of their own at home, but they were all young kids at the time. That the dads thought of me and Joe on game day was testament to how close-knit our neighborhood had become in a relatively short period of time, and being a Brockton neighborhood, it was only natural that our families bonded over sports. The McCoy boys would go on to play football for the high school, winning Super Bowl championships of their own under Coach Colombo, making the whole of Deanna Road proud. Billy McCoy was a state champion wrestler, too, earning himself induction into the Brockton High School Sports Hall of Fame for his multi-sport efforts. Not to be outdone, Frank Moore's two sons, Derek and Brian, who for years logged extra BHS track team road work by endlessly circling our half-mile block at dinner time, are both Hall of Fame inductees too for track, indoor and outdoor.

I remember standing in the beautifully sunny chill of early December, waiting our turn outside the Alumni Stadium box office, and I remember sitting high up in the stands, brimming with anticipation. The specifics of the blowout itself are long gone, but I distinctly recall the moment Brockton first took the field. One of the Boxer players dashed out onto BC's Astro Turf well ahead of the pack of black-and-red* teammates uniting in his wake.

I said, "Who's that?"

"It's not MacAfee," Joe told me. "Not a Colombo." I watched him scrutinize. "Definitely not Delancey. Bob, can I look at your program?"

Mr. McCoy and Mr. Moore considered it bad form on the part of the dasher to separate himself from the rest of the team like that, but I liked it. I was thinking, if it'd been me down there, I'd have probably done the same damn thing.

*[Boxer's Note: *Despite Brockton's team colors being routinely advertised as black-and-red, the true shade of the football team's helmets and game pants was considerably darker than Red; more along the lines of a deep Cherry, or a Blood. Black-and-blood does have a better ring to it.*]
—

I want to be sure not to give the wrong impression when I mention time spent watching television with my father. Although sitting on the floor with my back against the hassock was in effect my assigned parlor post, just as Dad's was in his wing chair directly behind me, everybody else of course spent a great deal of time there too; all eight of us Virgos jockeyed territorially for position on the couch or at the dining room table or sprawled on the floor with Gretchen, the sole canine in the clan (another Virgo), or at the turnstile refrigerator door. Eventually though, as the evening wore on, unless there was something special on TV, Dad and I would usually find ourselves the last men standing, or rather, reclining.

Old Lady Recall being such a cranky curator, presenting for display only those volumes her fickle taste deems singularly noteworthy, she has been patrolling the dusty Television Show stacks of yesteryear since way back when. With a squinting cataracted eye she annually winnows out unacceptably mundane artifacts so that at this point when I leaf through my mind's archives seeking specific broadcast content to tie in with this or that particular vignette, all I come up with are those landmark characters and events which everybody in the world recollects: Bobby Fischer -vs- Boris Spasskey (which sparked the decade's great chess renaissance in America); Spassky's indomitable countryman Vasily Alekseyev; the dazzling superstars Mark Spitz, Dan Gable, and Olga Korbut (who had each single-handedly sparked the booms of their own individual sports amid the mayhem of the Munich Olympics); the '72 Dolphins; Patty Hearst; Watergate; The Rumble in the Jungle.* I distinctly remember being in the parlor, bearing witness to all of them during those years. Otherwise, though, the golden moments of the everyday which my Dad and I lived on may as well have been accompanied by a mewling test pattern. So, for the purposes of fleshing out the mise-en-scènes of our little sitting room dramas, we can go ahead and assume that a ballgame was on, or the evening news, or *All in the Family* or *The Odd Couple* or *Columbo* or something.

"Let's see what else is on, Gregga."

If a segment on the evening news caught my father's attention, he was often able to use it as an object lesson for a valuable piece of real-world wisdom; and the brand of knowledge Dad was serving up was far from your standard boilerplate Honesty's-the-Best-Policy, Women-and-Children-First, Live-and-Let-Live kind of stuff. The pearls he cast were choice as truffles.

"See that," he said once. "Don't ever stay above the 8th floor in a hotel. If there's a fire, the ladders on our trucks can't reach you."

"They can't?"

"They don't go that high. Look at these people. If that fire's not knocked down fast, those people right there are goners."

In addition to other fire safety tips (e.g., "If you're in your room, or a hotel or something – anywhere – and you hear a fire alarm or someone down the hall yell 'Fire!' check your door knob before you open any door. If it's hot, do not open that door – go the opposite way, get out a window if you can. And if it's smokey in the room, hold a wet towel to your face, and stay low and keep your bearings. Crawl if you have to, but don't panic. You have more time than you think. When you get to a door, feel around for the hinges. If they're on your side, it opens toward you. If not, it opens out. You'd be surprised how many people we find on the other side of a door they could have easily gotten out through... But the room's full of smoke, and you're blind and you can't breathe and you panic."), Dad would say, "If it's the middle of the night, and you hear somebody creeping around the house, never turn on the lights. You know your way around the house, they don't." This was good common sense survival stuff that might not occur to a young man in the heat of the moment.

One night Dad told me, "When you get a little older and you find yourself at a party where some girl is having sex with a bunch of guys – leave. If you're stuck somewhere, call me. I'll come and get you."

"Okay."

"You understand? First of all, don't ever be one of the guys having sex with her. It could be a girl you know, it could be a complete stranger, laughing and drinking, having a good time. Doesn't matter, just make sure you get out of there. It's bad news. I've seen it happen – to a *couple* of guys."

*[Boxer's Note: The 1974 Ali-Foreman fight had been postponed about a month from its originally scheduled September date due to a cut Foreman suffered in training camp. This was unfortunate for one of our own because the original undercard for The Fight had included former Brockton Boxers defensive end and all around dangerous man, Dornell Wigfall.]

"Really?"

"A few days later she's sobered up, gossip's going around, someone calls her a name, or her friends are winding her up, or her family finds out – and all of a sudden the word around town is Rape. Then anybody who was even in the house at the time is guilty. 'Why didn't you stop it? You were there! You just let it go on?'"

Still facing the television, I remember nodding Dad my full attention.

"You don't want to be messing with the town pump anyway."

I shook my head of course.

"You'll see, though. It's going to happen," I heard Dad say. "That's why I tell you guys, when you're out in the world, you got to look out for yourself. Always keep your wits about you. You don't believe it now, but this kind of stuff's going to one-hundred-percent happen. To you or someone you know."

I was nodding at the TV again.

"One hundred percent for sure."

I turned my head around, nodding, so he could see I understood.

"It's just... *Life*. So be alert. And don't let the one it's going to happen to be you."

—

1973 turned into '74, and brought with it my final Little League season. If the sport of football was intent on having me toil in anonymity, overlooking my golden god-given gifts, such as they were, then so be it. I'd always have baseball – my first and truest love.

Regular batting practice with Dad at the playing fields around Southfield, with Rich and Steve now old enough to shag balls in the outfield, had me primed for a good final season on King's. The coaches said they'd be trying me on the mound this year, in addition to my usual catching duties, so I worked on that with Dad too. Fortunately, King's had a couple pretty good arms already, so I was only going to be used in relief when needed and the occasional spot start, which suited me fine. Pitching was never my thing. Dad didn't condone curve balls, anyway ("Too young. No, I don't care what their dads say. They can do what they want to do. Around here, it's no curve balls till high school."), and I struggled with sporadic control issues, to boot. We had a talented youngster join the team that year, Mike Holzman. He played shortstop and pitched too, with a nice little slidery curve that he could actually control. Mike was a good kid. He was going to be a great player one day, and I was glad for the opportunity to pass along some mentoring and positive reinforcement like Messrs. Abbruzzi, Loud and Crowell had done for me.

One night before supper, I was on the front lawn working on those control issues, with Dad as catcher. I used the edging of our driveway as the rubber. Dad was across the lawn squatting by the little stand of trees with his target open wide. "Keep your eye on my glove. Wind up, and step directly at me. Good. See? Don't try to steer it. Don't even think about it, just keep your eye on my target, step, and let it loose. Good. Don't worry, we're going to keep working on it. You'll get it."

After a while, Dad said, "Alright, now from the stretch. That a way. Good. Again."

When we were called in to eat, he said, "Nine out of those last ten pitches were strikes. And you're not losing anything off your fastball when you go from the stretch."

"I can't just go out of the stretch all the time, though."

"Why the hell not?"

"Everybody else goes out of a wind up with no men on."

"You're not everybody else."

—

Sitting home one night with my father, putting my back into the hassock, I heard him say, "That's a fire."

Sirens wound and wailed their way to our neighborhood, and then onto our street, and ceremoniously took over everything, right outside our house. Red fire truck lights were sweeping onto and off of our parlor walls amid the dissonant churning roar of heavy engines and air brakes.

Dad stepped into his untied sneakers and out onto the lawn. Next door where my Gilmore School classmate Roxanne Torrone lived with her pain in the ass little sister Janine and their mother, Big Roxanne (whose sobriquet belied her lithe, leggy, tanned, Mrs. Robinsonian physique while certainly paying apt homage to her luminous personality), smoke was streaming out of two front windows, and from somewhere up on the roof.

My father said, "Stay here," and strode off across our adjacent side lawns to consult with his firefighting brethren while I stayed there watching from our front stoop. I was guessing that some manner of quick identification would transact before this random neighborhood guy was granted access to the perilous work perimeter, a confidential high sign or watchword perhaps; because for all they knew, Dad, clad as he was in his preferred dad attire (sweatshirt with cut off sleeves and dungarees) rather than the smoky dark blue uniform of his comrades, was in all probability just some nosy rubbernecker.

After a brief conference, I saw him nodding. Then I watched as he walked up to the Torrones' front steps and, with the controlled audacity of a matador, or a magician, pulled the door open and stepped aside in one fluid move, releasing a rolling cloud of gray smoke into which – *POOF!* – he disappeared.

I like to think I'm pretty well versed in the basic laws of physics, but this was one of those moments where Time stopped and Space expanded; or Space shrank and Time leapt away: All I know is, without benefit of action or forethought, I found myself halfway across the Torrones' lawn and in a very bad mood.

One of the Brockton firefighters yelled, "Hey!" which stopped me and startled me. He yelled again, "HEY!"

I heard my own voice yell back, summing up the point of all things, "My father's in there!"

Alas, mighty mighty King's failed that summer in their bid to "three-peat" – mainly because a.) the term itself would not be coined until the end of the following decade, and b.) Allied Auto Parts had a much better record. I enjoyed a pretty good season personally, though, highlighted by a heated battle with Allied's Wally Allegro for the league lead in home runs. When all was said and done, with each of us having pulled into the lead and then fallen behind countless times, we had each amassed two round-trippers apiece (Hey – it was a different time; wooden bats; OPEC; etc.).

Much like my brother Joe, Wally Allegro was living proof of the cold randomness of the universe, especially when it came to the fertilization lottery. Although he and I were both twelve years old, Wally was already a seventh-grader in junior high when our Little League season started, while I was still in elementary school. I can remember him arriving for one of our games wearing his gray East Junior High uniform rather than his Allied blue, having come straight from an after-school game.

Although Allied Auto won it that year, King's did manage to give them a go in at least one of our matchups. Late in the season, tied 4-4 after regulation, we went to extra innings. In our half of the seventh, standing on third base with two outs, I spotted an opportunity to try one of Steve Loud's old tricks, the Delayed Steal. I had watched him get away with it three or four times throughout the course of my first year on King's (from my prime vantage point on the bench). The main prerequisite as I saw it was that the opposing catcher must not be throwing the ball back to his pitcher with any kind of zip on it. A few innings earlier I'd noticed a considerable arc on the Allied catcher's leisurely tosses to the mound. If I was ever going to try out this bit of chicanery, now was the time. When the pitcher delivered his next throw to the plate, I casually walked off third an inconspicuous five or six steps down the line, stopped as nonchalantly as you like, and turned obediently back toward the base once the catcher looked my way. Nothing happening here, sir! As soon as he released his throw back to the pitcher, I bolted for home. Having caught both catcher and pitcher off guard, it looked like I might have a chance. In a bang-bang play at the plate, I slid in, stretching the toe of my cleat between the kneeling catcher's legs. If the ump called me out, I'd have had no gripe, but – perhaps in accordance with the unofficial Tie-Goes-to-the-Runner rule, or the even less official Reward-the-Aggressor policy [*See Jackie Robinson's twenty career thefts of home, not to mention Babe Ruth's TEN!*] – I was declared safe.

The following night in our parlor, Dad said, "Hey, look at this." He was pointing out a tiny headline in the *Enterprise* Sports section: Dunn's Steal Gives King's a Win.

I felt all the flesh on my forehead scrunch together in bewildered amazement. What the hell…?

"How do you like that, Ma?" Dad announced. "Greg got some ink in today's paper."

"Let me see."

My mother read aloud, "Dunn's steal gives King's a win. Greg Dunn stole home in the first extra inning to give King's a 5-4 victory over Allied Auto who had come back from a 4-0 deficit to tie the game. Ah… then there's… Katz… Allegro… blah blah blah." Ma concluded, "That's going in the scrapbook!"

"What scrapbook?" I dared not presume that my bit of small town derring-do belonged among the feats of those legendary Hyde Park heroes, uncle Kevin and Uncle Jim.

Joe cleared it up for me. "The Dunn Family Scrapbook, fool."

"No, not that one," Ma corrected as I punched and Joe winced. "*Our* Dunn Family Scrapbook."

You mean there was another one? This was the first I'd heard of it.

Ma said, "I'll be back in a minute. I'm going to Mammoth Mart right now for a new one."

I was beaming. "Is this what you meant when you said everybody would know our name, Dad?"

He laughed on his way to the kitchen, "It's just the beginning, Gregga. Hey, who wants Christo's pizza?"

"YEAH!" we yummed. "Cheese please!"

"What's their number? Where's the book?"

I knew Ma had long since added Christo's in her perfect handwriting to the list of emergency numbers on the wall by the phone. "It's right—"

"Ah, here we go. You want your shish kebab?"

Whenever my mother said "yes" it came out almost sounding like "years."

"And a Greek salad?"

"Well done," Ma added. "Make sure you tell them well done twice. Julie, get Ma's pockabook?"

"Greek salad? Ah – yes, can I make an order to go. Marie, Greek salad?"

"Years. You have to tell them twice, or—"

"One well done shish kebab meal. A large Greek salad. A small Greek salad. Two cheese pizzas…" Dad cupped the phone: "Anchovies?"

"No!" "Naw!" "NO!" "Come on, Dad!"

"…and two pepperoni pizzas. That's it. Yup. Yup. Yup. Yup, you got it. And well done on the shish kebab, right? Right. And what's the total? Good enough, see you then." Dad hung up and told us, "Twenty minutes."

"I'll pick it up on the way back," Ma said.

"YEAH!"

"Need money?"

Ma patted her pocketbook. "Nope."

"The old Ma's alright, huh guys?"

We couldn't agree more. They gave each other a smile and kissed.

This cheerful episode had all the necessary ingredients: Good news, the element of surprise, our family enjoying great food together, and mild-mannered me at its epicenter.

The only possible improvement on perfection would have been if the newspaper account had mentioned my appearance on the mound as King's closer in the seventh inning, and the fact that, in what would be the last pitching performance of my baseball career, I

55

had struck out the side to end the game. Dad often coached me as a batter to lay off high fastballs with two strikes, tantalizing though they might be. "Pitchers'll try to get you to bite." He was right, and I brought that knowledge to bear against Allied, finishing off the last two batters (the dangerous Johnson brothers, Dana and Craig) with borderline high fastballs which they tried to hit onto Electric Avenue.

Coming off the mound victorious, I was hailed and jostled by my teammates and coaches. Mr. Dole's son (and former King's teammate) David came onto the field too, proclaiming, "From the stretch!"

—

My celebrated (at 134 Deanna Road, Southfield, at least) Little League career came to an end that summer and, storied though it had been (in the *Brockton Enterprise*, at least, which ran no less than three items pertaining to my evidently newsworthy run-producing exploits), there would be no such attendant fanfare during my second season on the Hercules Wrecking Co. football team, the reason being that offensive lineman not named John Hannah warranted the expenditure of very few drops of ink in these parts.

It was a fun season, though, playing alongside my buddy Tess on the first-string offense. Actually playing in the games changes everything! With me at center and Tess at right guard, we no longer had to roll around on the Marciano Stadium field during pre-game calisthenics to generate telltale grass stains on our game uniforms – which, by the way, consisted of cerulean colored jerseys with fire engine red lettering, numerals, helmets, and pants. (I know – sounds a little flamboyant, but those uniforms were by far the coolest in the league, trust me.) Upon my promotion to first team, quarterback Chuck Colombo welcomed me by jokingly lamenting, "Oh, no! The return of the cup!"

"What number'd they give you," Dad asked.

"Fifty-five."

"Good solid number."

Hercules enjoyed another undefeated championship season that year and, truth be told, our spotless record undoubtedly upped the coolness quotient of the uniforms – for nothing polishes perception like success. Had we gone winless, our disorienting 3D chromatic color scheme would probably have come across as, at worst, clownish, or at the very least unjustifiably bold.

Although Dad was confident that my days as center were numbered, he nevertheless tutored me regularly in the ways of the line.

"Never play the other guy's game; make him play yours. If he's your same size? Great: You're stronger, so muscle him. He's bigger than you? Fine: You're quicker, just get lower than him and drive. All things equal? Perfect, because you're tougher: Outlast him. The other guys'll always quit before you will. Remember that."

Throughout that season he kept the faith, believing our coaches would one day come around. Pretty much every night my father was home, we played long-toss catch on the street. I had to stay sharp because, in a case of mixed-messaging too strange to be fiction, I was not only the Hercules starting center, *but also the backup quarterback*. (Don't ask me, I have no frigging idea.) [*All inquiries should please be directed to Jack Watson, Ken Benoit, Richie Powers, et al.*]
—

Meanwhile, back at the hassock, Dad muttered, "Hut, hut," and lobbed a soft fade pattern over my left shoulder which I caught with arms fully extended after briefly bobbling it.

"Joe, please," my mother chided him from the dining room.

"See that, Ma? No glasses, bad eye and all."

"I'm just waiting for one of those to smash in a million pieces all over my floor."

"Hasn't happened yet," Dad reasoned, to which Ma just nodded with a "Yeah – *yet...*" kind of shrug as she put out her cigarette. "Where's your glasses?"

"In the room. I don't need them for up close."

"Ma, what was Greg's vision last time?"

"With glasses?"

"Yeah, with the glasses."

"20/20 in his good eye, 20/80 in his bad eye."

"20/80's not that bad," I said, suddenly defensive.

"It's lousy," Dad clarified. "That's why if you ever end up being a receiver for the high school, make sure they always line you up on the left side."

"I'll probably be a lineman, so I won't even need–"

"You're not going to be a lineman," he informed us. "Believe me."

I figured I'd give the old man the benefit of the doubt, his batting average thus far being somewhere around 1.000.

He went on, "So, 20/20 - 20/80. Not great, but way better than it was before."

My mother smiled, "You remember second grade when you had the patch?"

How could I forget? "Yeah…"

"What was his vision when you first took him to Doctor what's-his-name?"

"West's his name."

"That's what I said…"

Ma laughed at that for some reason.

"But what was it? Very first visit?"

"In his bad eye? 20/500."

"What!" I heard myself protest.

"Doctor West said it was probably worse, but that was as high as the spectrum went."

"That's why we tell you to wear your glasses all the time, Gregga. In school and out."

"But up close I see fine."

"Because you're doing all your seeing with your one good eye. Put your hand over your left eye right now and look at Ma."

I did as I was told. "No change. Hi, Ma."

"Hi."

"Right," Dad said. "Because your good eye does all your seeing for you. Now cover that eye instead. See? Big difference, right?

That's why they used to have you wear the patch over your good eye: to force your bad eye to do the seeing, to exercise it."

I remember nodding my hazy understanding.

"But now," continued Dad, "With no patch and no glasses, pretty soon the good eye's going to get worse and worse because it's doing all the work."

Ma said, "Remember that first day with the patch? As soon as we left Doctor West's office you walked right into a telephone pole?"

"Yes!" I teased her, "Thanks a lot, Ma!"

We enjoyed a nice reminiscing family laugh and I went down the hall to fetch my glasses.

—

I can't recall the epiphanic moment during that second Hercules pre-season when someone on the coaching staff first considered supplementing my duties as heir apparent to the Starting Center fortune with those of a Second-String Skill Position concern (perhaps it came as early as the lunatic forty-man scramble of humanity known as the "team race" on day-1 of tryouts), but whoever was responsible for this brainchild must certainly have been working his devious palms with gusto at our first preseason scrimmage against Bridgewater.

Very little of that year's actual gameplay remains afloat in the old memory pool, but for some reason I do distinctly remember stretching before the start of the Bridgewater scrimmage, and overhearing Chuck explaining to D.J. Bergeron how his sister Beth had spent that whole afternoon memorizing all the jampacked lyrics to the song "Life is a Rock (But the Radio Rolled Me)".

"She played her 45 all day up in her room, writing down one line at a time, lifting the needle, starting over, writing the next line, until she had the whole song; then she must have played that thing a hundred stinking times in a row learning it."

"That's your sister Beth," D.J. agreed.

Don't ask me why I remember that...

Anyway, after both teams' starting units had battled it out for two full quarters, a Bridgewater coach's whistle signaled the change of squads at midfield.

"B-teams up! Let's go! B-teams!"

With my first-string teammates jogging off to the sideline, and backups jogging in to replace them, all I had to do to prep for my maiden series as signal caller in a game situation was take a deep breath, spit-wash my hands, move forward one step in the gallery huddle and face the other way.

"Alright, boys," our offensive coordinator Mr. Benoit exhorted. "Here we go. Let's take it to them. Forty-one Buck on two. Forty-one Buck on two. Ready? Break!"

This particular play required me to perform a fancy little reverse turn after taking the snap, and hand off to the fullback for a straightforward running play through the right guard hole. It made sense; start out simple.

Once under center, I barked, "Ready! Set! Hut! Hut!"

Upon landing a pirouette of such balletic grace that Baryshnikov and Nureyev would have hung up their tunics for good and devoted their remaining years to its study, I was in position, poised for the hand-off, after which would follow a full-speed carrying out of my realistic option fake down the line of scrimmage (to freeze the defensive end and linebackers for that crucial split second of indecision).

The play ran like clockwork. There I was, poised. The fullback, however, had gone to the *left* guard hole, grazing my butt as he barreled past, the idiot! Or was it I who had made the wrong turn (much to the sniggering delight of the Bolshoi peanut gallery, no doubt)? No, it couldn't have been me. I was right there where I was supposed to be, poised and everything.

Poised, shmoised! I tucked the ball, cut up into the guard hole, and booked it straight down the middle of the field like Larry Fine on his way to save K.O. Stradivarius, scoring a fifty-yard touchdown for the good guys.

Back in the huddle, Mr. Benoit was greedily fidgeting with his hands. "That's the way to fix a broken play," he grinned. "Let's get another one!"

"Take it easy out there, will you, Dunn," Chuck joked later on the sideline. "Trying to make me look bad?"

—

Like King's in my final season of Little League that year, the 1974 Brockton High football team – despite some talented beasts on defense and a dynamic offensive backfield – was destined to have their hopes for a third consecutive championship unceremoniously dashed. Not one... Not two... Yes, three(!) away-game defeats would seal their fate. The shocking opening day loss by one touchdown to a determined Natick squad (whose revered head coach had died of a heart attack in the off-season, a source of bittersweet inspiration often cited by the Natick players that season*), left Boxer fans in a state of outright bewilderment, but it was the defeats in two of the season's last three games which gave rise to mutinous grumblings from the Done-for-me-Latelies around town who openly clamored for – if not the head, then perhaps at least one of the big toes of Coach Armond Colombo.

Attending a mid-season home game that year (Brookline, I think. We won big), Joe and I had found a couple open spots in the stands behind a group of halftime hooligans, the older guys who lived to torment our marching band and security. They were yelling at the players and coaches, heckling the referees, passing an old football back and forth directly over the heads of innocent paying customers. Having arrived a little late, my brother and I'd had no choice but to settle among these rowdies at the scoreboard end of the bleachers, high in the uppermost corner. The only alternative would have been to openly commit the high treason of visitors' side seating. When the whistle blew for halftime, the evil army of hecklers all stomped their way down the stadium stairs, scattering to storm the field in waves of precision mayhem designed to confuse and overwhelm the ill-prepared security staff.

"You hear those assholes," Joe said. "Still criticizing Colombo for the Natick game. It's only one loss. If they win all the rest, they'll probably still go to the Super Bowl. Probably win it, too."

"Really?"

"Morons. I can understand why the family sits on the visitors' side. Listening to that crap all game long would piss me off too."

"What family?"

"The Colombos, and the Marcianos. That's them way over there. See them? Mrs. Colombo... Beth, in the light blue coat... Peter Marciano."

I saw no such thing. Then again, my field of focus tested out somewhere between Harry Greb and Polyphemus. One thing I did plainly see, though, was that whenever the sun broke through it was solely to warm the Brookline side as its glow inched over their crowd (and the Colombo clan) momentarily, right to left. (Good call on the sweatshirts and windbreakers, Ma!)

"You should be wearing your glasses," Joe reminded me.

"But how do you know that," I squinted. "About the family?"

"That's the scoop. Everybody knows that."

"Not me."

"Well you must not be in the loop."

Evidently Joe's first semester enrolled at the high school had already promoted him to a broader scoop loop.

"Come on, let's take a walk," he elbowed me. "Get some popcorn or something."

"You read my mind."

It occurs to me now that Joe never had any intention of getting popcorn that day. We bypassed the snack shack without so much as an Austin nostril rising to take in the bounteous aroma.

*[Historical Note: *The Natick Redmen would go on to win that year's Super Bowl, although they were by no means a powerhouse, managing to score more than twenty-one points in a game just once in the regular season. Fortunately for them, though, their defense was rock stout, holding all but two of their opponents to a single touchdown or less and yielding no more than two TDs in any game.*]

"No popcorn?"

"We can get some on the way back. Will you look at this shit?"

Joe and I stopped to let the halftime trespassers dash by as they fled the field in a headlong huff, this week's interference presumably at an end. They howled and whooped through the endzone and hopped the track's surrounding fence at a dead run, en route to the wedge of lawn beyond the Marciano Stadium sign, their unofficial demilitarized zone.

"Good athletes," I said. "You got to give them that."

"They should put up netting out here, to snare these assholes when they come through, like in 'Planet of the Apes.' Look at them. Can't get over themselves."

In the clear now, they immediately threw themselves into a roughhouse version of Kill the Man with the Ball.

"Want to play," Joe asked with a sly twinkle in his eye, starting toward their triangular playing field.

"No, we don't even know them. Wait up. They're probably all in high school anyway."

"So what? I'm in high school. And you're just as good as they are anyway. Just pretend it's the Bridgewater scrimmage."

Joe had inherited from our Dad the ability to put things in a way that made sense to me.

"No..."

"Really? You sure? Well: I'm going in."

My brother strolled across the triangle right into the middle of the melee. I Followed as far as the edge of the grass, and could feel the shame of my apprehension along with my flat out admiration for Joe burning their way out of me.

Before you could say "forced fumble" Joe had stripped an unsuspecting runner and scooped up the loose ball. None of the gang objected. He took two giant steps, planted, and threw a thirty-yard spiral across his body *to me!* If I didn't duck or catch it, the beat up ball was going to hit me right in the face, so I caught it. Joe's maneuver elicited a general "Ah!" from the mob, as if to say, "Oh! So that's how it's going to be!" The would-be tacklers reacted as one toward the ball's change of direction like a Saturday morning soccer game of preschoolers.

The bloated football was worn to a pitch dark brown and smoothed of any texture it might have once had. Rather than starting out with some sort of evasive action, I took off directly at the pack. One of the first lessons I'd been taught about carrying a football was that running straight at a defender would either make him commit or would put him back on his heels. Either way, you would have the advantage. I kept going at them until they started taking aim to size me up, then I angled away as fast as I could around the mob's right flank, leaving some of them tackling air as I raced past and others flying right by me when I'd shift or hesitate. Those with a surer bead came in high, leaving their feet, sending me bouncing, twisting, quick-stepping along the perimeter of the throng until I finally shook free and left their cackling asses behind.

With the effort of sustained flight already starting to take its toll I reversed field, desperately pinballing my way back through the donnybrook.

Joe had apparently chosen to remain aloof, still as the Statue of Liberty, since throwing me that sink-or-swim pass a moment ago. Now, content to observe the proceedings from afar, he was applauding quietly as I rushed toward him, my horde in hot pursuit.

"Take it!" I blurted on my way by, thudding the ball in his bread basket. He promptly did an Eddie Popowski number, windmilling his arm and launching an underhand behind the back spiral to the area of sky high above the madding crowd, evoking more delighted jeers.

On our way back to our seats, with popcorn and Cokes in hand, Joe said, "Told you."

It would eventually come to pass, when I started playing running back my final year of Hercules, and again later in high school and beyond, that there'd be strange games now and then where for some reason I found myself galumphing through a pasture of orchard grass in cumbersome ill-fitting cleats; but then there were those rarefied times when I experienced that same sense of kill-the-man-with-the-ball unstoppability, crashing through tackles, tip-toeing by DBs with side steps and stiff-arms, finding wide expanses of open field at every turn— although, of course, such charmed afternoons would be few indeed, and very very very far between.

—

It would hardly be telling tales out of school to say that sports in general were a big deal in Brockton, and particularly so in our house.

That winter, Joe surprised us by going out for the high school wrestling team – a Dunn family first – instead of basketball.

"Maybe next year," he told me. "I've been thinking about this since the Gable Olympics. And Danny Kates [our cousin] wrestles for Duxbury. Figured why not give it a shot? I can always go out for hoops next year if I want."

Trying a sport completely new to him? Instead of playing one he already knew he was good at?

"Don't worry, I'll still go to the Y with you to work on your game."

Joe and Dad had been teaching (i.e., schooling) me on the Brockton YMCA courts for a year or so in preparation for my trying out for the South Junior High team. They would tutor me for a good hour, and then join in the nightly pickup games with the group of decent Y regulars, shirts/skins. In order to qualify for the five-man team who challenged the previous game's winner, they had to be one of the first five to make a shot from the foul line, which for Dad and Joe was pretty much automatic. I still remember one deft ball handler who played every night, a curly-haired six-footer, who strongly resembled in countenance and style former Providence College star and recent Celtics draftee, Kevin Stacom. (He even had "Stacom 27" written in marker just below the back collar of his green sleeveless t-shirt.)

I asked Joe, "That can't really be Kevin Stacom, can it?"

"How could that be Kevin Stacom when Kevin Stacom's got a Celts game in one hour? Come on, will you?"

"I don't know, I didn't think so, but…"

"If that dude – who I stole from and drove on last game – is Kevin Stacom, then I'm Slick Watts."

As a wholly inexperienced newcomer to the sport, I wouldn't have been surprised to be cut altogether but, along with my buddy Tess, I made the "seventh grade practice team" (aka the doormats over whom the varsity team ran roughshod at practice, and who were by no means entitled to dress for home games or travel to away games). The seventh grade squad was nothing to sneeze at, though. Just three seventh-graders – super smooth Manny Silva, big bad Mike Jackson, and world's greatest athlete Eric Abel – made the varsity team which went unbeaten that season (What can I say: championships in those days came like fruit from the refrigerator), and at the end of the year when the annual Seventh-vs-Eighth intrasquad game was played – and we got to use our three varsity guys – the lowly seventh-grade team actually won it on a controversial last-second off-balance one-handed heave from the corner by (no it was not a travel!) little old me, Underdog. (I know: Laughably lame self-promotion, but hey – you grow up in a sports town, you take your victories where you find them.)

As for Joe, he made the JV team as a freshman that year, which was not bad at all considering the Boxers starting lineup included some of the state's top-rated wrestlers.

Rich and Steve were looking forward to starting Little League in the spring, but both of them showed immediate interest in Joe's new venture, partly because it was right up their rough-and-tumble alley (e.g., A few years down the road, when Ma would go food shopping and leave Rich and Steve in the station wagon to watch their little brother and sister, the twins would pit young easygoing Gary and younger wirier Julie against each other in the way-back for no-holds-barred rounds of utter mayhem, best out of three falls. They called it "Crazy Larry & Sadistic Sally."), and partly because it was taking place right then instead of several months hence.

We all started going to the BHS gym with Dad to watch the Boxers wrestle. Joe told us which varsity guys to pay particular attention to.

"If all our best weights do well in the States, we'll have a good shot at winning the whole thing. That's Steve DeGiso right there. There's Donny Colombo."

"That's got to be Murray," Dad said, pointing to the sinewy pitbull pacing behind the team bench, smooth of gait, flaming orange hair, sliding low on one knee, shadow-grappling.

"Yup, Mitch Murray. Number one in the state last year. Look, here comes Mr. Colombo…"

It was indeed the man himself, striding up to the back row of the gymnasium bleachers.

"…He comes to all the meets."

Brockton wrestlers swept the first eight weight classes that night, with Ainslee, DeGiso (Steve), Murray, DeGiso (Mike), and Packard all winning by fall. Next up, athletic and brute, Don Colombo pinned his guy in forty-five seconds.

Watching him shake hands, I said, "So he's the linebacker on the football team?"

"Yup."

"Number forty-…?"

"Four," Joe nodded. "Danny's forty-three."

"Right."

Mr. Colombo was standing, ready to leave, moments after the referee's slap of the mat. I saw Donny glance up at him in much the same way I checked the left field foul line for my father during baseball games.

"I don't blame him," Dad said. "Guy probably has a million things to do."

"Can we stay for the whole match, Dad," Steve asked.

"Why, you want to see the heavyweights?"

Rich, Steve and I said, "Yes!" "Yeah!" "Of course!"

"Good. Me too."

"You guys want to go in town with me tonight to see Dave Cowens," Dad asked us one day. "And Havlicek?"

"Yeah!" "Where?"

"Boston Garden."

Joe squinted at me. "Where do you think?"

My question wasn't so unreasonable, was it? After all, hadn't Dad taken us to the K-Mart on South Main Street last year to see Bobby Orr and Mike Walton (we lined up at one of the registers to shake their hands)? And to Sal's Pizza in Codman Square to see Don Nelson and Satch Sanders when we were living in Dorchester (they mingled without fanfare among the customers as if caught ducking in for a quick slice – although both were dressed formally in dark suits with vertiginously long neckties)?

On the drive into Boston that evening, my father made sure to remind us, "Watch the way Havlicek hustles the whole game."

"That's alliteration," I pointed out. "We learned that in english. *Hav*licek *hus*tles the *whole* game."

Dad glanced at the rearview and went on, "He never stops moving without the ball. By the end of the game the other guy's going to be gassed."

I figured calling attention to my dad's phonological choice of words again wasn't absolutely crucial.

He had taken us to games at the Garden before and, along with the popcorn and peanuts, had always fed us some nugget or other of insight to chew on. I remember "Chamberlain's a cry baby" in particular because I simply couldn't reconcile in my mind the idea of that gigantic guy at the foul line (actually well back of the line) breaking into tears right there on the court. Another tough one to picture was, "Russell would stick him up his ass any time he wanted."

Joe and I enjoyed climbing with giant strides the tightly coiling ramp that led to the balconies. Settled in our seats, with the game underway, I said, "Look, Joe. Super Super John John!"

We always got a kick out of seeing that the same little sign was in the same place every time we came, hanging from the first balcony's front row railing, presumably by the season ticket holders of those seats, up behind the basket, off to the left:

>Super   Super
>John   John

"Dad, can we go walking around?"

"These stairs are steep," he understated paternally, cupping a match to light his El Producto (Blunt), sending a few precursory puffs toward the rafters and banners to mingle with the carcinogenic cloud hovering high above court side. "Be careful." (Over the years, when it came to admonishment or advice, Dad had developed a propensity for reserve worthy of your most laconic postgame press conference coach. When he deemed something "not bad" it was most likely excellent; "okay" meant it was a good bet it sucked; if he used the word "steep" you'd do well to assume that there was a perpendicularly sheer drop off involved, and in the case of Boston Garden's balcony stairs you would of course be right.)

"We will."

"You got your tickets?"

This was a veiled reference by Dad to an ignominious disappearance of mine several years earlier when he and uncle Jimmy had taken my brother and me to Harvard Stadium to see the Boston Patriots face Johnny Unitas and the Colts. High up in the concrete stands that day, Joe and I had sat in wonder, trying to estimate how many people the stadium could hold. Rows of concrete bench seating ran from one end of the giant horseshoe to the other, with vertical aisles dividing the rows into wide sections. Out of the otherwise unpunctured sprawl of solid concrete, a narrow entryway was cut near the base of each aisle, creating portals (of which we agreed to disagree after several countings there were thirty-eight in total) that resembled the crenels of a great military battlement. We watched fans swarm out of every portal until the pure grey canvas of the stadium stands was completely colored in by the capacity crowd.

At one point in the game I went to the men's room, and on my way back to our group I had somehow lost my bearings in the packed stadium. ("Should've let me go with you," Joe would joke for years to come, whenever a blunder of mine of any kind arose.)

Believing I was in the right section, with a view that seemed just about the same distance from the playing field as that of our seats, I respectfully excused myself one-by-one past fifteen, twenty, thirty tolerant fans in a row, only to discover that Dad and Jimmy and Joe were nowhere in sight; so I continued through to the next section the same way, "Excuse me," "Excuse me," "Excuse me," "Oh, I'm sorry!" "Excuse me," "Sorry, ma'am" "Excuse me," clambering my way sideways along an endless range of sneakered, shod, hard turned toes.

In the separating aisles I would pause to rest, scouring the crowd which was now chanting "We want Kapp! We want Kapp!" (in reference to Boston's newly acquired free agent quarterback); from there I'd push on for another section's worth of polite excuses until each successive section became a new case of déjà vu in Etiquette Hell, bearing me farther and farther afield.

Have you ever been out somewhere and had your car stolen? For a while your brain refuses to accept the evidence. You keep returning to your parking space again and again, bewildered. That's how I kept gazing up toward the place I'd been sitting, but where was everybody? They should have been right *there!*

I am not kidding when I say that I then deemed it the wisest course of action to simply go back, retracing my every step, excusing myself to the same rowfulls of somehow less tolerant spectators on the way, again, and again, and again, all the while craning in search of my long lost family. (Hey, maybe I'd missed them the first time through because they'd gone off looking for me! Or perhaps they, too, had to go for a pee… all of them… at once…)

Anxiety ratcheted up audibly in my quavering voice as I finished off each unsuccessful thirty-pack of begged pardons. To collect myself, I took refuge through one of the portals, descending to the ground level concourse beneath the stands. Down there I recognized the door to the men's room I had used earlier; or was mine the one farther down?

I wished I had brought Joe with me. From underneath the stands, all of the evenly spaced portals looked exactly alike. Rather than hunching and shuffling my way around the ankles and knees of any more seated Patriots patrons, I determined to take a more strategic tack. I ascended to the nearest portal in order to scan the sea of faces from a stationary position. Failing to spot anybody, I went back down and, one by one, tried every portal in the place until I was obviously standing on the opposite end of the stadium's horseshoe looking back across the field for any sign of a Dunn.

Well, what was there to do but start back in the other direction? If worse came to worst, I guess I could try to have Dad paged over the intercom like Ma sometimes had to do at Bradlees when I'd wander off. Okay, here we go; next portal. Let's try the one marked... Section 34.

Aha! What section were they sitting in? Was it written on the ticket in my pocket? Holy heaven... Yes! There it was: Section 4! Do the numbers go in order? Yes!

As soon as I made it to the other side and stepped through section 4's portal into the light of day, I heard Joe yell, "There he is! Greg!"

The pent-up anxiety was too much. Before I'd even reached them, I was overwhelmed with relief.

"Where you been," Dad asked.

"I got lost..."

Joe said, "On the way to the bathroom?"

"It's alright. Take it easy. Nothing to be upset about."

"Yeah, Gregory," Uncle Jimmy joked. "Calm down. Taliaferro's not *that* bad."

Although Joe and I were no longer little kids anymore, Dad made sure at the Celtics game that we did indeed have our tickets on us.

Wandering the ramps and stairways of Boston Garden, we would loiter at the Loge entrances to watch the game from different angles for a while up close.

"Joe, look," I remember saying. "That guy at the Y does kind of look like Kevin Stacom."

"He wouldn't have 'Stacom 27' on his back if he looked like Jim Ard, would he?"

On the highway out of Boston it was always a special treat to catch a glimpse of the shows playing as we passed the twin drive-in screens off the highway.

"Hey, the drive-ins!"

Dad said, "Okay, what's playing?"

"That one's... a... bunch of girls at the beach."

"Okay."

"And that one is... boring. A bunch of guys talking."

No matter what was showing, Joe and I couldn't tear ourselves away until the last sliver of screen had disappeared from sight.

—

In case my heavy hand hasn't sufficiently hammered it home... Brockton in those days was an ideal place for a sports-playing kid to grow up, particularly if his chosen sport was baseball.

The four junior high teams (scrappy North, talented West, also-ran East, and perennial power South) provided a very competitive transition from the prior summer's Little League ball to the upcoming Pony League's larger dimensions. Our South team my seventh grade year was one of the best I would ever have the frustration of riding the bench on, going undefeated as league champs. Even if I am the one saying so, my substitute status owed more to our team's overall talent than any difficulty I might have had with longer base lines and mound. Bob Johnson, John Sullivan, Mike McGillis, Joe Pomerleau, Eric Abel, Don Tessier, Chuck Colombo, Chris Gormley, DJ Bergeron were a tough lineup to crack. All-stars all, they would go on to distinguish themselves at the next level – with the strange exception of Bobby Johnson who for some reason decided to eschew high school varsity baseball altogether despite having been our talented team's best player.

In addition to the junior high circuit, Brockton's thriving summer programs too provided between Little League graduation and the advent of tryouts for the BHS and American Legion Post-35 teams four years hence a vehicle by which young ball players continued to sharpen their skills. Thirteen and fourteen year-olds moved up from Little League to Pony League, while the Colt League program fostered those in the next age group with aspirations to one day secure a spot on the exceptionally selective Boxer varsity and/or Legion squad.

Brocktonians simply loved their baseball, to the extent that the Pony League's annual citywide player "auction" was faithfully reported in the *Enterprise,* listing by name and team (and home address in some cases...) all of the eighty-five players worthy of being drafted. (In our first year of eligibility, Chuck Colombo was chosen first overall by Stall & Dean Company, to the surprise of no one. Drafted second by the Lions Club was Downey's own Wally Allegro, and to the double-taking surprise of yes one (i.e., me!), with the third pick in the 1975 Pony League draft, Teamsters Local 25 selected... *Yours Truly.***)

**[Acknowledger's Note: *By virtue of the Brockton Pony League's father-son rule, which decreed that an incoming player whose father happened to coach one of the ten teams would automatically be assigned to that team, power-hitting Steve Tuite went straight to Stall & Dean Co. without being involved in the draft, per se (thereby resulting in a much envied coup for Stall & Dean). As my brother Joe matter-of-factly apprised me, had Mr. Tuite not been head coach, there is no doubt that his son Steve would have been drafted ahead of me, and most likely Wally too.*]
—

As challenging as the transition was from Little League to Pony League that summer (distances of the mound, baselines, and outfield fences all lengthened greatly), it was my new role in the fall on team Hercules that took the most getting used to.

During the off-season, my father had assured me that this year I would be moved to the backfield, and probably linebacker too (although I'd never to that point played a single down on defense). In fact, he talked as if the matter had long since been settled, to the extent that I wondered – as I had in the case of the Bozo miracle – whether Dad had somehow colluded with the powers that be to make it so.

"In every game you're going to be one of the fastest guys on the field," he regularly reminded me in the parlor. "So when you get in the open, take off. Use your speed. Make them have to catch you, I don't care if you're running for the goal line or the sideline."

I would nod at the TV.

"And when the play's between the tackles, be sure you always hit the hole hard. No fooling around with stutter steps or any of that shit."

"Yup," I'd nod.

Sure enough, after the Hercules team race on our first day of practice, which, without Eric and Tess to contend with, I happened to win (those two guys had both ineligibly turned fourteen in the months prior to the start of the season instead of waiting until after September first as Chuck (9/5) and I (9/9) had wisely done), our offensive mastermind Mr. Benoit informed me that my services as starting center were no longer required.

"You're a linebacker now."

Fair enough, I thought. I could probably still wear my same number 55.

"And you're my starting tailback."

Oh well: there goes that. But hey – maybe I'd be given 43!

Chuck would later joke, "The best thing about you moving to running back? Kissing that freaking cup goodbye!"

At home, Dad seemed pleased. "Tailback. Good. That means it's just you and a lead blocker in the backfield, no other halfback."

"Aha..." With it being my first day at the position, I hadn't wanted to expose my ignorance to Mr. Benoit earlier by requesting clarification as to my new job title.

Dad gave me one of his curt nods. "Means more carries for you."
—

That fall was a landmark season in our house. My mother, who had always been the methodical yin to Dad's more spontaneous yang, made good on her long-standing desire to pursue higher education.

"Ma's going to nursing school, guys."

"Yeah, Ma!"

"So when it's time for homework or studying for tests, it's up to everybody to keep it quiet around here."

"Yeah!" "Of course!"

Our heartfelt but wholly unrealistic pledge of silence turned out to be moot because Ma had by this time mastered the maternal art of noise cancelation. All of her studying took place right there at her usual dining room table spot amid the usual household hum all around her.

One rainy day, Steve and Rich and I were lolling on the rug with our Doberman Pinscher Gretchen, goofily singing along to *The Banana Splits* while Ma studied.

"Tra la laaa," we sang. "Tra la la laaa…"

My mother looked up from her studies to turn a bemused smile on us. "Has everybody in this house gone crazy or is it just me?"

"You!" "You!" "You, Ma!" "Probably you!"

Shaking her head, she tapped the end of her cigarette into the ashtray.

"One banana, two banana, three banana, four…"

"Dad's home!"

"…Four bananas make a bunch and so do many more. Over hill and highway–"

"Hi Dad!"

"It's really starting to come down out there. How you guys doing? You letting Ma study?"

"Yup." "Good workout?"

"Three games of handball with Sully. And a nice sauna."

"D'you win?"

My father sneered at the silly question and said, "I was talking to Murray in the sauna [i.e., Mitch Murray of Brockton Wrestling fame]. He said he ended his workout today with a thousand sit-ups."

"No way." "All at once?"

"All at once."

Sitting on the rug in his BVDs, my ten year old brother Steve was not impressed. "So? That's not that much."

"It's not? You ever do a thousand sit-ups?"

"No," Steve confessed. "But I could."

"In a row?"

"Yeah in a row."

Dad said, "You sure about that?"

"I could do a thousand sit-ups right here. Right now."

Without missing a beat, my father called his bluff. "You do a thousand sit-ups right now, I'll give you a hundred dollars."

Steve looked at me. "Hold my feet and count?"

I grabbed hold of his ankles and my brother Steve was off.

He did the first hundred like he was rolling out of bed.

"Looking good," Dad had to admit.

A couple minutes later I said, "Two hundred!"

Although this performance was taking place in the center ring of the Dunn Family Circus, other routine business went on normally.

"You want something to eat, Joe? I was going to make burgers."

"You read my mind," Dad smiled. "You're studying, though."

"No, I'm almost done. Guys? Burgers?"

"Yeah!" "Cheese please!"

Joe moseyed into the parlor and took a seat on the couch to view the goings on. Even Gary was lured from his laboratory, carrying one of his notebooks.

"Three hundred!" I announced. "Actually, I'll wait on mine, Mum."

"I'll make them all now," she said. "Then you and Steve can heat yours up later if they need it."

What can you do but bow in the presence of perfect sense?

"I want mine now," said Steve. "I'm hungry."

Dad said, "You can't just stop in the middle to eat!"

"I'm not stopping."

"I'll put yours and Greg's on last," my mother said. "And you can just warm them up in the microwave after if you want."

"Why can't I have mine right now?"

"Not while you're doing sit-ups."

"Why not?"

"The man knows what he wants, Ma," said Dad, perhaps anticipating a timely C-note-saving cramp.

"Three ninety-eight... three ninety-nine... four hundred!"

At some point in the low eight hundreds, Ma said, "Ketchup, Steve?"

"Yuh."

"Here you go."

"Thank you." Steve held his burger in both hands, biting at the apex of his Up, and chewing right along for a few fluid down beats. On a rise he took another chomp and then with his mouth full he said, "Kayave some melk?"

Now he was just showing off, but the kid didn't spill one drop.

At the stroke of a thousand, he and my father both sighed and stood up. "Here's twenty bucks for now," Dad said, emptying his wallet. "It's all I got on me. I'll owe you the rest."

Steve promptly gave all the cash to me in return for holding his feet.

"I got to hand it to you, Steven," Dad announced. "You said you could do it and you did it."

I sat down to my big (still plenty warm) (ketchuped, mayoed, and relished) burger, while Steve walked stiffly to his room to remove with care his abrasion-stained underwear in order to check out the two burning raspberries glowing away on the bottom of his victorious butt.

The sighs of collective relief shared in the stands of Marciano Stadium in September, 1975, must have been something like what Yankees fans were feeling in the mid 1930s when their young center fielder, running third leg on that championship relay team of Ruth-Gehrig-Dimaggio-Mantle, picked up the pennant and flew it full mast all the way into the 50s. With pretty much all of Brockton's Super Bowl stars having matriculated, the new-look Boxers were intent on staking their own claim, and in so doing they proceeded to outscore their first two opponents 75-0.

On opening day against Natick, Joe and I found ourselves in our usual spot halfway up the home side stands on the forty-yard line. We saw reassured fans all around us nudging one another, nodding, "Yup, okay. That's better. That's more like it."

"This Damiano kid looks pretty good," someone said. "Throws a good ball. Good feet. I mean, he's no Pete Colombo…"

"Yeah, but who is?"

The big story that first game was how decisively we avenged last year's still-painful loss to Natick, but I was just as impressed with the emergence of the best running back that I had seen yet in a Boxer uniform. Big number 42, Phil Johnson, was sprinting and jumping his way around, over, and through the Natick defense, an adult among kids. Those well-oiled Wishbone offenses of Boxer teams past were formidable and unquestionably successful, but they hadn't featured a singularly explosive back like this before.

"Wow Joe, give me that program. Where they been hiding this guy?"

"Phil's been on the team for a couple years."

"Where? He looks like frigging O.J. out there. Leaving these dudes in the dust."

"No," Joe corrected, "O.J. scoots. Phil runs upright."

"What – he's a senior!" I couldn't believe it. "How the–? Why wasn't he out there last year!"

"He was, at DB."

"This guy's a running back, man! Look at him: big, fast, smooth. We could have used him. Against Natick!"

Joe turned to me. "Playing in front of who? Those backs were all seniors."

"I don't give a shit what grade somebody's in! Phil Johnson is exactly what we needed – somebody explosive."

"We had Delancey," I was reminded.

"Delancey wasn't doing this, Joe. Look – another nice run! O.J. better watch out."

As was his wont, my brother preferred to take the long view. Toward the end of the 35-0 thrashing, he said, "He's having a great day alright; two hundred yards at least; multiple TDs. But it's only one game against a shitbum team. Natick obviously sucks this year." As opinionated as he always was, though, Joe kept an open mind. "But actually, if he does keep this up all year, our Phil Johnson will rush for even more than 2,003 yards in a season."

The following week, on our way to the stadium for the Durfee game, my well informed brother said, "Should be no contest. Durfee's great hoops, great baseball. Shitty football."

After play had gotten underway, I wondered out loud, "Where the hell's Johnson?"

"That's him down there by the bench, in street clothes," Joe told me. "In the baseball hat. Blond hair. Holding – it looks like – a lollipop, of all things…"

I squinted a bit to narrow the focus. "Blow Pop?"

"Cherry, if I'm not mistaken," eagle eye Joe concluded. "No red-blooded male his age would be seen in public with a blow pop in his mouth!"

"Sheesh, okay, take it easy. What's so bad about Blow Pops?"

"It's right there in the name. Looks like you're slobbering all over a dickhead."

I laughed, but then realized he wasn't joking. "Come on, Joe," I said. "And hey – what about Kojak?"

"First of all, that's not reality. It's an idiotic gimmick on a stupid TV show."

"I like Kojak…"

"And second, those are Tootsie Pops."

"Oh. Yeah."

"And Phil Johnson, as you can see, is not fictitious."

"So that's him?" I squinted again. "You sure?"

"That's Phil."

"And you know him?"

"I don't know him but I see him in school, we're in the same building. I know who he is."

"So how come he's not dressed? What's the story?"

"Some kind of injury to his leg, they said. Thigh or something."

As it happens, senior halfback Dan Colombo filled in quite ably for Johnson that day, scoring on a pair of first half touchdown runs and looking good doing it en route to spearheading another Brockton blowout.

"What do you know," Joe quipped. "Number 42's out injured? Enter number 43 to replace him. No problem."

"I know," I had to agree. "Colombo looks pretty good out there."

"He does. Credit where it's due; he stepped up."

"Hell yeah."

"But I mean, we're not talking a Wally Pipp situation, or anything. He's never going to unseat Phil."

"No, but still…"

"And don't get me wrong, Danny's a great athlete. But running a football's not his true thing."

"Oh, no?"

Joe frowned, "Not even close. That boy was put on this Earth to play Baseball. Natural born hitter, pure and simple."

I had heard our South Junior High baseball coach say pretty much the same thing. "Mr. Fitz said that too."

"Mr. Fitz was right."

"He told us once at practice last year that Dan Colombo was the only blue chipper he had ever coached."

Throughout the remainder of the Durfee game, being of somewhat similar build as Colombo, I had little difficulty projecting myself vicariously onto the field, sporting his same jersey number in classic Dunn family tradition, and hearing my own name booming from the press box speakers during all the rest of his runs.

———

"That's why I always say," Dad reminded me over my shoulder one Sunday afternoon in the parlor. "If you're ever in a position where you know it's going to be a fight, and you can't avoid it: Make sure you throw the first punch."

I knew that like I knew my last name. "Yup," I nodded.

"That'll give you the advantage right off the bat." I sensed he was nodding too.

At the dining room table, my mother looked up from her studies. "Always be ready to defend yourself."

Dad agreed. "That's right, at all times. And landing the first punch is the best self defense there is. Ends a lot of fights right then and there."

My father and I had been watching Joe Namath pick the hapless Patriots apart.

"He's hobbling around, but he's still great, huh Dad?"

"Oh, Namath's a winner."

Memory's a funny thing. After all these years, I haven't been able to forget a particularly weird little tidbit about the game. For some politically abstruse reason, Japan's emperor was conspicuously in attendance that day in one of the Shea Stadium private boxes. (My mother, with her Sicilian sense of grudge, marched into the parlor. "Hirohito! What the hell are they doing letting this son of a bitch into our country? He attacked us!") Also, come to think of it, Jim Plunkett was benched that game, if I'm not mistaken.

My father heard me groan a bit when I shifted position to scooch a little lower against the hassock. The weekend previous, after a street-clothes and cleats walk-through practice, I was riding my bike home when I realized that the flat of the pedals happened to fit perfectly into the spaces on the bottom of my cleats at the arches; cool. Unfortunately when I popped too much of a wheelie off the sidewalk and tried to right myself by hopping off the back of the bike, my cleats stayed stuck to the pedals for a second. The wheelie continued its rise, rearing like an unbroke bronco. All I could do was hold on until I collapsed ass backwards (alas, no sissy bar), pulling the bike down on top of me, smacking the bend of my back on the corner of the curb. Eight days later and it still pained me a little when I coughed or laughed. (By the way, that *lime green* monstrosity of a bicycle was the Herculean joke of the season. Teammates complimented me on it relentlessly, and just in case the banana seat, chopper handlebars, speedometer, and ridiculous choice of color failed to catch your eye, you couldn't possibly miss that majestic insignia emblazoned across the chain guard in vivid black script: **The Dill Pickle**.) (What can I say? It beat walking.)

"How's your back?"

I felt okay, actually. "It's alright."

"You took a couple good hits out there today."

I nodded.

"Take yourself a nice hot bath before supper."

Ma said, "I think I got some good pictures today. I'm getting the hang of Dad's camera."

"Really?"

"On your first touchdown for sure. And then catching a punt. I was out of film on the last one, though."

Dad said, "You got to stop using up the roll on plays Greg's not getting the ball."

"I would if I knew when he wasn't getting it and when he was."

"Know what?" my father suggested, hopping up from his chair to fetch his own beer. (Apparently my having exerted myself well and truly in the name of Hercules earlier that morning was enough to warrant my taking the rest of the day off.) "Greg can signal us from the huddle whenever he's about to get the ball."

"I could whistle. Whippoorwill! Whippoorwill!"

82

My little joke made both my parents laugh. Dad said, "No, just something simple, in plain sight. Like, when your number's called, scratch the back of your calf with the other foot, or…"

"Or I can just pull up my right sock."

"Good, that's better. Do that," Dad decided. "Ma?"

"Got it."

"Yeah," I said. "And everybody else will be busy with their own stuff, so nobody'll be watching what I'm doing while I'm still in the huddle."

Dad sat back down. "That's right. But you know who will be watching? Because he was watching you today and asking about you?"

"Who?"

"Colombo."

I turned with a little groan to look back at my father. "Really?"

"He was at the game with Marciano's brother, and I was sitting a few rows behind them. And the whole game he was asking about you. How old you were, what grade you were in."

"Did you say I was your son?"

"No, one of the kids sitting near us told him all about you."

"Really?" This was another one of those uneasy yet somehow pleasing anonymity-puncturing realizations. "Wow…"

"I'll get a bath going for you," he said, on his feet again.

That sounded pretty good, actually. "Thanks, Dad."

While my father was running the bath, Ma said, "You know what I figured out about photographing punts?"

"Pray tell," I smirked.

My mother clarified, "Well, punt *returns*."

I nodded her along.

"When we got the pictures back from last week's game there was a good one of you catching a punt and another one at the moment right before the actual catch."

"Yeah, I like that one."

"Me too. And from what I can see, the punt returner is at his least…" she paused to weigh a few different terms, deciding on, "graceful... at the impact of reception. But a picture taken in that last fraction of a second before the catch captures all the movement and atmosphere of the play much better."

"I like that, Mum. You always put thought into what you do."

"Otherwise what's the point of doing it?"

"Touché, Madre."

That last season on Hercules was a fun one: my first time at running back, and my first time ever playing on defense. I was installed as our left linebacker, and Chuck was on the right.

"How you liking defense so far," Joe asked one Sunday night at dinner.

I nodded, "It's alright."

In our game earlier that day against the west side team, Howard Johnson's, I had come *that* close to my first pick-six. With their quarterback forced to throw under pressure from midfield, he sent a desperate Garo Yepremian pass fluttering directly toward me in the hook-to-curl zone without a HoJo's receiver in sight – without a HoJo's player of any kind in sight. In other words, the only things standing between me and the Marciano Stadium sign yonder was the golden H of goalposts welcoming me with open arms. As often happens in moments of such heightened clarity, time abruptly stalled to a crawl. Waiting under it like a kick returner, I zeroed in on the wounded duck's twisting tailspin as it floated and flapped for dear life in hopes of making it to Christmas in one piece.

Then, with visions of Mike Bass dancing in my head, I finally felt the abrupt chuck of my fellow linebacker as he knocked me aside and made the interception. Despite my stumbling efforts to help him keep his feet, he went right down untouched by the opposition. I couldn't really blame Chuck, though. He was making a play for the ball and he probably didn't expect that last second collision any more than I did; although we were quite obviously on my half of the field...

"There's a school of thought in football," Joe explained, twirling his fork in the gravy of his mashed potato volcano, "It holds that the best athletes are on the defensive side of the ball."

"Oh, yuh?" I was interested. Joe had never been a guy given to guffaw, but whenever he spoke up with a smirk, something sharp was usually on the way.

"And that's debatable," he went on. "Although I can certainly see the argument. They are great athletes, absolutely. But on the other hand, there's no doubt whatsoever that the smartest players are found on the offensive side. Know how you can tell?"

We were all waiting. Joe looked at me and I shrugged.

He said, "Because *they play offense!*"

We had ourselves a good laugh at the expense of all the dumb defenders.

If there had been any doubts as to which side I preferred to play on, they were well dispelled during the game earlier that day, courtesy of Wayne "Skip" McGee. Stocky and fast, he comprised the bruising bulk of the Howard Johnson's powerful running attack. At the beginning of the second half he took a toss sweep around his left end, bouncing off tacklers, as I hustled my way toward a point downfield on the far sideline. When he did break loose I was glad to see that I had anticipated correctly the proper line of pursuit. He might have been a bit faster than I was but I had the angle on him as I closed in to knock him out of bounds. When I launched myself at his numbers, full force, center mass, he had absolutely no room to maneuver. However, what Skip McGee evidently did have was a concealed lead pipe stiff arm with which I was abruptly poleaxed. I felt the shuddering *shock* and saw the sudden *flash* of completely unexpected exploitation. The next thing I remember being aware of was my fingernails clawing ineffectually at his thigh pad, and of him almost stumbling when his heel kicked me in the facemask. Then, lying there flat on the field, I had nothing to do but admire my ground's eye view of the perfectly undeviating chalk sideline as it ran, along with streaking number 32 in orange and white, the final forty-five yards straight to the endzone.

At our house on Deanna Road, Julie had a room to herself of course and my three younger brothers slept in one room at the end of the hall across from our parents. Joe and I were still sharing a bedroom, as we had always done, but despite our being very close in age and very close in general there was a definite sense of divide developing which never felt greater than at this particular point in our lives. Already a sophomore in one of the largest secondary schools in the country, brother Joe was blazing his own trail of independence while I was still pacing the familiar humdrum hallways of junior high as an eighth grader. I couldn't help but envy all the worldly experiences he must have been enjoying out there on a daily basis.

Don't get me wrong, I don't want to sound complaining about that year's scholastic experience because although I wasn't rubbing elbows with the athletic elite of Brockton High School as was Joe**, and while it was true that I had been condemned to trudge essentially the same three perpendicular courtyard-flanking corridors of South Junior High day after day from pillar to post and back again (the weary trudging of which at times felt like some kind of infernal – or at the very least purgatorial – penance), my burgeoning adolescence was nevertheless hard at work occupying my full attention most waking hours, keeping me inquisitive and alert to a host of hitherto unknown quandaries, realizations, and downright delightful earthly diversions.

**Joe routinely referenced his conversations with Donny Colombo, for example, who according to my brother would frequently show up for class during wrestling season wearing vinyl workout gear, having just come straight from a session of jogging the bleachers of the swim team's indoor pool; or he would relate to me his lunch periods spent in the Green Building cafeteria with quarterback Mike Damiano where they would peruse together accounts of the Boxers' latest football game in the Monday edition of the school newspaper. (Once, late in the season, Joe told me how Damiano had cracked up laughing but seemed genuinely taken aback while reading aloud from the Sports section of The Permanent Press, "The boxers responded when much-maligned quarterback, Mike Damiano, led a

ten-play scoring drive..." Every chomping mouth in the cafe turned on them, Joe said, when Damiano blurted, "MUCH MALIGNED?!")

It was during this seminal school year for instance that I first consented to the carbuncular clinginess of a fanatical teenage girlfriend (about which and whom the less said the better), and it was also this eighth grade year, I'm pleased to report, that the cement was poured for the formation of my lifelong friendship with good old Chuck Colombo. It is axiomatic that the regular gathering together as a group of any kind of athletic team cultivates an immediate and surprisingly amnesia-proof camaraderie.

So it was that on the Hercules Wrecking Co. practice field our camaraderie took root. Having since participated as a member of many such close-knit groups over the years on a variety of different teams (baseball, football, basketball, spring track, winter track, lacrosse), I can say with firsthand personal experience that each sport produces its own peculiar type of bond (yes, the vibe on an indoor track team is *very* different from that of its outdoor counterpart), none more cohesive than the one forged in football; and nothing in sports approaches the intimacy found in a football team's huddle, not even the holy union of pitcher and catcher; and further still, within the crucible of the huddle lives the most unbreakable brotherhood of all, that of the offensive linemen (sorry, D-line, it's not the same). Although Chuck and I were never members together in the fraternity of the trench, we were fortunate enough to become joined, for the first time that season, in the Order of the Most High But One: backfield mates.

"How does it feel to be fourteen," I remember kidding Chuck during our first week of school. His September 5th birthdate was hard to forget since it fell on the same day as my mother's and preceded my own by just four days. (I laugh now when I recall sometimes resenting his advantageous head start; if our birthdays had only been reversed I could have benefited from those *four extra days* of batting practice instead of him!)

—

The faithful supporters who filed into Marciano Stadium on those autumn Saturdays in 1975 were the furthest thing from frontrunning fair weather fans. On the contrary, the collective mindset in our home side stands was one of cautious optimism and healthy wait-and-see skepticism, but even the most discriminating followers soon ended up gnashing and keening, consumed with misdirected umbrage and the bitter bile of comeuppance, cursing themselves for their embarrassing hubris, because after having steamed full speed ahead over Natick and Durfee to the tune of seventy-five points to zero, the USS BHS suddenly foundered (seemingly overnight!), sputtering through the next four games, posting scores so feeble that they barely registered as scores at all: 0, 8, 6, and 6. (Yes, you read me right: three touchdowns in four games!) Only by the grace of good old Weymouth North did our Boxers somehow win one of those games, 6-0.

Much like their 1974 brethren, the '75 team found themselves at the two-thirds mark of the season all but out of contention. It was too bad too, because they'd definitely had their moments throughout the year, on both sides of the ball. Even with that titanic gash in the middle of their season, they still outscored their opponents 155-102. Although this statistic fell well short of their predecessor's dominant 241-131 point differential, '75's team finished with a win-loss record which was identical to '74's, a respectable but highly unbrocktonian six-and-three.

"Something's not right," our fans could be heard muttering on the way to their cars, downcast. "I don't get it."

"Damn sure missed Johnson those games he was out."

"Obviously. But it's not just that."

"Oh, no doubt."

"Colombo better do something, though," they agreed. "All's I know."

"Bet your ass."

—

Fortunately for Hercules Wrecking Co., we fared better than the big team that year, posting another unblemished record (unless you want to call our 12-12 tie with Howard Johnson's in week three a blemish, which we won't and I ain't asking). At the league banquet, all the Hercules players lined up to receive red windbreakers with our team name and the year and the word "CHAMPS" printed in blue on the chest (a sly color combination which as you know confuses the eye into seeing the letters hover and float in place and which entertained us to no end). A nice picture of me, Chuck, and lineman Tom Thibeault smiling next to the championship trophy in our fashionable bell bottoms and polyester print shirts appeared the following day in *The Enterprise*.

"Scrapbook time," Ma announced and turned her attention to the phone at her ear. "Ah – years: An order to go, please. One greek salad... large..."

"No anchovies, Ma!" "Cheese, please!"

Joe said, "So any time Greg gets his picture in the paper, we get to have Christo's? I'm going to start following him around with a camera and sending them in."

"Want to take the ride with me to pick it up," Dad asked him. "Practice for your driver's test?"

"Yes I do," Joe affirmed.

On more equal footing with Chuck since joining him in the backfield that year, it seemed inevitable for the two of us to hit it off. In addition to our temperaments registering within a few degrees of one another on the low-key end of the personality spectrum, we appreciated each other's sense of humor and we shared similar tastes, in music for instance. Winter and spring saw us spending pretty much every school day together since we were taking the same geometry class and we both played on South Jr. High's basketball (1-loss league champs) and baseball (undefeated league champs) teams. It wasn't to the point where we hung out after school or ever showed up at each other's house on weekends for pickup games (I had no idea where he even lived and, as far as I knew, Chuck had never set foot in Southfield), but as school friends we got along very well. I would liken our relationship at that time to the kind struck up in later years with certain guys at work, or with the joking regulars at the Y or the health club.

—

[Author's Note: *As of this writing (spring, 2022), Mike Trout is "mired in a slump", as they say. His 0-for-25 drought is certainly a frustrating inconvenience, but it will represent by year's end, beheld through the rearview of four hundred at-bats hence, a nearly insignificant depression in the season's endless highway. Major League ball players' seasons last forever; not so little boys'.*]

I became acquainted with the baked-in benefits of New England's comparatively brief youth baseball season during that eighth grade spring while playing shortstop for South. We had a very good team, to put it plainly. In fact we fancied the meat of our order to be the Murderers' Row of the junior high circuit. Chuck was our reliable rally starter batting second, followed by the incomparable Eric Abel. Hitting cleanup I was Gehrig to Eric's Ruth, if you will; in the Tony Lazzeri role was my line-driving buddy Tess. At the end of the season, Coach Fitzgibbons even arranged for us to play against the high school's freshman team. Many of our Pony League peers were on that team: Mike Barry, Wally Allegro, Mike McGillis, Dana Kerr – all-stars all. The game was held at their home field, a fenceless windswept pasture across from Marciano Stadium. I only remember two plays from the whole game. One was a routine line drive to short which ticked off the webbing of my glove when I mistimed my leap. I was already awkwardly on my way back down by the time the ball reached me. On the only other play of note, I was made beneficiary of an inside-the-park, as it were, home run after hitting a sinking liner which barely stayed fair and skipped past the left-fielder's outstretched mitt (i.e., future great friend Mike Barry's, whose balls I would occasionally enjoy breaking for years to come over this very play). Since the granite and grass outfield dropped off in a shelf in deep left and then ran all the way to the Shaw's parking lot on the horizon, the chase was on. I crossed the plate, retrieved my bat, and expressed to the opposing bench my wholehearted disagreement with their claim of "foul!" – all before the ball made it back to the infield. We won by one run, I think; or tied; or lost by one. I don't recall exactly, but it was a close low-scoring game, I know that. We made our point.

That junior high season lasted something like fourteen games, during the entirety of which I was hot at the plate. Had I fallen into a several game slump, it would have represented a sizable chunk of the season, seriously harming my on-base percentage and batting average but, truth be told, the word "slump" was as abstract a concept to me at that time as "pregnancy" to a virgin. Having never experienced one, I could only imagine what slumping might be like (if I thought of it at all), and since I possessed the extraordinary foresight and prudence of a suburban fourteen-year old, I spent precious little time pondering its wherefores.

Please indulge a moment of somewhat self-congratulatory digression: The tail end of that spring's South Junior High season happened to coincide with the fortuitous addition of home run power to my swinging bag of tricks. It first manifested itself at Nelson Playground, our home field, after a rare Saturday morning practice. While we were all dispersing to our waiting parents' cars or our bicycles parked against the backstop to go our separate ways, I saw that Chuck and Eric were lingering on the infield in conference. I slid my glove onto my handlebars. They were waiting for a man wearing Bermuda shorts and a long-sleeve undershirt who was walking to the mound with a catcher's mitt full of balls. Although stockier of build, he bore an uncanny resemblance to Rocky Marciano. It had to be Chuck's (maternal) uncle Peter, whom I had up to that point often heard of but never met.

As team batting average leader, I was not about to let those sly dogs gain any ground on me by sneaking in extra batting practice right under my nose. I removed my glove from my handlebars.

"A little extra BP?" I queried, jogging out to join them. "I'll help shag."

Eric and I set up shop in the outfield while Chuck took his place in the batter's box. He was a good hitter to all fields and he kept us busily roving the outfield for a solid fifteen minutes.

When it was my turn at bat, I wanted to show those guys that they had their hitting work cut out for them if they thought they were going to unseat me for the team batting title. I stepped into the batter's box.

"Where do you like them," Chuck's uncle asked, wiping sweat from his brow with his sleeve. I held out my left hand, palm down, in front of me and he nodded.

My dad's countless hours of batting practice had taught me to cover the plate well. When he'd work the outer third I would drive the ball to right. When he threw down the middle I'd send it straight back at him or into dead center field, but my preference was inner third, waist high.

True to his nod, Chuck's uncle Pete started grooving pitches right there into my wheelhouse.

"Give us something to do out here!" Chuck razzed from deep left field.

Even deep left field at Nelson's wasn't all that deep, but very few home runs were ever hit there thanks to the imposing fence in that part of the park. Nelson's entire outfield was enclosed in sturdy chain link, most of which stood seven feet tall whereas that section from the left field foul pole to the left-center power alley featured a triple-stacked facade which reached every inch of twenty feet high. Kids who played there called it the Chain Monster. Many a screaming liner chinged off of it during games, turning what would have been sure extra-base hits at any other park in the city into close plays at second if the left fielder played the ricochet properly and came up throwing.

After a couple long fly balls, I pulled one down the line over the Chain Monster. It bounced high off the pavement of Keith Ave. and clattered around on the front porch of the house across the street before Chuck collected it and threw it all the way back to his uncle on one hop from the porch. Other than a towering Eric Abel blast during the season, it was the first time I had seen a batted ball actually clear the fence.

"You caught that one nice," Chuck's uncle told me.

The next several pitches were popped out, grounded out, lined out. Then I sent another one over everything. This time the lady across the street gave Chuck a piece of her philosophy on the principles of privacy and trespassing. I flew out deep another few times, then launched a moon shot onto the lady's lawn. Where had this home-field power been all my life?

Trudging around the fence again to fetch it, Chuck groused, "Come on, Dunna!"

Of course I loved that he thought I could suddenly jack home runs at will, and far be it from me to disabuse anyone who overestimated my prowess at anything, even one of my friends – *especially* one of my friends.

"Sorry!"

Thank you for your indulgence because it was this newfound potency at the plate that served as the tipping point for my decision to bow out of football and its concomitant lower back ailments in favor of a year-round devotion to my first love, hardball.

It was something I had been debating for a while, along with whether to attend Brockton High at all. My classmate Mark Boone frequently talked about his older brother who had been a star football player for Cardinal Spellman. Brockton's "other high school" was set off by itself, tucked away at the top of a hill somewhere on the east side of town. We had lived in Brockton for years and I had never once seen it. Surprisingly neither had Joe although he seemed to know all about it.

"Their football coach, Pete Ambrose, has a good thing going there. He lives in Southfield, actually."

"Really?"

"On Paulin Ave. Right by the Tessiers."

"Mark Boone's brother was the running back there," I mentioned. "Or still is."

"Yeah, Joel Boone. He played in '73 and '74. Very good back. And they had Earl Strong before him. Strong was great."

"The two of them, one right after the other?"

"Yeah. Ambrose has a good program going."

"They Division-Two or -Three?"

"I think they're in Division-Four."

"Oh."

"But I remember Boone. Seemed like every other game he was *Globe* player of the week. Putting up crazy box scores. Four rushing TDs. A touchdown *pass*. A couple two-point conversions. Two hundred yards on the ground. All on fifteen or sixteen carries. And he would have rushed for a lot more yards, but the endzone kept getting in the way."

"So if Joel Boone had been going to Brockton instead, we would've had—"

"He wouldn't have played."

"Whuh?"

"Not at running back."

"Really?"

"Who's he going to start in front of? He would have been a receiver or a DB."

"But, I... You just—"

"Greg, you got to take those big stats that running backs post with a grain of saltpeter. First of all, it's Division-Four for a reason: Premeditated murder by stampede is against the law, and that's exactly what Colombo would be charged with if they let Brockton play Spellman. Secondly, it's all about the offensive scheme. If you're fortunate enough to be the feature back on a run-heavy I-Formation offense, and you're any good at all, you're going to put up some hefty numbers. You see USC last year? Ricky Bell barely had five yards a carry, but he led the country in rushing – almost 2,000 yards. Because he also led the country in carries, and every time they ran Student-Body-Right, Student-Body-Left, he was the student they gave it to."

Joe looked like he was about to go on a riffing roll.

He said, "Same thing with O.J. Simpson his senior year. He actually averaged *less* than five yards a carry. But give that dude the ball more than anybody else in the country? In that offense? No doubt about it, the rushing title's his. The Heisman Trophy's his. Shit, give *me* the ball 30 times a game behind that line and I'll guarantee you a thousand yards rushing myself."

"Heh!"

"Minimum!"

Joe was the best. I prompted him back toward his point, such as it was. "So…?"

"So this is why I've told you: We will never see a legit thousand-yard rusher at Brockton as long as they keep going Wishbone. When that triple-option's humming, it's too well balanced for any single running back to really stand out – statistically, I mean."

"Unless…?"

"Unless nothing. That great Boxer team of '73 put up something like 370 points, the vast majority of which came on the ground."

"And not a one of 'em rushed for 1,000 yards?"

"Nope: no feature back. And there's only so many yards to go around. So all three backs ended up with seven or eight hundred yards apiece. And I'll bet Pete Colombo had 500 yards himself that year, as QB."

"Wow," I said, considering that. "Oh, plus they had MacAfee."

"He was a monster of course, but the Wishbone limits its receivers too. Because MacAfee only caught nine or ten touchdowns that whole year. All the rest of their offense came from the backfield through that beautifully run option machine. In a different kind of Pass-First / Run-Second offense, MacAfee would have led the state in TD receptions, easy. It's all about the scheme."

"Right…"

"So that's why it might actually be smarter, from a strictly Dunn Family Scrapbook perspective, for you to do the Spellman thing… as much as I'd love to see you wearing the badass black-and-red of a Boxer."

My back ached just thinking about it. "Speaking of which, what's Spellman's mascot?"

Joe gave a quick chuckle. "Cardinals."

"Cardinal… Spellman… Cardinals?"

"I know."

"You mean the bird, I hope."

"Yeah, not the College of Cardinals cardinal," Joe laughed. "The bird cardinal."

"What's their colors?"

"Same as USC's."

"Ah, that's not bad."

"Yeah… cardinal red…"

"Come on now."

"… and gold."

"Wow. Cardinal frigging overkill."

"But come to think of it: Even though Ambrose does have a good thing going, we really can't do any better than Armond Colombo, right?"

"Yeah, no."

"And hey – you put your time in, you're going to get your shot."

I didn't know if he meant any guy in general, or me in particular. "Me?"

"Yes!" Joe spat. "You!"

"Alright, okay. Take it easy."

"Listen to me, Greg. You're a good baseball player."

I believe I shrugged.

"But you," he said, "are a natural born running back. You just don't know it yet."

Be that as it might, I was becoming fascinated with the idea of attending this mysterious little school on the hill. The boys wore jackets and ties to class, for Christ's sake! Also, I figured that I'd have a much better chance of playing varsity baseball as a freshman or sophomore at Spellman. You know: Bigger fish / Smaller pond.

—

I don't recall ever mentioning any of that to Chuck, but I must have somewhere along the line (or maybe Joe had let it slip to Donny – I really don't know) because out of the blue one day that summer, my father called me to the phone, "Gregory!"

Perhaps Noah was more dumbfounded when he received his fateful call. *Perhaps!*

"Hi Greg. This is coach Armond Colombo."

I heard myself go "Uh–" Then, "Hello. Good, ah… afternoon–" I stretched the phone cord into the bathroom, under the door for privacy.

"Greg, I heard you're thinking of going to Cardinal Spellman. Maybe playing soccer instead of football."

I don't know how soccer got in there, but I said, "Yes."

"You've been to Marciano Stadium to watch Brockton play football, right?"

"I have. A bunch of times."

"Then you know: Only the best of the best play football for Brockton High."

I felt myself nodding.

"I don't know if you've heard, but Eric Abel's family is moving to Florida."

I had heard about that.

"We're missing out on a very special player."

I said, "Eric was… he's…"

"We don't want to miss out on you too, Greg. Because I see you doing great things at Brockton."

"–Oh."

"And I want you to know, if you do decide to come out for the team this year, I can guarantee you'll be on the sideline, dressing for varsity games, home and away. As a freshman."

This was stupefying, to say the least. I honestly don't remember how the call ended. Maybe I said, "Where do I sign?" In addition to the above dialogue, all I do remember is a buoyancy inside that has in my experience only been rivaled by the epiphany of love.

Other than my parents, Armond Colombo would ultimately exert the greatest influence on my life's course of any person I've known, an influence and impact that began right then with those two minutes on the phone.

'Back ache, schmack ache' I thought. 'Brockton Football here I come!'

―

Late one evening early that summer, watching TV in Dad's chair while Ma studied in the brightly lit dining room, I heard my father pulling into the driveway so I hopped up and took position in front of the refrigerator, poised.

As I would sometimes do, I pulled a bottle from the fridge, spun on my heel in that patented quarterback pirouette of mine, faked to the fake fullback and finessed my way out of the kitchen to deliver the handoff to Dad when he came through the door.

With arms held parallel on the horizontal, forming a spacious breadbasket strike zone, Dad bent forward to hug the handoff and paused there to say, "That's the way. Direct with two; give with one; look it in."

You could've smelled the wood smoke on my father from down the hall, but at such close quarters the pungent emanation was about to absorb me bodily.

Dad took his seat with the sigh of a working man ready for rest. I slouched on the rug, backed up by the hassock.

My mother came over to give him a kiss and a pat on the chest. "Hungry?"

"I had something at Florian Hall."

Ma said, "We saw that fire on the news last night."

"Which one?"

"Roxbury."

"We had a few in Roxbury."

"It said Humboldt Ave."

"Oh, yeah," Dad nodded, swallowing a swig of beer. "Working fire. Everybody already got out but it took a while to knock that one down. Good fire."

"All the guys alright and everything? Nobody hurt?"

This was a fair question of genuine concern, but it clamped my gut. Ever since the tragic Hotel Vendome fire of 1972, when nine Boston firefighters perished, most of whom my father had known (including one that I myself had met at a department softball game), I'd made it a point of never again inquiring. Firefighters, it turned out, could die in oh so many ways: 5-story hotel walls collapse, floors fall away, roofs cave in; explosion, smoke inhalation; on the way *to* the fire, on the way *from* the fire; *ambush* ("They threw a box spring down at us from the roof across the street as soon as we pulled up."), even false alarms ("Remember I told you about that time with Vinny Dimino?").

Dad kind of laughed, taking another swig. "Nothing about the fire hurt anyone, put it that way."

"Huh?"

"We were the first house in. It was already going real good when we got there. It took a while just to get up the stairs. So we made it to the second floor and were on our bellies in the hallway–"

"Who was with you," I asked.

"Me, DeGrandis, Stanton..."

"Uh-huh." These were guys I'd come to know from cookouts at our house. They'd all end up carousing in the backyard at the picnic table long into the night, laughing and drinking and cracking us up with hilarious firehouse stories, one more outrageous than the last, until it was way too late for anyone to leave.

"...Damon, Buckley, Jimmy McDonald, Paul Moore."

"Oh," I said. "All of engine 42."

"From our group, yeah. So, half of us were laying in the hallway, and the rest were behind us on the stairway. Then another engine got there and tried to climb by our guys on the stairs."

"Oh..." said Ma, understanding. "No..."

"What?"

Dad said, "When you're the first house in, you never let another house overtake you. Lead house is lead house, start to finish."

My mother attested, "First in, last out."

"That's right."

"What happens, though? If another house tries to get by you?"

"Heh!" Dad scoffed. "What do you think happens?"

I felt my head shake and my shoulders shrug. "Aono."

"Brawls happen."

I said, "No... *Fist* fights?"

"Bet your ass."

"Right then and there?"

"Right then, right there."

"Inside the burning building?"

My father started laughing. He chucked the hassock with his heel to reset my equilibrium. "Yuh, Greg!"

I was laughing now too. "Well I don't know!" I could feel my face fighting a gape. "So– Hold it hold it... Sheez... Hold on... So... Did they– Heeh... Did they get by?"

Some of Dad's swig came spitting out. "Hah! *You* try getting by Donald Damon!"

I said "Wow" again. When I looked at Ma she just raised her eyebrows.

Dad said, "Remember that time, with the fire next door?"

Of course I did. "Yuh."

"Remember I went over there and went right in?"

"Yup."

"Fire in Boston, that'd never happen. It'd– it's... unheard of."

"They'd have kept you out?"

"Bet your ass."

I was mulling that over when a barely heard "hut-hut" came out from somewhere under Dad's breath. He tried to handcuff me with a quick shovel pass but I trapped it against my chest for a short gain.

After a while, Ma wrapped up her studies and the dining room went dark just as the sky outside was doing the same. My father nudged the hassock with his wool-socked foot, rousing me.

"Huh?"

"Sleeping?"

"*No...*"

He said as if repeating himself, "I said, I thought Ma told me you were staying over your buddy Conrad's tonight."

"Oh." I growled to clear my throat. "We were supposed to." Again I gave a quick clearing cough. "But then he remembered, he had to leave for football camp today."

"Colombo's camp?"

I yawned, "Awww... yuh."

"That starts today? Why didn't you say something?"

If I hadn't been stretching my arms over my head I might have shrugged. "Aono."

There was vexation in my father's voice. "I thought you wanted to go to that?"

I said, "I don't know," and then clarified, "Not really."

"What town is that?"

"Brewster, wasn't it," my mother offered, stopping at the kitchen doorway on her way through the parlor.

Dad stood up. "How long's it take to get there?"

Ma shook her head. "Hour, hour and a half down the Cape."

Whoa, whoa, whoa, whoa, whoa. Unless I was badly mistaken, my father was actually considering crashing Armond Colombo's Cape Cod football camp without so much as a registration, invitation, or even prior conversation. My gut clenched up again.

Dad said, "Isn't he expecting you to be there?"

"No. We never–"

"What'd he say when he called you that time?"

I said, "Nothing. About the camp..."

"Are you sure?"

I knew that conversation like the Pledge of Allegiance. "Yes."

"I thought you told me he did."

I was trying my best not to doubt my account, but... had he? Or was it possible that I had been somehow unclear in relating that unforgettable phone call to my father? "He talked about trying out for the team," I mentioned tentatively, replaying the words to myself in my head so as not to mislead or misquote, "but he meant the actual varsity team tryouts at the end of the summer." I added more for my benefit than his, "The regular tryouts."

Since rising a moment ago, Dad had stepped into his boots, walked to the bathroom, and urinated with the door open, all the while holding up his end of our conversation. It eventually occurred to me that my carefully parsed wording was unnecessary and altogether beside the point. Everything was settled: Brewster or bust.

"Pack a gym bag with some shorts, socks, underwear, and t-shirts. And sneakers, and your cleats, and your cup. You got a mouthpiece? Rose, you want to take a ride?"

"Years. I'll drive."

"Let's go, Gregga. Hustle up."

I had been a Dunn for a while at that point, so I knew that our leaving was already a foregone conclusion. The best I could do was concoct a subtle time-buying stall, perhaps until morning, and hope for some miracle to come in the form of an overnight theft of our car, or flash flood, maybe a death in the family.

I practically yelped, "We're leaving now? It's starting to get dark already."

"I'll be in the car," Ma said helpfully.

All subtlety forsaken, I declared, "We should go in the morning, bright and early."

"I got errands first thing tomorrow." "You can't show up on day two!"

An hour or so into our road trip, I had my head leaning flat against the backrest and my eyes closed. I could feel places under my arms where the anxiety had soaked through.

Rising at a suddenly alarming angle, I heard my voice come out just shy of a whine, "What bridge is this?"

"Sagamore," Ma said, snapping the map. "Indian for Algonquin chieftain." She opened the passenger fly window to breathe in the breeze of the canal. "Something like that. At the bottom get on 6-East, Joe."

Our Pilgrim predescessors had navigated the narrow trailways of Cape Cod without benefit of electrified street lights to guide their way, like it or not, and so did we.

"It's kind of nice down here," Ma said. "Quiet. No place for your car to break down, though."

"Not at night," Dad agreed.

When we finally pulled off from the darkness of the road into the darkness of the wooded campgrounds, the only visible light was high in the night sky. The rhythm of Brewster's vociferous crickets rang through the amplifying trees, their busy signals boomeranging back and forth.

"Here's a few bucks for your pocket," Dad said. "Try to get a ride back with Conrad if you can."

I managed, "Okay."

"You made it here on day one, so you're all set. Just find a bunk in one of the cabins and you'll be fine."

I nodded.

Ma said, "Have fun, honey."

"Yup."

"Play hard, Gregga. Show Colombo what you got."

As my parents quietly pulled away I saluted them, touched by their overall modicum of fanfare, as if such pain-in-the-ass midnight rides were par for the parenting course.

The first cabin I came to was dark and still so I was as cautious as could be when I pulled the plank door open and stepped inside.

Then, tangibly close to my now contorting features – practically tooth to tooth – a brutish nose guard of the NFL's leather helmet era in quasi-female form somehow *became* in my path.

Have you ever been truly startled in the dark? Shocked by an unseen life-size thing shrieking in your face from out of pitch blackness? Odds are most likely not; so please take me at my word on this one: Some kind of hellbent banshee will, quite on its own and without exception, explode from the top of your throat cavity with a cry the likes of which you've probably never heard and by the grace of all that's good in the world one you've never had occasion to make yourself.

Italics, capitalizations, and the pedestrian glyphs of conventional English language keyboards can hardly do justice to the menace contained in that counselor's choice of curses. Suffice to say, her screams made the heat leave my body all at once and made the crickets instantly hang up on their calls. Fortunately, I was able to fend and parry and plead my innocence before any really harmful blows were landed.

From that dubious *entree* I was ushered off to a separate darkened cabin of wisecracking bunk-bedded teenage guys (obviously teammates all) where I was allowed to occupy a vacant bottom bunk for the night. Their jocular repartee played harmony with the call backs of the undaunted crickets to, quite to my surprise, lull me at last into a dreamy sumptuous sleep.

Apart from that actual first impression, my next first impression of football camp was positively pleasant in the form of a kickass breakfast buffet, presented as a panoply of inviting bright colors and fulfilling aromas, everything laid out in a long row of big metal rectangular trays. There was tray after tray of scrambled eggs, crisp bacon, sliced cantaloupe melon and honeydew melon, country sausage, browned home fries. Each different food lay separated by a single tray of toast (white toast; rye toast; pumpernickel toast; wheat).

"Take all you want, but eat all you take. Nothing goes to waste!"

I helped myself to all of it, including two huge ladles full from a mountain of the whitest fluffiest tapioca dessert I had ever seen. I don't have much of a sweet tooth, but I couldn't resist piling it high and heavy on my plate. When I sat down, it was the first thing I tried, scooping up a great big mouthful which prompted the kid sitting next to me to declare, "Wow, you really like cottage cheese, huh?"

It turned out by week's end, most unexpectedly, that my much anticipated first ever meeting with coach Armond Colombo did not come to pass. Whenever I saw him running players through their drills, he always happened to be working with the older kids, or leading drills at the opposite end of the playing fields. After a couple days it occurred to me that he might very well have not even known I was there at all and, come to think of it, why would he have?

By the time our instruction had culminated in the big final day scrimmage, I had – in another discouraging instance of coaching caprice – been assigned to share second string wingback duties with a rah-rah kid from Milford. I ended up with zero carries for the game to go along with zero catches on one red zone target which was intercepted as I prepared to catch a sideline pass in stride at the pylon. The Milford coach scolded me for not trying to catch the ball at its highest point.

What had been achieved?

—

The next time I was to see Armond Colombo would come later in the summer, and once again it would take place from afar.

Earlier that August afternoon, my father and I had gone to lunch at the Maui.

"If you get a chance to play this year, it'll probably be on special teams."

"This year? No…"

"You never know," Dad said. "Someone gets hurt? You got to be ready."

That was true.

"If it's on punt returns, always catch everything. But watch out. Even on a fair catch, refs almost never call interference. So be ready for guys to be right in your face or to get bumped a little. Unless you're flatout pancaked before you touch the ball they won't throw a flag. Like how umps look the other way on double plays when fielders don't touch second. Nobody ever gets called for it."

"Okay."

"And remember, the other team's going to be flying down the field so to give yourself the advantage make sure your first couple steps are straight upfield if at all possible. That way you're making it that much harder for their outside guys, cutting off their angles. Afterwards make whatever cuts you have to."

That made sense. I nodded over my chicken lo mein (don't ask how I remember the food).

"On kickoffs, too. Same thing. No matter what direction the return's going, your first few strides should be straight up the field. And remember, on a kickoff you're going to be running at full speed. As they approach, most of them'll be getting blocked or be back on their heels, so don't get cute with that jitterbug crap. You're running full speed all you have to do is lean a little to one side and keep on going. You'll blow right by them."

This would turn out to be a very useful lunch.

Later on at home I was hanging out with Gretchen in the back yard when my father called me in to the phone. It was Chuck informing me that I had missed Brockton High's first captains practice of the season which had been held the night before.

"What the– nobody told me!"

"It's Monday through Friday at six, at Eldon B. This week and next."

"I had no idea!"

"No problem, just don't miss any more."

"Are you sure?"

"It's fine."

I hung up and gave my father the details. My consternation was obvious. He said the same thing Chuck had said, "Don't worry about it, just don't miss anymore."

"If I had known…" I groused.

"Forget it. Six o'clock?"

"Yuh."

"Alright, we got time. Got to go to the bathroom? Do it now, then let's go."

At five minutes to six we pulled up at Eldon B. Keith Field. Two blocks west of downtown, it was actually the varsity baseball team's home field, and I had played several Pony League baseball games there over the past two years. The entire infield was made of dirt, and the outfield fence fronted West Elm Street down the left field line and ran all the way to a very deep center field.

Apparently this was where the varsity football team used to play too before Marciano Stadium was built. Legend had it that upwards of 10,000 fans used to pack this place for games in the 30s, 40s and 50s, but I couldn't see how. There was just one small section of dried out wooden stands (you couldn't very well call those things bleachers) along the third base line behind the Brockton bench. Nowadays, such sparse seating could accommodate no more than a few hundred fans, tops. Judging by the position of the stands, and the one remaining set of goal posts behind the visitor's bench on the first base side, it looked like the third base / left field foul line must have served as one of the football field's sidelines, so the other team's side line would have been out in right.

There must have been a hundred guys in shorts and t-shirts congregating on the outfield grass casually horsing around and limbering up. So these were the players my brother and I had watched at the stadium last year. I wondered which of them was Damiano, which was Lalli, which was Saba.

"I'll be back in an hour."

"Thanks, Dad."

"Go get 'em."

Chuck was the only one I would have already known, so I sought him out as I walked across the infield. By the time I reached the group at the edge of the grass in shallow left field, I saw him talking to some older guys. They looked like football players, even larger in real life than I'd expected, and considerably hairier too, with full mustaches and beards. They were all commenting on an elegant white 2-door coupe pulling up outside the fence in right center field.

"Does your father know how much it fucks with everybody having him sitting out there watching?"

"Absolutely," Chuck laughed.

"Watching. Lurking. Looming," another guy intoned ominously. Then with a suave Latin American accent he purred, "Driven in luxury. With fine Corinthian leather. In our new... Chrysler Core-dough-bah."

"Somebody's got to keep an eye on you hoodlums. Make sure no one makes off with the stinking goal posts."

A clock somewhere must have struck six because a bunch of guys lurched as one into a jog toward foul territory and everybody fell in behind them. We did a lap on the perimeter to warm up, approximating a typical quarter mile track, which took us down the third base line toward home, around the backstop, past the goal post ruins, up the right field foul line, and along the entire outfield fence. One of the leaders ran the latter half with his shorts pulled down, mooning us.

Jogging beside me, Chuck laughed and shook his head. "Fucking Damiano."

According to the Massachusetts Interscholastic Athletic Association (our state's governing body), it was against the rules for teams to hold formal practices prior to the official start of preseason which was still a couple weeks away. This explained why Chuck's dad was posted clearly outside the bounds of Eldon B. Keith Field, and it perhaps also explained why there were no footballs in sight on the field itself. For all the world we young men could have been gathered this evening for the sole purpose of taking part in some good old group calisthenics among friends. And that gentleman parked in the car out there? Oh, just your average Brocktonian, citizen Colombo. It could have been anyone minding his own business in a non-coaching capacity, relaxing of a summer evening on public property, enjoying his car's luxurious A/C. A few other cars pulled up during our exercises to observe alongside the Cordoba. In fact, these same vehicles returned night after night. Could they have been assistant coaches? Interested dads? Who knows?

Chuck had referred to these nightly gatherings as "captains practice" but a more accurate name might have been seniors practice.

After our warm up lap all the seniors formed a line twenty abreast with a couple arms lengths between them. The rest of us fell in, facing them in several evenly spaced rows, juniors up front, then sophomores, then freshmen of which there were three including me.

Once again the shelter of anonymity suited me just fine, thank you. I was perfectly content to remain within its cozy confines, performing my stretches, squat thrusts, sit-ups, leg lifts, push ups and such from the safety of the back row.

It's nice sometimes when you don't know what to expect; just like that week spent at football camp, even the most mundane feature comes alive with the novelty of it. I remember enjoying the coolness of the grass during three-man weaves with Chuck and John Millett (a beast of a freshman and the son of legendary lineman-cum-coach, Chet Millett), and its rich smell, too.

"Alright, wind sprints!" a burly senior commanded after calisthenics were completed. "Ten to a line! Let's go, sophomores! Get up here!"

We all merged with the forward rows, abandoning the hierarchy of seniority.

"220s! To the goalposts and back! It's your ass if you come in last!"

Someone called, "How many?"

"Six of them!"

"Ah, fuck…"

"Go!" the burly one shouted at the first row. Then to the next row, "Go!" Then the next, "Go!"

The wind sprints suddenly transformed our leisurely frolic into something rigorous, more along the lines of what might be expected of such a highly competitive program as Brockton's.

When my 10-man flight took off on the "Go!" I almost immediately clipped heels with another runner, just like in the Hercules team races. I barked, "Sorry!"

In case you didn't know, the gods of Sport, just like their capricious big brothers who oversee War and Fortune, are a tricky bunch. That is to say they like to play tricks on you, and not necessarily in the spirit of good clean fun. I think they get it from their father. They'll set traps and throw up obstacles for no greater reason than sheer boredom it seems. They're partial to irony, too, and their trickery is legend. You can find it writ large on a global scale (as with the wicked prank pulled on women) or writ inconspicuously small (as with the mind of your friendly neighborhood bigot).

During that first captains practice their trickery alighted on me in the form of clipped cleat heels. I had stumbled for a few steps, but managed to regain my stride. How awkward would it have been for coach Colombo to see me plant myself face first into the grass by way of salutation?

Somehow a moment later it happened again. "Whoa!"

Then, for a third time our feet got tangled. I looked behind me. The laughing hyena pulling this particular trick was one of the larger mustachioed seniors. "The fuck you looking at," he scowled, trying once more to swipe at my cleats. Although I had been sprinting already, I turned and really took off to add a layer of separation. You have to understand, at that point in my life I was still very much the naïf. As far as I knew, oaves* were neither good looking, nor athletic, but here was this guy, oafish in every regard except physical.

For every one of the 220s, he made it his business to trail me to the starting line and kick at my feet once we took off. At one point I heard Chuck behind me yell, "Hey, cut the shit!"

There wasn't much recovery time between sprints. Pretty soon wind got short, mouth got dry. I remembered an old workout hack my dad had told me about: A couple pebbles under the tongue helps generate moisture.

*[Coining New Currency: When it comes to the plural form of "oaf", I prefer "oaves" to "oafs". Anyway, I cleared it with my brother, Joe – or rather, he cleared it with me – so you need not turn to the OED or your trusty Strunk & White usage manual. Joe says, "Fuck them. Professional "I" crossers and "T" dotters. It is not too late in the language to coin new words, Greg. Not even close, remember that. It's never too late."]

After the last 220, we were told, "Mile warm down!" by which the burly senior in command meant four times around the perimeter. "Let's go! Rest when you're dead!"

Toward the end of our third lap, the Maui's chicken lo mein surged out of me (and I guess *that* is why I still remember so specifically my earlier lunch choice). In a few totally uninhibited convulsions I retched up one colorful outpouring after another in gooey intervals onto the grass in deep left field.

Upon our completion of the mile, Chuck came over. "That asshole's an asshole," he said. "Don't mind him."

"Where are the Ralph Abbruzzis of yesteryear?" I spit out my pebbles. "What a fucking clown."

"I know. Look at the size of him. He doesn't even start!"

Chuck's a good dude.

When I got in the car, my father said, "How was it?"

I smirked, "Puked on the mile run."

"Yeah, I saw that. Wouldn't have gone to lunch so late if we knew."

"Chuck never told me!"

"Nah, nah," Dad corrected me. "Don't try to blame Chuck. You got something going on, it's up to yourself to make sure it's all straightened out."

"Yeah."

I was just hoping he hadn't caught my little heel-toe tap dance with Emmett Kelly out there.

"And how did the rest of it go? You run any actual plays? Wishbone?"

"No, we just did stretches and cals and stuff."

My father nodded. "Let's hope Colombo saw you throwing up."

I said, "Let's hope? Why?"

"You never stopped running while you were doing it. Shows him you're a tough kid."

—

All through the remaining captains practices, my wind sprint tormentor kept after me. As far as I could tell it wasn't due to any organized team policy for the razzing or hazing of newcomers; I was the only one it was happening to. Then again, no senior in his right mind would haze Armond Colombo, Jr., aka Chuck, and you'd be taking your life in your hands messing with John Millett. So maybe that just left little old me.

I had recently read Lance Rentzel's book which detailed the raunchy initiation rituals he was subjected to while playing football at Oklahoma. The stuff I was enduring at Eldon B. Keith Field paled in comparison, but still – it's always disconcerting to be singled out for harassment, regardless how lame it is.

During one of the last captains practices, Chuck stuck up for me again, "Cut the shit! What's wrong with you?" It fell on deaf ears.

During our warm down jog, I said, "Thanks back there."

Chuck scoffed, "Course."

"What the hell's up with your paisan? What's he, drunk?"

"He's not *my* paisan!"

"Well, I mean, insofar as you are both 'of Italy.'"

"In so far as? Who are you, Mr. Twomey?" [In Ref. to dry-humored South Jr. High English teacher William Twomey.]

"Heh!"

Coming back to the point, Chuck said, "Of Italy? If that dude's 'of Italy' it's in name only, believe me." He scoffed again and laughed, "My paisan..."

This was my first ever experience with such monkey business. Knowing that Chuck had my back helped a lot, but to this very day I don't know what it was about me in particular that rubbed my man the wrong way. It was certainly something, though. Still, as much as it unnerved me, it was mostly just bewildering. What depths of sadness and abuse must this poor clown have undergone at home to make him focus his misdirected anger on a much younger, much slighter, complete stranger like me? I could only imagine.

—

On the Saturday following our two weeks of captains practice, all players were outfitted with helmet, pads, practice jersey and practice pants in preparation for the upcoming start of double sessions on Monday. Grueling two-a-day practices would comprise the varsity football team's tryouts proper. On Sunday night I went to bed as early as I could.

At 7:30am the next morning my father, brother Rich, and I pulled up to the Store 24 outside Eldon B. Keith Field. Dad gave Rich some money. "Here, go get Greg a juice and one for yourself, and something to snack on later."

"What kind of juice?"

"Anything," I said. All I had in mind right then was how my first meeting with Coach Armond Colombo was going to go.

"Supposed to be a muggy one today," Dad mentioned. He could sense my preoccupation, I think. He said, "So, remember – you go to the front of the line on every drill. Blocking, tackling, it doesn't matter."

"Yut."

When Rich came back out he had two small bottles of apple juice and two Devil Dogs.

"Want yours now?"

Drumming my thigh pads with my thumbs, I asked him to hold onto mine for now.

We pulled the car around to the back of the store to park right next to the field itself.

"Play hard, Gregga. Show 'em what you got," my father nodded.

I nodded too.

"You sure it starts at eight?"

I looked around. Dad was right, there should have been players idling on the field already; coaches arranging things. "Yeah," I said unconvincingly.

A car speeded to a stop beside us, skidding over the gravel. Four older guys I knew by sight from captains practice piled out in shorts and t-shirts. From the trunk of a dull black Pontiac they pulled their helmet and pads. The facemasks protruding through the neck of the shoulder pads formed convenient carrying kits for the young stevedores to hook and hoist high on their backs. I guessed these easy going fellows were fixing to suit up right there on the field. Maybe that was the Boxer way, I noted for next time.

From the back seat, my trusty brother offered, "Want your helmet?"

"They're all heading over toward the building," Dad said just as the same thing dawned on me. "Follow those guys."

Rich was already outside of the car, my helmet riding his hip. He was more nervous than I was I think, chewing on his Devil Dog, looking off toward the building.

My father gave my shoulder pad a smack with the butt of his fist. "Go get 'em."

"Yut."

"You're good at this game. Have fun."

As the stevedores strolled toward the brick building's basement door, we fell in behind them. Arriving at the pool party in a tux, I was making a point of trying not to over exaggerate my feigned nonchalance.

Rich handed me my helmet outside the door. "Should I wait out here," he asked.

"Ah... yeah, probably."

"Want your drink?"

"Actually, yeah, give me that." I put my arm around his shoulders. "Thanks, Richa. We should be out soon. It has to be getting close to eight."

The heavy dent ridden door was in the rear of the great Mass. Volunteer Militia building, better known locally as the Armory, whose street-facing side presented a faux fortress battlement to loom over the vehicle and foot traffic of Warren Ave. Its entire basement level now evidently served as the locker room facility for our dear old high school football team.

I entered on a wide stretch of hallway, repurposed by virtue of four parallel training tables and shelves of supplies into the team training area. It was bustling with coaches fast at work taping players' ankles. I couldn't see how so many guys could already be experiencing discomfort to the extent of necessitating such attention, so I guessed this level of proactive care was SOP for elite teams such as the one I was now attempting to join.

The mood in the training area was relatively loose, I thought, although the players were the ones responsible for most of the jokey chatter. Coaches were bent intently to their tasks, taping at a rate of one ankle every one-and-a-half to two minutes and slapping the feet of each completed pair. The whole coaching staff was at it, Mr. Colombo included. Each table had a stack of white adhesive tape close by. The brusque stridence of constantly yanked and torn strips lent a not altogether unpleasant cacophony to the proceedings. The hollow thump of spent tape rolls in the big Brute barrel added to it too. When feet were slapped, you'd hear, "Next! Let's go everybody! Let's go-o-o-o!"

I watched taped players hop off the tables and barefoot players hop up in their place. They all looked like upperclassmen to me so, rather than presuming to join their line, I opted to err on the side of reserve-and-observe.

A doorway on the right connected the training area to the locker room proper. I could hear "Sympathy for the Devil" playing and being sporadically sung along to. Rather than loitering outside on the off chance that I might make eye contact with Mr. Colombo, I peeked my head into the locker room. It was a long grey rectangular space lined on both sides and one end with wall lockers. I was neither pleased nor surprised to see a hundred guys in various stages of undress, not a one of them as completely outfitted as I was.

A bunch of their heads turned toward the new arrival.

"Who? Who?" some of them sang.

As the new guy holding his helmet with no place to put it down, it was a little tricky trying to come off cool and casual. "Who! Who!" I almost put the fucking thing on my head. "Who– Who–" Perhaps they thought I'd been among them all along and had simply been one of the first players taped, hence already fully dressed. "Who... Who..."

"Look at this one," I heard a voice snigger. "Got all gussied up at home."

"Ashamed of showing off his nude little noodle," another announced.

"Mummsy dressed him real nice though."

Ah! Locker room wit at its finest.

Paul Duford, the baby-faced Kiwanis man-child of Little League rivalries past, walked in behind me from the hallway. I had noticed him at captains practice because he looked exactly the same as he had as a precocious twelve year old power hitter in the City Series. I wondered if he recognized me as the guy who robbed him of extra bases that time in our game at Producers. Maybe so, actually: he gave me a friendly wink on the way by.

Then I heard, "Dunna!"

"Huh?"

"Come here!" Chuck waved me over. "I called these three lockers for us," he said. "Me, you and Millett."

The team lockers were the second piece of understated proof positive that I was now truly entering the big time (the first piece having been that whole business-as-usual ankle taping thing going on out in the training area), although referring to them as 'lockers' was a misnomer. They didn't have little doors on them, nor locking mechanisms of any kind. Instead they were individual open-ended closet spaces like those seen in the locker rooms of professional sports teams, tall enough to easily accommodate all of our clothing and/or equipment, spacious enough to easily accommodate a pair of shoulder pads, with a top shelf for toiletries and sundries. Of course, at that moment I had nothing to store in the way of sundries or clothes.

"Oh, hey, nice going," I thanked Chuck.

"Johnny's in the middle. This is you."

"Cool." I put my helmet on the shelf for lack of anything better to do with it, and then I got right to the point. "So: I guess we suit up in here, huh?"

"Yeah. I didn't tell you?"

I combed my vocabulary for the exact right wording. Aha – got it: "No."

Chuck burst out laughing, more at my solemnity, I think, than his monstrous gaffe.

Then we heard coaches announcing from out in the training area, "Okay, five minutes! Everybody out in five!"

I asked Chuck whether lowly underclassmen like ourselves were expected to have our ankles taped, or were even allowed to, or what?

He just smiled, shaking his head as if my question were the silliest thing he'd ever heard of.

Assistant coaches shooed us out with instructions to wait by the building's rear entrance before taking the field. Coach Colombo was going to address us all as a group.

Outside, up on the outfield grass, I saw my brother Rich shooting double leg takedowns on a tackling dummy.

While we waited for our fearless leader to emerge, it occurred to me that a fair amount of my fellow aspirants were making their official debuts this day. I counted heads twice. Whether 120 or 123, a lot more of us were definitely now assembled than had been at any of the captains practices. I mentioned it to Chuck. From this group, he figured, about half would quit or be cut.

I recognized several of the new guys as good athletes and hot shits with whom I had played baseball over the years. Strict observance of the annual practice of captains was apparently considered non-mandatory by these free thinkers, or maybe they simply hadn't gotten the memo. Either way, although I knew that none of them were mere incoming freshmen like myself, I couldn't help feeling righteously holier-than-they in our newcomer hierarchy by virtue of the commitment I had so devoutly demonstrated lo this fortnight past.

The patch of flattened gravel in back of the Armory might once have been the site of a busy loading dock, or some other utilitarian service area, but decades of disuse had transformed it into an open air stage of sorts, especially if you squinted a little and put your imagination to use; and as if to bolster the concept, long tiers of arcing wooden steps had been conveniently set into the earth along the outskirts of the gravel many many seasons ago, creating an open stairway leading up to the ball field's ground level and lending a visual impression quite amphitheatrical in its effect.

Come to find, this oddly situated stretch of low-slung stairs/bleachers accommodated an audience of one hundred twenty-something fully outfitted football students just right.

Coach Colombo's inaugural address was breathtaking in its brevity, as blunt and audacious as a Bukowski poem.

"One goal: Undefeated Super Bowl champs."

He slowly trod the width of the whole gravel stage, wing to wing, nodding to himself. "Chicopee wants to stop us," he nodded. "Chicopee's coming... How long, Gene?"

By far the most physically imposing member of the coaching staff, Gene Marrow stated, "Twenty-seven days from today."

Mr. Colombo nodded. "On this practice field right here, there's one topic of discussion for the next month, and only one."

Cat calls began to flutter about, giving voice to our new common scourge, fixing fast in Boxer lore the accursed name of "Chicopee."

"That's it," Mr Colombo confirmed, his twinkling eyes aflare. "Right here... nothing else matters." He pointed us to the field. "Helmets buckled! Two laps!"

As we clambered up the steps, everybody was barking, "Chicopee!"

—

The morning session of day-1 was dedicated to all things offense. Quarterbacks broke off into drop-back drills overseen by Mr. Colombo himself. Linemen followed Mike Donovan, Joe Antone, and Mr. Marrow to the blocking sleds while the JV coaches (O'Connell, Miller, Bradshaw) led running backs and receivers through a host of agility and ball handling drills.

On hot summer days like this, the first thing you felt was thereafter the least thing you noticed: constant dripping sweat. My brother Rich found the shade of a leafy foul territory tree a refreshing home base, but as the August sun made its slow ascent, pulling the temperature and humidity up with it, he made sure he was never far from anywhere I was.

Resourceful Rich had discovered a handy spigot on the back wall of the Armory from which he continually refilled his 10-ounce apple juice bottle.

When it was convenient I would dart over to him between taking my turns at something.

"Good man, Richa."

"I'll keep filling it up!"

When the players vying for starting positions on offense were practicing their new plays for the first time, we underclassmen were enlisted as non-contact stand-ins on defense to lend a measure of realistic proportion to their run-throughs. It felt great just being there on the field with the first-string guys, but a couple of times, running stride for stride with a receiver, I wished I was allowed to make a real play for the ball.

My position at faux cornerback was the closest I had come to Mr. Colombo since we took the field at 8 o'clock. I eavesdropped on his every instruction, my diabolically simple plan being to store this information for as long as it took – two years? three? – until I got my chance to compete for a starting job. Like as not, I would have his ear by then, so I'd come out with it, Iago-like, at just the right moment, proving myself the ever apt and indispensable pupil.

Perhaps if I had played quarterback, some of Mr. Colombo's pearls from that day might have paid off down the road; like on running plays when he'd reiterate the fundamentals of proper handoff protocol ("Direct with two hands! Give with one! Look it in!"), but as pertains to a halfback I found little practical benefit in such rubrics.

However, all of us had our last names scrawled on a strip of athletic tape across the front of our helmets, so on sweeps to my side I made sure I was squarely facing our head coach when the pulling tackle came at me or when the halfback made his deke and turned upfield. If the offensive guy was obstructing my sight line I would hop to one side at the end of the play for a peek over his shoulder like an ambitious extra in the background of a movie scene. This nonsense too paid $0.00 in dividends. Maybe I should have made the block letters of my name larger, or used a red marker as some players had been clever enough to do.

When break time was announced, every sweaty helmet came right off and our whole slow herd huffed across the field, hoof dragging. Coaches reminded us all to avail ourselves of salt tablets when we got inside.

Making my way over toward my brother I saw Chuck.

"Four hours already?"

He said, "I know, wasn't too bad. Now let's get our butts inside, see if that A/C's working."

"Sorry, A.C.," I quipped. [No reaction.] "I'm going to chill under that tree over there with my brother."

"That's your brother?"

"Yep."

"I was wondering. Make sure you get some oranges and chocolate milk."

An unusually specific adios, I thought. "Okay…" [For all I knew, I had just inadvertently snubbed a quip of his, so we were even.]
—

On our walk to Store 24, Rich offered to carry my helmet. After a minute he decided that the best way to do so, despite the wobbling, was on his head. Then, with a child's enviable aplomb, he went right into the store like that.

When he came out he was carrying two more juices and a couple Drake's apple pies in my upturned helmet.

"The lady's nice," he explained

Swinging his makeshift pail by the buckled chin strap, Rich led the way back to our shade tree.

When we were done, I told him I was going to go in to use the bathroom. "You want to come in with me?"

"I peed already behind the tree."

"Yeah but you want to come in, take a look around?"

He thought for a moment. "No. I'm going to fill these up." He gave me a big grin, "Now we got three!"

Inside, most guys were relaxing on the long bench that bisected the rectangular locker room lengthwise, or slouching in the lockers themselves. Chuck and John Millett were seated in our section, talking and drinking chocolate milk from half pint cartons.

"Grab a couple milks," Chuck said.

John nodded, "And oranges before they're gone. Got to replenish."

Looking around, it appeared that the seniors had staked claim to the rectangle's cul-de-sac and settled there exclusively. Apart from that, though, the locker location pecking order seemed pretty much catch-as-catch-can. For instance, even though it was still only Day-1, we had thus far been allowed to coexist peacefully since moving into our little freshman neighborhood on the outskirts of seniorville, with no sign of overt hostility or prejudice despite our lack of social standing. I hadn't even encountered my churlish trickster anywhere yet. His campaign of ill will was probably suspended now that our exercises were taking place directly under Mr. Colombo's watchful eye.

A guy somewhere called, "Hey, Chucky!"

"Whucky?"

You could hear the smirk in his voice. "Out on the field, is it okay to talk about Farrah Fawcett?"

"Not if you know what's good for you."

One of the slouching senior linemen cleared his throat. He assumed the diction of an orator while wisely projecting just loud enough to be heard by those in the immediate area only. Tongue in cheek, he mimicked, "What matters other than Chicopee? Not one thing!" Then, for the benefit of those who might be unclear on the literal meaning of "not one thing", he rattled off a shortlist of henceforth taboo practice field discussion topics. "Not *Rice and Lynn!* Not *Bruce Jenner!*" He ran the back of his meaty hand across his chin to wipe away the dripping sarcasm. "Not *Archie Griffin!* You want to talk about Kenny MacAfee, go right ahead," he grinned. Huzzahs of exuberant esprit-de-corps rose up from everyone around him, including me, John and Chuck. The big guy finished strong. "Not your girlfriend's bushy little *thang*," he scoffed. Then, evoking more cheers of solidarity, "Not *schoo-ool!*"

I asked Chuck, "Which way to the bathroom?"

"That away. Just keep walking."

Following instructions to a T, I passed the coaches office at the far opposite end from us, beyond which were located the showers and the team restroom (containing several urinals and open commodes which, if you've never experienced this level of excretory candor, fosters a special kind of fellowship indeed, believe you me).

———

When we came out for the afternoon session, already stiff from sitting around, Rich was waiting with his little bottles of water on the amphitheater stairs.

Our agenda was pretty much a mirror image of the morning's with a defensive slant. Linemen were off by themselves doing hard core full contact drills, of course: one on ones, two on ones, bull in the ring, madman across the water. Meanwhile we "backs" ran through form tackling drills and tip drills until the starting linebackers and DBs were told to take their positions to face full-speed pass patterns. As had been the case in the morning session, these exercises were non-contact run-throughs, promoting mental muscle memory and recognition through repetition.

With Mr. Colombo handling the calling of our pass plays, I now found myself almost literally rubbing elbows with him. A couple times I was tempted to speak up and just introduce myself with a hearty handshake, smiling through my mouthpiece. Might I have misread or misinterpreted the unspoken bond I imagined we had between us? Then again, maybe I was just learning a hard fact of life at the bottom of the totem pole.

The comforting cloak of anonymity to which I had so often retreated in the past provided cold comfort indeed when you wanted to shuffle it off but couldn't.

Ah, well. Remembering my father's parting words ("Play hard, have fun. You're good at this game."), I took encouragement from the curl and slant passes I had caught in traffic. Now, since I was standing in as a receiver, I was entitled to make a genuine play for the ball. In fact, I had beat a linebacker to the boundary for a nice gain on a wheel route, to which Mr. Colombo barked, "Same group! Same play!"

The second time around I got behind the cornerback and I was battling the sun a little but Chuck hit me in stride for an obvious touchdown.

"–the hell! Have an idea! Same group, same play!"

I felt a little bad for the DB. He lived one street up from us, and he and my brother Joe hung out sometimes.

I knew I'd have to dig a little harder on this one, being the third time in a row we were running the same exact play. When I circled out of the backfield, Chuck lofted a beautiful timing pattern just as I crossed the line of scrimmage. The soft spiral disappeared into the sun spot and came out right on target. Just as I'd figured, I had to turn on the jets to catch up to it. I managed to barely get there on the dead run. As I tracked its arc into my outstretched hands I had absolutely no idea the burned DB had given up altogether on the ball, not to mention the non-contact rule. *Wow* went my wind right out of me. I was flat on my back, unable to breathe in or out. I have no memory of what became of the ball. Maybe I caught it, but I don't think so. Who cares! **Football Survival Rule #6: Always protect yourself in drills, "non-contact" or otherwise. Always.**

This was no emergency, of course. I just couldn't breathe. I knew it would pass.

Players came over and stood huddled around me as I lay there squinting for breath at the blinding sun.

"Dunna, you okay?"

"You alright, man?"

I mutely waved them off, assuring them as best I could.

The huddle grew until all I could see above me was the sun and the dark shadows of shoulder pads and helmets. Then in an unbelievably cinematic reveal, Mr. Colombo leaned into the huddle, eclipsing the sun but for the aura surrounding his own head. [This is no exaggeration!] He said, "Welcome to Brockton Football, Greg."

—

At home, Dad said, "Hop in the shower. I'll have some nice BLTs for you when you get out."

I'd take Dad's BLTs over most lunch fare anywhere.

Although I assume it was the newness of everything that had kept me energized and alert throughout my first day of double sessions, standing there under the heat of the beating shower I could feel the very last remnant of my physical strength washing right away.

"Was it hard running those sprints at the end," Rich asked me while we ate.

I shrugged, "Yeah, but…"

"They're supposed to be hard," said my father. "At least the last few."

"Right."

After lunch Dad suggested we kick back for a while in the coolness of my parents' air conditioned bedroom, to which Rich and I readily agreed.

Awakened in the disorienting grey of twilight, I felt bodily embedded in the mattress, sore all over.

"Whuh. Uh…"

"Good sleep?"

I nodded up at my father.

"Come on guys."

Beside me, Rich looked as groggy as I felt. He read my mind: "Time is it?"

"Time to get up."

It looked too light out for my parents to be going to bed. "Already?" I didn't care how early it was, though. My ass was going right to my room and straight back to sleep.

"Time is it," my brother asked again.

"Six," Dad said. "Breakfast is all ready for you. It's on the table."

Breakfast? I was crushed, feeling as hopeless as the wrongly accused. "Whuh the–" Such disappointment on our faces made my father crack a smile. "Let's go, Rich Van Winkle."

Still bewildered, my brother whimpered, "Who…?"

Sure enough, Chuck was right about the cuts and quits. A shitload of guys didn't even make it to the first cut. They just abandoned ship. Admittedly, the week of double sessions leading up to cuts proved to be the most physically taxing experience I had ever undergone, but the thought of quitting never entered into it. Finally, so many guys bailed on their own that there wasn't even any need for a second round of cuts.

In the process of determining the starting game day lineups on offense and defense, our JV lineups took shape too. The junior varsity proving ground was as competitive as could be because after that first day of doubles we were tasked on a daily basis with taking on the first-string units in live scrimmage.

Running plays against our starting D led me to realize that a.) those guys on the other side of the ball were some badass dudes, and b.) the JV squad being affectionately nicknamed "hamburgers" made more and more sense every day.

I also realized that my recently dormant *bête noire* might merely have been playing possum during our détente because there he was again alright, rearing his ugly head in the direction of my ribcage whenever possible. If I was stopped at the line on a dive play, he'd be sure to yell "Hold him up!" and fly into the scrum knee or forearm or said head first to my groin and gut. If I was already on the ground, his would inevitably be the dead weight piling on at the whistle.

Be that as it may, during those first few days of double sessions I must confess to privately nursing the admittedly pie in the sky notion of possibly being named to the starting kickoff return team or punt return team. No, I know! I know. But, hey – stranger things have happened, right? Haven't they?

I don't know how close I actually came, or if I was close at all, or was getting closer or not, but I had to give Mr. Colombo credit. He kept his own counsel, as usual, playing the crucial kick return card close to his the vest until the very last, so that every one of us hopefuls would remain scurrying hungry right down to the wire.

The only return man lock, as far as I could see, was electrifying junior letterman, Mike Parham, a jitterbugging track star. If we had one secret weapon on the team, he was it. Simply faster and quicker than everybody else, and good-sized to boot, he could go the distance untouched on any given play. As part of a primarily two-platoon team, he was one of the rare exceptions, playing starting safety and also being utilized as a change of pace running back; although if you asked me he should have been our clear feature back, like Phil Johnson the year before.

One day during double sessions this dynamo decided to remind everyone just what he was capable of. He bounced a routine dive play outside, racing to the near sideline before doubling back all the way to the far sideline, only to triple back the other way again. Except for the exasperated line of trailing defenders, everyone on the field was laughing, including all the coaches. Mike Damiano was kazooing "Yakety Sax" until Mr. Colombo mercifully whistled the Benny Hillian farce to an end. It was really something to see.

—

One night in the darkness of our room, I confessed to Joe the perplexing harassment I'd received from that oafish senior adversary of mine.

"Really," he said. "Who?"

His bedside lamp came on.

When I told him, he said he hadn't met the guy. "Yet. But I know who he is. Class-A asshole. Kind you read about."

"Yeah."

"I'll let Damiano know."

"No, Joe—"

"Guy's screwing with you, right? I'm sure Donny wouldn't mind having a word with him too."

"Ah, come on, it's not like *that*."

"*That's* the only way it ever is, Greg."

"Yeah, but—"

"Hey: Listen: It's always like that. Period."

Joe was the best; preternaturally direct. He rarely had use for peripheral considerations or niceties. All of a sudden, though, I was more uncomfortable with this conversation than I was with the conflict itself. "And anyway," I argued, "Donny Colombo's already graduated."

"So?"

'Hard to argue with such airtight logic,' I thought. ' Touché.'

Even so, I didn't want the situation to escalate any further if it didn't have to. "Joe," I began.

"*Greg—*"

With that, I knew I'd heard the last word on the subject for the night. His light went out. I heard him roll over to sleep. After a while of lying there thinking, I began timing the intervals between blinks of my wide open eyes.

The next morning in the shower I heard the bathroom door open. "Yo!"

"It's me."

The sink faucet went on and Joe started brushing his teeth.

"You know…" he began, correctly assuming that I knew exactly what he was talking about as he spoke between spits. "What I always say…" My brother's ultimate solution was a predictable variation on a common problem-solving theme of his. "Start throwing a few elbows around, that shit'll stop quick."

—

Once the official roster had been finalized, we were given our game uniforms (red game pants and visitors white jerseys) at the beginning of practice one day to sit for team photos.

When my turn at the counter came, our irascible equipment tzar demanded, "Name!"

"Dunn."

He consulted his clipboard. "Running back."

"Yut."

By Luck's good graces, the excellent high school football career of Dan Colombo had come to a close the previous fall, thus ending his four year reign as Boxer #43. Consequently, I was hopeful that I might don the venerable mantle this season and in so doing carry the Dunn family torch and perhaps launch a distinguished quadrennial of my own.

I was suddenly and truly shocked to see that my wish was coming true as the neatly folded game jersey bearing number forty-three got frisbeed my way. My elation was not only short-lived but also unfounded. Upon further review, my assigned number turned out to be an imposter, not 43 at all but its hunchback lookalike: 48.

"Oh, hey," I surprised myself by speaking up. "Is forty-three available? Instead?"

Like a Dickensian workhouse master apportioning gruel, our red-faced equipment tzar went deep purple, astonished by my impudence.

He cried, "Direnzo's 43!"

"Oh…"

"Okay? Yuh?"

"Yuh."

The color all around his addled eyes receded in beats toward its regular rosé. "You're Dunn, right? You're 48 for Christ sake."

I nodded and he got back to business, addressing the next guy, "Name!"

Outside the Armory's rear entrance we were seated in the sun for the yearbook picture in three tightly arranged rows shoulder to shoulder, elbow to elbow, knee to knee on the curved amphitheater steps, captains and seniors up front, juniors behind them, sophomores and freshmen rearmost, all of us posed with hands on knees. The photographer took his work seriously. He climbed to the fire escape's second story perch for a bird's eye view.

"Alright everybody, up here!"

For some reason, this bright well-composed shot of our nicely shipshape group was not used for the game day programs. Instead, the following week we were once again assembled in our visitors whites but this time we were seated in the shade of the bleachers along Eldon B. Keith's third base line. Rather than three tight tiers of identical length, we spread ourselves across five unevenly paired rows, producing a darker and altogether inferior presentation; not to mention that the decision to have us sit with arms folded across our jersey numbers suggested, here and there, sickly belly aches more than bravado. In either case, you'd need a genuine jeweler's loupe to make out me, Millett, and Armond, Jr., tucked away in the back corner.

———

Exactly why it is that the few isolated details of one ordinary day can continue to stand out, apart and vivid on the beach of your memory all these years later, while scores of identical others have washed away forever with the ebbing surf, is way past me. All I know is, for better or worse, there they stand, and I'm glad of it because without them this collection wouldn't be possible.

Several such unforgotten particulars took place that season on a normal night at home. It was right around my birthday because the school year had already gotten under way but we had yet to play our opening game against Chicopee which was to take place in the third week of September. So, datewise, we're talking somewhere right in there...

Dad came in from work and we told him we'd seen on the news how a Boston fire truck had been damaged under a bombardment of rocks when it arrived to answer a Bowdoin Street call in Dorchester only to find miscreants laying in wait on the rooftops.

"Happens all the time over there," my father said. "At least it wasn't another box spring. A couple weeks ago, Heath Street projects, they just missed our truck with a king size box spring off the roof. Came crashing down right next to DeGrandis. He's lucky he's not in the ground right now."

I went to our room to tell Joe about this remarkable box spring incident which was apparently so all-in-a-day's-work at Dad's firehouse that it hadn't warranted so much as a mention when it originally happened a couple weeks prior. Joe was standing in front of his record player listening to Funkadelic's *Let's Take It to the Stage* album, admiring the cover art.

"Bootsy..." he said to himself. "Oh, hey. So you guys going to be ready for Chicopee? I heard they're ranked number nineteen nationally in one preseason poll. That's what Damiano said."

"Really? Shit."

"Speaking of which, what's new with your stalker? Anything?"

"Nah, same crap," I told him. "But I've been thinking. You got to figure this dude must have been forced to eat some big time shit somewhere along the line. And now he's doing his damndest to pay it backward in the form of hatred toward me, misguided though that hatred might be."

"Oh, he was fucked with as a kid, no doubt about it," Joe theorized.

"Yuh?"

"Bet your ass. But he's not targeting you out of hatred."

"No?"

"No way. On the contrary, the bastard likes you."

"What!"

"Oh yuh. That doesn't let him off the hook for being an asshole about it, though. If he's got a hard-on for you, he should just make a pass at you and get it over with. No need for these grade school histrionics; pulling your hair at recess."

—

A couple days before Chicopee, the training staff scraped and peeled off the worn Boxer decals from all of our helmets and carefully applied brand new ones. Of course Brockton's Boxer Dog logo has since become acknowledged as hands down the coolest helmet mascot of all time (not to mention the baddest assed most universally feared team emblem since the swastika), but even way back then, two score and some-odd years ago, in the ever-changing yet naively innocent seventies, its mystique was not lost on us. Though only recently adopted as our trademark at the dawn of the decade, it had become as instantly iconic as a Van Gogh self portrait — its stern lined face similarly rendered, too: standoffish in ¾ profile, bearing visible tell-tale signs of auricular severance. It's hardly exaggerating to say that whenever we "donned the dog" for practice or games, we did so with a pride bordering on military.

By the way, it was around this same time that, as unexpectedly as it had started, the strange intrasquad harassment directed at me ceased, and a great relief it was to finally bid goodbye to such puzzling malevolence. I have no idea what's ever become of the guy, bless him. I hope, perhaps, for his sake, he found God.

—

Not to worry, folks — I have no intention of boring everybody with a detailed game by game, or incident by incident, account of the 1976 football season. It would take too long, wouldn't it, what with the exaggerated sense of wonder inherent in every little thing along the way as viewed from my neophyte perspective.

So, to very briefly summarize, we finished with another 6-3 record for the season, once more matching the decade's low-water mark, making it three consecutive years of identical underachievement. We were again led by an unsung but staunch defensive unit. It gave up just 77 points the whole year while registering shutouts in three games and surrendering more than two touchdowns in a game only once all season (to wit, the Newton fiasco, a black comedy of special teams errors, foolishly untimely penalties, an *air fumble,* which taught me something about our steely head coach: In the unlikely event of a Boxer blowout, no matter how lopsided the score, Armond Colombo is NOT about to pull his starters in the waning minutes of a losing cause – so, cool your cleats, second stringers.).

It's too bad we didn't do better that year because the seniors, for the most part, were high quality dudes, generally letting the underclassmen go about their business unmolested. Steve Goulding, Duford, Tom McCann, Tom Tully were always civil; Mark Baker. In fact, cheers to Mark Baker! One day as the JVs were heading out of the Armory for an away game, Baker clapped me on the shoulder pads in good natured support, urging me to, "Go get 'em." I appreciated that.

Unfortunately, despite victories versus perennial powers Chicopee and Leominster (12-0, 19-14, respectively), the ultimate blame for our three-loss season must be laid at the door of our anemic offense (sorry, fellas) which exceeded 20 points scored in a game just once that year (21-0 vs Quincy – of which more later) on their way to barely breaking triple-digits in total points for the nine game season. Over the course of our three defeats we scattered exactly 13 pitiful points, including the indignity of a Thanksgiving Day goose egg against arch enemy Waltham. To put it into perspective for anyone new to the sport of football, our odds of winning those three games while averaging just 4.3 points scored per game were worse than those of lightning striking the same goal post twice and the other goal post once *in the same quarter* of a single game…

After the debacle in Newton, Mr. Colombo didn't say one word that Monday as we watched the entire game film straight through from start to finish. His silence echoed off the locker room walls. The 16-millimeter film ticked continuously through the projector in real time in stark contrast to the customary ¾ speed we used in order to better study each possession as it played out in dreamy rich black and white. (Something I particularly liked during films was when, at Mr. Colombo's behest, defensive coordinator Mike Donovan would rewind the film which resulted in portraying the ball carrier's reversal of direction in balletic tiptoe.)

Mr. Colombo addressed us as a group the following day at practice. "It's very easy to win after you've won," he said. "And it's very easy to lose after you've lost. The hardest thing in sports is to win after you've lost. The Super Bowl is still within our reach as long as we win the rest of our games, and that's our one and only goal right now. Let's get to work."

—

As previously promised, we shall not be reviewing the Boxers' 1976 football schedule with anything close to a game by game scrutiny. There'll be no analysis of gutsy play calls, nor cataloging of down and distance, so fear not.

That being said... ;) I would be remiss indeed if I didn't make mention of one landmark game in particular. In many ways it best represents Brockton being Brockton.

Yes, I'm referring of course to our late season clash with Suburban League rival Quincy. I like to refer to it as the Score-One-For-The-Good-Guys Game. In addition to its being one of our staunch D's stellar shutouts, this 21-0 contest also featured a halfback option pass for a touchdown by versatile Duford.

Later, good man Baker came up with a fourth quarter TD reception to close out our scoring for the day. Having obviously been brought up right, he'd been cool to me all season. When he scored that touchdown, my emotions got the better of me, I guess. In the heat of the moment, I found myself out on the field by the near hash, smacking his shoulder pads and banging celebratory chests with him.

Shortly thereafter, not a single person at Marciano Stadium that crisp bright Saturday was more surprised — I daresay more dumbfounded – than ole number 48 in your game program when Coach O'Connell shouted, "JV offense! JV offense!"

"Shit! This is it, Dunna," Chuck elbowed me, buckling his chin strap. "We're up."

If you asked me, I'd have said this game's outcome was by no means assured. The good side of a 21-0 score halfway through the fourth quarter was a nice position to be in, but such a lead was hardly unblowable, let's face it. Nevertheless, our unpredictable head coach was entrusting us with its keeping. Unless I was mistaken, we would be tasked with running some straight handoffs, and with any luck, as long as nothing went drastically wrong, we might register a first down or two along the way.

Incidentally, years earlier one summer day at a roadside MDC playground pool when Joe and I were kids, I had defied our grandmother's admonition against trying the higher of the two gleaming metal slides while our bathing suits were still wet. Gram was always dispensing such nonsensical advice. While I climbed the ladder to the top of the slide her words went in one ear and for all I know went bleeding right back out as I came-to some time later, heavy-headed, sick to my stomach, sprawled there on the burning macadam below. Then there was another time, kids again, on family vacation, playing two-on-two tag football outside our cottage, when uncle Kevin sent me out long. I had a step on Joe, and it would have been a perfect scoring pass if not for a young inconveniently placed oak tree abruptly interrupting my wakefulness. I mention these shocking knockouts (and there've been just the two in my career thus far) because on the field in the huddle against Quincy I was as close to experiencing that same type of daze as I ever would while still on two feet. For the first and only time before or since, my knees were nervously and very visibly shaking. I tried to wrestle them under control by casually clutching them. Meanwhile, Chuck had evidently called the play because our other halfback said, "Is that to me or Greg?"

He was a junior who on more than one occasion had tried to make a fool of me in front of the upperclassmen; unsuccessfully, but still. Nevertheless, I was thankful he'd spoken up. Otherwise I might have missed the play call altogether. Chuck scolded him, "It's Dunna! Pass number three!"

So much for conservative running plays to kill the clock. Go, Chuck!

Pass number three was a backside wheel route to the halfback where the QB rolls right and throws back left. To sell the play, the left halfback bides his time in the backfield for a two-count, chipping the defensive end if necessary, before breaking into his route. I patiently feigned pass blocking for what must have been "one-Missi–" and then took off. Chuck hit me in stride for a twenty-one yard gain. I might have gone all the way had I not made a desperate beeline for the lone safety as soon as I caught the pass.

That one reception served to demonstrate an oft misattributed dictum which nicely sums up our delightful human tendency to mislead by way of data whenever possible (i.e., "There are three kinds of lies: Lies, Damned Lies, and Statistics." [Credited variously to Mark Twain, Benjamin Disraeli, Lord Beaconsfield, et al.]), by establishing mild mannered newcomer G. Dunn as the 1976 season's team leader in Yards Per Reception (minimum 1 catch).

Cue drum roll...

Player	Pos.	Class	YPR
G. Dunn	HB	Fr.	21.0
K. Lalli	TE	Sr.	11.1
P. Duford	HB	Sr.	8.7

[One Final Note to Oddsmakers and Statisticians: *For the record, Quincy had shut out Weymouth North 26-0 earlier in the season. We in turn shut Quincy out the following week 21-0. In most galaxies, per the laws of transitive properties, or averages, or some such, the above data would ensure an orderly Brockton victory over Weymouth North when the two teams played each other, right? Right!? Right. Actual final score in our Milky Way that shameful day in 1976: Weymouth North 8, Brockton 7*]

—

Winter of that year marked the introduction of weightlifting to my off season workout routine. Chuck and I would take the BAT bus to the Y every day after school, and we'd meet up on Saturday mornings too. The immediate and regular gains we made on the bench press were a revelation. To warm down we'd jog a mile on the indoor track or play a couple games of handball.

"That's one more game that's harder than it looks. Jeepers."

"No kidding," I said. "My father's been playing for years, he makes it look easy."

"My uncle Peter, too."

We overheard some guys in the locker room discussing *Rocky* which had recently opened to pretty much unanimous acclaim.

"Paul Bradshaw's supposed to be really good," I mentioned.

Chuck threw a nod at me. "You hear that?"

"They say the boxing scenes are great."

He kept nodding dubiously.

"Why," I asked him. "You seen it?"

"My uncle said he's going to have some t-shirts made up: 49-0 The *Real* Rocky."

Back home, Rich and Steve occupied a cushion at the end of our couch, sharing one of Joe's *Scholastic Wrestling News* magazines. Joe was slouched at the other end as I was too against the hassock. My father said, "Hut hut." Then he said, "Good hands."

I couldn't disagree. Joe confirmed, "First down."

Twisting off the cap with a courtly bow, I delivered Dad his beer. "There you are, sir. One Miller High Life. Will there be anything else?"

"Another one every half-hour till they're gone?"

Returning to my slouchy post, I sighed, "Considerate Dunn."

"You guys have a good workout?"

"Actually yeah."

"Still getting stronger and stronger, right?"

"We are!"

"See?"

"Especially on bench."

"It shows, too. You're looking bigger. Through the shoulders."

I agreed completely, but it was very good to hear it coming from somebody else.

Dad said, "So what do you think about wrestling next year?"

My inner voice was shaking its head, 'Ah…'

"You're strong and you're tough. With your long arms you'd be hard to handle."

"I've never even done it before," I said.

"Well, when we turn the playroom into a wrestling room, you can work with Joe anytime you want. As soon as we get the mat in there."

"And I don't want to have to suck weight in the off-season. I'm trying my best to put weight on."

"The Colombo kid did it in the off-season, and it didn't hurt him. He wrestled great then put it right back on for football."

I nodded.

My father let it drop. "So, what were you guys working on tonight?"

"Oh, you should have seen! This guy from the team walks in, he sees us doing curls and starts laughing. 'Curls for the girls,' he says. 'You know, there's other body parts other than biceps. You guys are all the same. Every day without fail you two are standing in front of that mirror doing curls.'"

"Because he's probably only there every other day, so to him–"

"That's what I told him! 'Monday, Wednesday, Friday we do arms, as you've noticed. Then… *Tues*day, *Thurs*day, *Satur*day – you listening? – we do *chest*. And we do *back*. Get it? Because the rest of the world continues to go about its business – whether you show up or not… Yuh!'"

"Shut him right up."

"Yup."

Technically, it was Chuck who shut him up. He's always been a hair quicker on the draw with a spontaneous riposte, but I figured my anecdote would work better in the moment with me in the lead role.

When we heard my mother's car pulling up the driveway, everyone in the room under thirty-five hopped to. My brothers and I made short work of unloading the dozen or so brown paper grocery bags packed in the back of our big blue Buick station wagon (known affectionately as The Tank), the once and future site of legendary "Crazy Larry & Sadistic Sally" brawls.

While Ma was putting everything away, she said, "Oh, I left a bag from the bakery on the front seat. Can someone grab it?"

Joe had returned to the couch and was just sitting down when he bounced right back up to fetch the bakery bag.

"Good news and bad news, Mum," he said, returning. He held the white bakery bag open for her. She removed the cob loaf of bread.

"What? Oh, no! Mold?"

"Didn't notice it, huh?"

"Well I didn't think to look underneath it."

"Let me see," my father said. "Oh, that's not bad. We can just cut it off. No need to waste the entire loaf."

"No…" Ma dropped the whole thing in the kitchen trash. "That was going to be for dinner tonight with the spaghetti. Shit. Looks like I'll have to find a new bakery."

"Not necessarily," said Joe. "It's actually a good sign when you find mold on a bakery loaf of bread. It means they're using fresh ingredients with no preservatives. From now on you just got to make sure you check before you buy. It's when you got rolls or bread in your pantry for a week or more and you still *don't* have mold that it's a problem. Then you know they're shooting it full of preservatives galore. And that stuff's worse for you than if you ate the damn mold."

We all chewed on this theory for a while.

Eventually my brothers wandered off to other parts of the house or outside. Ma went back to the bakery for a fresh loaf of bread, bringing the moldy one with her.

Dad nudged the hassock with his heel. "So I haven't seen that girl around you've been going with."

I shrugged a little to nudge it back.

"You two break up?"

"Ah…"

"Yuh?"

"I don't know… I think she's a little crazy. Like… in a medical textbook crazy."

"You don't need that."

"No."

"But all women are crazy."

"Hmm!" I laughed. "Yeah."

"That's not bullshit. You can't blame them, though. Women in this world got the shit end of the stick from Day-1. We'd be crazy too if we were them."

I nodded, and I could sense Dad nodding too.

—

Every new baseball season, thanks to my dad's timely batting practice regimen, I was at my very best when it came time to show up for tryouts; peaking, as they say, at the right time. Nevertheless, I had no delusions about making Brockton's varsity team as a freshman. It was pretty much unheard of. I was a good player, an all-star at every level so far, but I didn't possess the transcendent talent of, say, an Art Sullivan, nor was I ever considered a "blue chip prospect" as my junior high coach Mr. Fitzgibbons once put it describing the precocious Dan Colombo. These recently graduated Boxer superstars might have been good enough as ninth graders to make the cut but, ah… I wasn't them.

I'd be perfectly content freshman year getting my feet wet as a member of the JVs; absolutely no shame in that.

As far as I knew, the only ninth graders other than myself trying out for the varsity team that year were Steve Tuite and Chuck, and I'm sure they would admit that earning a spot on the big team was a more or less Kingmanian long shot; for the veteran competition was fierce and deep, and it was unlikely that either

Chuck or Tuite had received off-season roster assurance in the way of a thunderbolt call from on high – I know I sure hadn't.

Tryoutwise, the three of us were hanging in there after the first week until one rainy day when the drills and exercises had to be moved entirely indoors for what we assumed would be an easy day. Head Coach Tom Pileski was nothing if not resourceful, though. He started practice by having us warm up in the gymnasium stairwell by jogging single file up and down the three narrow flights, seniors leading the way, underclassmen falling in behind. By the time the frontrunners were headed back down, those bringing up the rear were just getting started. Some of the seniors mugged as they passed us going the other way, reverting to exaggerated high steps or feigning exhaustion.

"Aggeehn!" Mr. Pileski instructed.

Now for some reason the continuous parade gave rise to silly camaraderie. A unanimous laughing chant of "Oh-wee-oh wee-oh-oh!" echoed in the stairwell for a couple laps, but the fourth or fifth time Mr. Pileski commanded "Aggeehn!" the only sound was your own panting and the spanking of sneakers on stone steps. With each successive lap, Pitching Coach Doc Kostka's inscrutable smirk took on a more sinister cast. Reaching the bottom on burning quads, I heard him mutter, "Once more unto the breach…"

Later in the gym, as a treat we were all given five swings versus the JUGS pitching machine. This was the kind with opposable spinning hard rubber wheels, between which Doc would feed tennis balls one by one, holding each ball up for the hitter to acknowledge before loading it into the hopper.

Matty Walsh immediately demanded "first crack at the jugs!" (Not only was Matt the best baseball player in my time at Brockton, but he was also First Team All-Silly.) Like everything else he did, he made it look easy, stroking line drives every swing while explaining by way of narration his obvious facility with jugs.

For those unfamiliar, hitting balls from a pitching machine is not hard at all once you get the hang of it. In fact, it's much easier than hitting live pitching; but facing a pitching machine for the very first time is tricky, no doubt about it. Without the benefit of a human pitcher's usual throwing motion against which to gauge your swing's rhythm, it is frankly shocking how quickly the pitched ball is *on* you, and flat out *by* you. If you make the mistake of offering at the first pitch, you will feel and look as childishly overmatched as you ever have been since your diaper days.

When my name was not one of those read off by Mr. Pileski as having made the first cut, I was frankly amazed. I had harbored no illusions about ultimately making the big team, but failure to survive the opening round of cuts meant I wasn't even eligible for JVs anymore. I had been hitting the ball well in batting practice, and hadn't looked clumsy in the field. Meanwhile all the underclassmen moving on to the next round were guys I'd been playing with in Pony League and junior high and, honestly, I was just as good or better than most of them. I don't know… Maybe it was those five whiffs that day in the gym versus the JUGS pitching machine.

———

My father said, "Just do the best you can on freshman. That's all you can do."

"Yeah…"

"Hey, they made a mistake, they were wrong. But who knows? You play the way you can play, hit the way you can hit, maybe they bounce you back up to JVs."

"Yeah," I disagreed. "Ever heard of a coach admitting he was wrong about a roster move?"

"Not yet," Dad teased, nudging the hassock. "Want to get some BP right now before supper?"

"Yeah, I do."

There were no takers for the thankless job of official shagger, so Dad and I drove to the Davis School by ourselves. On the diamond nearest the school I set myself up just in front of the backstop and Dad estimated a reasonable facsimile of mound distance about halfway between home plate and the actual pitcher's mound.

"Right through the ball. That's the way."

A few minutes later in deep center field on the opposite diamond a young father showed up with his kids and was underhanding softballs to the little one.

"Try to pull them," Dad said.

"Yup."

He started throwing only inside fastballs to help facilitate my pulling. My father had always had excellent control, so I knew I could dig right in.

"Nice," he said as I drilled one. When he put the next one in the same place, so did I. "That's the way."

We had five scruffy batting practice balls until I pulled one a bit too well into the woods over the left field fence.

"Whoops."

"And then there were four..." Dad announced.

After another one went into the woods, he started working the outer half of the virtual plate. When he grooved one right down the middle I sent a line drive right back through the box.

"Sorry!"

Never being one to pitch around power, he sent the next pitch to the exact same spot with a little extra hop on it.

I hit a bomb to dead center field. It came down around second base on the other diamond and skittered past that dad's ankles.

"Little help!"

The guy attended to it like a piece of poop to be scooped, and lobbed it in our general direction underhand.

"I got it, Dad," I said, dropping my bat and hustling toward the outfield. When I reached the ball, the other guy said, "You know, I got little kids here."

"Sorry about that!"

A minute later Dad grooved another one and I drove it deep to the opposite infield again.

"Little help!"

The other dad ignored us.

My father nodded to me, holding the baseball up like a JUGS machine loader. "Alright, last one."

I had my best swing ready for his best effort to my best spot, and... *boom!*

The other dad yelled, "What the hell!"

"Sorry!"

"Now you're doing that on purpose!"

"If he could do that on purpose he'd be on the Red Sox for Christ sake!"

The guy said, "Better not do it again!"

"Oh, I better not?" My father started walking toward the far diamond, letting the catcher's mitt drop after one or two steps. I shouldered my aluminum bat and trailed about sixty feet six inches behind.

We retrieved our remaining baseballs without incident. Walking away, we heard, "I got little kids out here."

"We were here before you even showed up, shithead."

—

The wound of being cut from varsity was as deep and immediate as a girlfriend's betrayal; all the more chastening for being so completely unexpected. It was just – next thing you know, the world is not as you always took it to be. That's humbling, to be sure, and most confusing. Ordinary currency is suddenly worthless? Yes. Start taking all new measurements. Updated blueprints are called for everywhere.

Come to think of it, the pain of that cut was actually worse than the loss of a duplicitous girl. It hurt like the disloyalty of a good friend.

Then again, you know what? Playing ball on the freshman team was fun. I knew pretty much all the guys from common leagues and teams over the years, and anyway – I myself was a ninth grade freshman, right? Plus, who knew how much playing time I would've gotten on JVs? For the freshman team I was starting at short and batting third. What's wrong with that?

Thanks once again to Dad's aforementioned pre-season batting practice work, I got off to a great start at the plate, going nine for my first ten at-bats with two home runs. Actually I was 9-for-9 through four games when I made my first out trying to launch a chest high fastball to Alpha Centauri. The pitch had good speed and zero movement, like ideal BP, the kind I routinely used to send center fielders sprinting to the fence for; but I just completely missed it, no idea how.

I was never a home run hitter, per se, but I had good power so I did hit my share of homers, and my first one that year on the freshman team is among my all-time favorites. At a Saturday morning away game, I was going to be leading off the inning so I took some practice swings in the on-deck circle while the pitcher warmed up, and I saw that when he threw a curve, there was a decided snow cone effect in his grip of the ball, with a good half of it visibly protruding above his hand. Sure enough, a couple pitches into my at-bat, he reared back in his windup and came out serving me that nice slow cone.

Later on between innings, a couple other players and I went to the water bubbler behind the backstop for a drink. A little kid rode up on his bike and asked. "Are you the one who hit that ball to kingdom come?"

—

I honestly don't think it's a case of sour grapes for me to say, without even minute reservation, that playing freshman baseball that year was definitely the best thing for me, and furthermore I actually preferred it.

My blazing hot start didn't hurt, obviously. After all these years, I don't pretend to recall the exact figures of every offensive stat, but 9-for-10 is easy to remember. Knowing my own strengths and weaknesses on the diamond, I'm sure I registered several walks during that torrid streak, probably two or three steals, a few RBI of course, and a bunch of runs scored. Full disclosure: I wouldn't be surprised if an E-6 or two weren't penciled in the scorebook either, but we're talking Offense here, and 9-for-10 is 9-for-10, I don't care who you are. I don't care if you're playing Wiffle ball in the backyard. 9-for-10 speaks for itself.

Fine, you might say, but why does it seem like we're undergoing some major 9-for-10 overkill here? We get the point – hot start (on the *freshman* team). Copy that. And then…?

Good question, glad you asked.

I am pleased to report that my entire stint of freshman ball that year was no less distinguished than that lightning HOT start of mine. However, nor was it more so because, in point of fact, with such a HOT start (Come on, 9-for-10 warrants a little uppercase gloating, doesn't it?), I was shaking the dust of that crummy little team off my feet and I was going to see the world through a JV's eyes – because I had gotten my ass called up!

Ah, the deliciousness of vindication!

Now with the world set to right I could get on with the business of achievement. On the following day, I joined the junior varsity team coached by the great Dave Fouracre. Along with Messrs. Colombo and Fitzgibbons, Coach Fouracre completes my triumvirate of all-time favorite coaches. They simply tower above the rest.

Unlike many other Brockton assistant coaches whose playing days had long since secured them eminence among the pantheon of Boxer greats, Mr. Fouracre was a rare expatriate in the City of Champions. He came to us from the Borough region of central Mass. where, yes, he had distinguished himself as a Hall of Fame baseball player for Algonquin Regional High School.

In the 1970s when the two of us first met as player and coach, he had yet to skipper a single varsity baseball game. However, by the time he took over Brockton's top spot in 1988, he was fully prepared to meet and exceed the lofty standard set by his legendary predecessor, Tom Pileski.

It was a quickly established axiom that Coach Fouracre ran a tight ship. His teams were invariably well-drilled and fighting fit, and they were *good*. Year in and year out his troops contended for Eastern Mass. supremacy, and in 1997 he led them all the way to the Division-1 state title.

The outstanding Fouracre coaching career has since garnered him well-deserved induction into the Brockton High School Athletic Hall of Fame as well as the Massachusetts Baseball Coaches Association Hall of Fame. It's always nice to see validation paid where it's due but, truth be told, even back then at the junior varsity level it was clear to all of us that he was the real deal, halls of fame or no halls of fame; and in addition to his tenacious baseball (and football) tutelage, Dave Fouracre also happens to be one hell of a guy.

"You're low man on the totem pole, Dunna," he told me on my first day as a member of the JV team. "This club we're playing today is struggling, so it should be a good chance for you. No pressure, get your feet wet, take some healthy cuts at the plate. You'll start at short and bat fifth today."

"Great. Thanks."

Previously in these pages, I have made mention of the baked in benefits in the northeast part of the country associated with such short youth baseball seasons. You go on a little run and, next thing you know, half the season's over and you're leading the league in a couple different categories. In fact, in my eighth grade year for South Junior High, I registered just thirty official at-bats for the whole season. I had always walked a lot – granted – but the main thing was that the season went so damn quick. (By the way, don't even bother asking how many hits I had, because you wouldn't believe me if I told you, okay? I'm serious.) (Suffice it to say, I led the team in Batting Average that year.)

Taking infield before my first JV game, I could feel myself literally licking my chops in agreeably anxious anticipation. I forget which nearby town we were playing in, but I liked it. The outfield fence was considerably shorter than most of the Brockton Pony League's vast unsymmetrical parks, so visions of dingers were dancing in my head for sure.

We opened the top of the first with three straight hits, including Dana Kerr's tomahawk home run to deep center, and a walk. "Aggh, you beat me to it, Dana," I thought. "Ah, well."

From the on-deck circle their pitcher didn't look like he had much. From the plate he didn't either.

"You and him, Dunna," Mr. Fouracre chattered. "You and him!"

If I were to rank the pitchers I'd faced thus far on the season, freshman included, this guy would come in dead last. Nevertheless, I whiffed at his tantalizing meatballs like a piñata. On my way back to the bench I was shaking my head, almost laughing for embarrassment. I already knew several players on the team and got along well with them; Chuck, Wally Allegro, Mike McGillis from the old days; Michael J. Barry (self-proclaimed "Jock Waste of the World") more recently. The looks on all their faces were a little embarrassed too, or befuddled, or just outright entertained. They probably attributed the fiasco to nerves, but I wasn't nervous at all.

With two outs, later that same inning, I stood on-deck again. We had batted around the order one and a half times. That's all I needed – to make the first and last out of the inning. There must be a term for pulling off that level of ignominy. If not, there should be; named after some oddly loathsome creature: "Way to go, Dunna. Nice platypus!"

Thankfully, Dave Kriteman flied out.

In the bottom of the inning, their first batter tapped a slow roller toward short. Nice! Redemption! I charged it and double clutched the throw to avoid hitting our pitcher with the ball, ultimately pulling Steve Tuite off the bag. So far, so bad: 1 inning, 1 K, 1 E.

They changed pitchers to start the top of the second, so from the on-deck circle I watched the new guy warm up to see if he would unwittingly reveal something, like the kingdom come snow cone dude. The only thing he revealed was that he had no business being on the mound in a real game facing a lineup as good as ours.

That inning we batted around the order again, technically. I went down chopping to lead things off, and then I bagged the first official platypus of my career by striking out again later to end the same inning. This would mark the only time I had ever been struck out three times in a game. During that third at-bat, I began to sense... something... vaguely dreadful, like the inevitable, like those late-for-the-game never-going-to-make-it dreams I sometimes had.

By this point nobody on our team would look me in the eye as I passed, nor in the neck or chest for that matter, nor the knee. Nobody wanted to see any part of the guy who might soon be going up to the plate for a chance at negative four-for-four in his big debut. Feigning distraction, their friendly smirks gone, they puttered around behind the bench or sat on it kicking at the dirt, fussing with the laces of their A2000s. Chuck was absorbed in a very deliberate game of catch with himself. I did notice Mike Barry glance at my spikes once but I think he was just admiring my new Pumas.

Somehow the other team's bullpen got their shit together and put us down in order a couple times in a row, dragging out the dread until the fifth inning whereupon I found myself once again alone in that rectangular no-man's land, the batter's box, *pressing*. You may ask, Aren't we over-dramatizing this? In response I may ask, Can we ever over-dramatize dread?

So this "pressing" is what I'd been hearing about all these years. This was that unignorable obstacle you put in your own way inside your own head. I had never been able to relate to it before, but from this day on when players or announcers would casually mention the infection by name *("Well, I don't know, Scooter. Knoblauch just seems like he's really pressing out there."),* or worse, if left untreated, its sinister yet deceptively innocuous sounding disease, "slumps", I couldn't help but feel for the poor guy.

It turns out that here in New England the swift sword of our baseball season cuts both ways. Three cheers for a strong start. May its favorable gusts secure you safe passage to the horizon. Conversely, woe to him who is pulled into the sucking vortex of a slump because, hey – he might not make it back out, people!

By the way, part of a slump's insidiousness lies in its ability to infect one's entire game. Unexplainable throwing errors turn into hapless strikeouts, and, trust me, vice versa.

I think we all know where this is going. The less said about my fourth at-bat that day, and by extension the entire JV season, the better. (Although, perhaps as a cosmic consolation prize, one shiny pebble has remained amid the rubble of that season. On the bus ride home from an away game, a panel truck pulled alongside us on the highway. The driver gave a modest nod in response to our gestures of approbation regarding the rare comeliness of his passenger, a pretty blonde in black turtleneck. After a wink or some other unspoken signal between them, he leaned back in his seat and she turned toward us in hers, pulling with both hands the hem of her sweater up to her chin. Were school buses of the day equipped with seatbelts, Mike Barry's head might not have literally hit the ceiling. As for those players in the back of the bus who missed the show: Tough titty. The panel truck slowly accelerated away, never to be caught up with again despite our unanimous exhortations for the bus driver to floor it. There was real desperation in some of our cries of "Melony!" and "Come back!" and "Please!" and *"Melonyyyyy....!"*)

—

It was around this same time that Chuck and I first took to hanging out socially, i.e., after and apart from organized school- and/or team-related activities. Looking back as I write this, it strikes me that the blossoming of our friendship proper, as opposed to our relationship as mere school chums or teammates, feels somewhat belated considering our similar dispositions and how regularly our classrooms and countless shared playing fields threw us together in the same specific circles.

A couple other characters from those circles making tardy yet everlasting marks back then were the one and only Mike Barry and the equally inimitable Budweiser beer. Over the years I have loved Chuck and Mike and Bud with the equal but alternating ardor of a dad for his triplets, to the extent that ranking the three of them would be a proverbial splitting of hall of fame hairs, like choosing between Griffey, Ichiro or Bonds? Take your pick.

Those heady times of intoxicating bonhomie, when we kicked it through the city's nights like Heismans, remain white as light in my memory, eternally aglow.

Mike Barry was a grade ahead of us in school, though, so the natural order of things would bring Chuck and me together during our high school years, making us each other's go-to guy when, for instance, it came to a weeknight's impromptu jaunt to the movies. Of course the more elaborately planned excursions (to the Garden in town or Coliseum on the Cape or Civic Center or Centrum in Providence or Worcester) for a concert, would include additional others of our ilk such as Matty, John Berksza, Wally, or Bobby Burchard to ride shotgun with Bud.

Throughout the numerous seasons of my ball playing youth, I was fortunate indeed to avoid the arbitrary winds of injury, all the while standing near enough to them at times to feel the chill as they blew past.

One such evening, from the front row of the high school's gymnasium bleachers, I witnessed my brother Joe's elbow dislocation which ended his wrestling match in forfeit, his season in recovery, and his career in effect.

Later that night Joe would wake the whole house with what can be best described as a human's howl. His hand was in the process of turning from blue to purple. Back at Brockton Hospital, the same doctor who'd applied the cast earlier promptly sawed it off, somewhat perplexed. He certainly hadn't foreseen his patient putting on nine pounds in the few hours since having been fitted for a cast.

"He wrestles for the high school," my mother explained. "Should have told you."

"Ah!"

Several of my school friends, too, suffered serious season-ending breaks or tears that led to multiple surgeries; and of course, in keeping with the way these things seem to go, they were all good players. In the cases of Paul Cashin, Bob Burchard, and Don Barlow the injuries turned out to be too severe to play through with anything resembling their former prowess.

—

Memories of sophomore year's preseason football workouts, apart from a handful of specific instances and incidents, have blurred during the intervening decades into a hodgepodge of similar drills and sweaty sprints from that very sweaty summer and the next one and the one after that. Having left the wide-eyed novelty of freshman experiences behind me, I was able to enjoy the familiarity and comfort of the commonplace in my second season. You'd be surprised how nice and easy everything seems in the absence of an upperclassman arbitrarily tripping at your heels.

One of those handful of unforgettable instances was a true "Where Were You Then?" moment. As we lay back on the grass of Eldon B. Keith Field one evening, doing leg lifts at the start of captains practice, our heads all turning like sidewalk strangers unable to pass someone staring skyward without looking up too, one after another stealing glances at our exalted cynosure in the distance who kept watch over us from his air conditioned throne of Corinthian leather, I overheard one of the guys say, "You hear Elvis died today?"

Another big deal that year, for me at least, was my inclusion in the daily procession of players having their ankles taped before practice. There were always multiple taping tables going at once on a next-available next-serve basis, so you were as likely to have Mr. Colombo himself handling your tape that day as any one of the assistant coaches; and every coach had his own personal taping technique. Some would apply a straight stirrup as a base, starting on one side of your shin with strips of the white athletic tape and pulling them tightly under the bottom of the heel and up the other side. Other coaches would start from your instep, wrapping the first few bracing strips around the back, just below the Achilles, and tearing off the tape at the instep again in a cross hatch design.

"What's with that spray before the taping," I asked Chuck sideways while waiting our turn.

"Adhesive. Helps hold the tape in place once you start sweating."

The first couple days at the end of practice, with players using surgical scissors to cut through their tape, you'd hear a lot of "agg!" and "fuck!" when they tore it off, hairs and all. (To this day, the hairless area partway up my shins and calves is a desert of barren follicles, the result of such recurrent depilatory trauma back then, I'm guessing.)

In the tape line that first day, I noticed some players had a layer of stretchy gauzy nylon wrap applied before the tape. When I asked about it, Chuck just shook his head. Behind us in line, Don Barlow snickered, "Yeah, that's just for pussies."

My Day-1 double sessions ankle taper turned out to be our hulking line coach, Gene Marrow. Despite the heat, he was wearing a gray Idaho State sweatshirt, his alma mater. Rumor had it that he returned kicks back in college, but I don't know how that could have been true. How the hell were you going to tackle this guy, especially once he got a head of steam going? All I do know is, when Coach Marrow held your lower leg steady in the tightening vise of his thumb and first finger during taping, you could instantly feel the bruises setting in as your fibula and tibia were pressed unnaturally nearer and nearer to one another, and you could perhaps better appreciate the universe's flair for humor as the relationship of the word 'marrow' to its own self took on a painful irony. (Though I would never sink to jockeying my way out of position so as to avoid his ministrations, as some unabashedly did, I must admit it required no small degree of preliminary girding to maintain a straight face throughout until he mercifully released me with a whap to the the feet and a booming, "Next!")

Testing out my tape job before practice, cutting back and forth on the grass, side to side on the dirt, I was immediately determined to never again take the field without being tightly taped afoot. What an advantage! How had I been able to avoid a common roll or sprain all this time with no tape support? Shit luck, that's how. I'd been performing without a net and I never even knew it.

According to a *Boston Globe* preseason forecast, the 1977 Brockton Football team was "l-o-a-d-e-d." With our overall size, and eleven returning starters coming back for their senior year, including five on the offensive line, favorable comparisons were being made to some of the great Boxer teams of the past. Spirits were high.

When I looked around the Armory, I can't say that what I saw struck me as greatness. I saw a bunch of fairly regular guys from whom I myself was separated by maybe one degree either way, or maybe two. The lofty preseason acclaim was spreading, though, echoed by the other papers and by opposition coaches too. 'Then again,' I thought, 'Maybe this is how greatness looks from a couple lockers over.'

Running as first-string halfbacks were Donny Barlow, a junior with whom I had played last season in the JV backfield, and senior superstar-in-waiting, Mike Parham. Unlike the previous year, I started out being tried right away at various positions at practice, rotating in as a substitute running back, receiver, and even defensive back, in addition to returning kicks and punts. Following my father's advice, any spot on the field was fine by me. Dad was always ready with a timely affirmation, like a quarterback reminding his guys in a fourth quarter huddle to hold onto the ball and stay in bounds to keep the clock running. When he had dropped me off that first morning of doubles, he reminded me, "You already know it, but pay attention and stay ready. Any chance is a chance, so go as hard as you can every time." I think Mr. Colombo saw things the same way. He never came out and said "Okay, let's see what you can do" but you got the feeling that every time your turn came in the rotation was another opportunity for you to tryout for the team.

—

As is so often the case, the last thing anyone could have wanted to go wrong was the very first thing to occur. One day at practice, Parham twisted his ankle.

"Doctor said it'll just be a couple weeks," I heard him say, limping into the locker room the next day on a crutch.

"So you'll be ready for Chicopee?"

"Oh definitely."

I remember there being a collective sigh.

To his credit, after just a few days he was back at the taping tables. Although still unable to run on it, he wanted to be suited up out there every day with the rest of the team.

Our general loss turned out to be a personal gain, albeit temporary, for me and a few other players who were able to take turns with the first-string backfield as replacements in his absence, though none of us as far as I could see were really standing out from the pack.

Parham's status soon became a popular topic of speculation, at practice, around town, and in school corridors once classes started. At an end of summer cookout at our house, my uncle Kevin said, "I heard your running back's hurt, number twenty-one. You might be getting some playing time?"

"No, he just twisted his ankle. Not serious."

"Oh, I was going to say... I'm looking forward to seeing what that kid can do with fifteen, twenty carries a game."

I know uncle Kevin didn't mean anything by it, but it always rubbed me the wrong way when a friend or family member suggested that any of my teammates were better than I was – even when they were. Do me a favor and keep it to yourself is all I'm saying.

During my time at Brockton High I was never privy to or even aware of the existence of any kind of depth chart, per se, posted or otherwise. To determine the hierarchy at a position, I had to see for myself on game day, just like everybody else. (As it has been said of A.J. Liebling's superlative essays on the sweet science of bruising, wherein he humanizes mythic legends of Boxiana like Marciano and Louis and Liston by relating to them in lace-loosened repose instead of lathered and en garde in the tensity of ring ropes, "the obvious goes unmentioned."** Evidently Mr. Colombo held to similar convictions.)

**The Sweet Science* by A.J. Liebling, copyright © 1951, 1952, 1953, 1954, 1955, 1956 by the Estate of A.J. Liebling; Foreword copyright © 2004 by Robert Anasi

Ever on the lookout for clues, with our opening game at Chicopee less than a week away, I hopped up onto Coach Marrow's taping table, adjacent to Mr. Colombo's where sat Mike Parham, naked but for gym shorts, receiving the finishing touches to his tape job.

Among the usual intimate odors of the locker room, I thought I caught scent of something almost sweet in the air. I remember hearing somewhere that the best Italian marble carried with it a mild vaguely vanilla smell. Glancing at Parham I told myself the new scent must surely have more to do with someone's cologne than any marble or onyx in the vicinity but, glancing again, all I could do was shake my head. Unlike my uncle Kevin, I was in no particular hurry to see what manner of havoc this sculpted specimen could wreak unleashed on the unsuspecting Suburban League.

Mr. Colombo patted down his handiwork. "How's that feel, Michael?"

"Good," he nodded.

Maybe by the time I was a senior our head coach would be calling me Gregory...

"Ready to get back at it?"

"Oh no, I was going to give it another couple days."

A sudden scowl equal parts rage and disbelief alerted Michael that his timeline of prognosis might be a little off.

"I'll absolutely be ready for Saturday, though," he assured all interested parties in the fragrant area.

At that point, his assurance might have been irrelevant already – a candidate's campaign promise with 100% of precincts reporting and the opponent's advantage insurmountable. Then again it could have just been my imagination. Sometimes I tend to read into these

things. However, when Coach Colombo called "Next!" and slapped Parham's feet away, there was no doubt in my mind that he assigned more to his gesture than met the eye, and a hell of a lot more to that monosyllabic order than met the ear.
—

Offensively our '77 Brockton Football team made a piss-poor accounting of ourselves that whole season, I must say, never coming within sight, let alone smelling distance, of the bicentennial team's modest 106 total points scored. Did I refer to that 1976 offense as "anemic" earlier? Well, gentlemen*, I humbly and sincerely beg your pardon.

If the '76 team had been truly anemic, then we must have been downright hemophiliac in 1977. I'm embarrassed to admit we managed a pathetic 88 points that season, establishing a new nadir of offensive ineptitude at Brockton, while amassing just three measly wins. A 3-6 record stinks, of course – *PATHETIC!* – but it's all the more disappointing because other than our opening loss to Chicopee we were ahead or tied at halftime in every game that year. By rights, we coulda, woulda, and most definitely shoulda posted a respectable won/lost record. Our inability to finish teams off can be attributed mainly to the inexperience in our backfield and the lack of senior leadership.

Tut-tut! Don't worry, friends, I won't bore everybody now by recounting the long litany of mishaps from our whole dismal campaign... but whenever I do happen to unlock the door, as it were, to descend to the cellar of that Brockton Football decade and poke through the cobwebby boxes of dented cardboard down there, a few old souvenirs do still stand out.

*[CONFESSIONAL: My Heartfelt Apologies to the Entire 1976 Boxers Offense, including but not limited to: *Damiano, Duford, Horton, Heger, Bergeron, Baker, Lalli, Tzikas, McCann, Goulding, Malcolm, Kechejian, Sullivan, Volta, Johnson, Frenette, Parham.*]

For instance, on opening day at Chicopee (a sunny Sunday following the unnerving limbo of a Saturday rainout), as luck would have it and frankly to my surprise, the very first play of our entire season was a screen pass to... you guessed it! Rather than knee-shivering jolts of nervous adrenaline when I heard my number called, the sensation filling me was the empowerment we feel at an idol's show of faith in us. If I was ever going to come through on the field of play for somebody, it was going to be right there right then for Armond C. Colombo, Sr., thank you.

As we clapped out of the huddle and broke into our traditional Wishbone formation, I set down to a three-point stance at halfback, touching one hand to the cool playing field grass. A breeze tickled over everything, including the growth of blades between my forked fingers. It's funny the way the solitary stillness of such moments leading up to the real action stays with you even more vividly than the ensuing act itself. In that fraught moment I remember the bending and buffeting of my blades of grass and thinking *This is the kind of random detail you'll end up remembering forever.* As I say, the overarching feeling then was not the knocking knees of a fledgling, but rather the strongest game energy I had ever known – crackling, quick and unstoppable. Here we go! Just get me the ball and get out of the way!

Evidently Chicopee's cornerback on the short side had faithful idols of his own to hail. He dropped me for a loss as soon as I caught the pass, four yards behind the line of scrimmage. After this inauspicious start, my debut actually went south from there. I would end up losing a fumble deep in Chicopee territory, and another one deep in our own territory. (To add insult to injury, as I trudged off the field after my second fumble, at barely a jog, head hanging, I heard, "Greg!" Then a moment later, "GREG!" It was my old junior high coach, the great Ed Fitzgibbons, who volunteered as the BHS game day statistician, yelling for me. In his fire engine red windbreaker, he was easy to spot on the crowded sideline, pen in hand, cradling his clipboard. When he saw that I'd heard him, he shouted, for all the world to hear, "Who was it?" If I wasn't so pissed

I would have laughed my ass off. Instead I punched myself in the chest and barked, *"Me!"*)

As southly as things were going, they could have been much worse, so I really can't complain; to wit, it was very lucky later that I managed to regain possession of a bobbled punt at midfield. This turned into another one of those freeze frame images you never end up forgetting.

Having been bent backwards and sideways by the oncoming tacklers, I saw for an instant from the bottom of the pile my unclaimed fumble just lying there in arm's reach and harm's reach away. On the brand new football's curvy face, its laces seemed to smile at me through clenched teeth ("What are you *waiting for...*?" it was trying to say. "Can't keep this up much *longer...*") as if it knew – like I knew – that there was barely time for me to shoot one hand out to spank the ball and snatch it back, preventing fumble number three or else having my elbow broken trying.

I was lucky as hell in that moment to avert the worst, pure and simple; not to mention that the world lucked out too, ending up richer by a good many Boxercentric vignettes thanks to the success of that far-fetched snatch of mine.

Needless to say, though, nobody would have argued if reservations for a sixty-day / sixty-night stay at the Boxer Dog House Kennel & Resort were booked and confirmed forthwith in my name. Honestly, if I were my coach I probably would have benched me. (The day wasn't a complete failure, to be fair. I did make one pretty good spur of the moment play, even if I am saying so myself. The second half kickoff came bouncing toward me. Its final surprisingly high bounce took every inch of my vertical leap with one hand stretching straight up to put fingers on it. Gathering it in, I carried out the first leg of our designed kickoff return reverse, handing off to Jon Lowell who then handed off to my fellow sophomore Owen O'Connor. From there, Owen took it eighty yards untouched to the endzone for our only score of the day.)

One more thing... The next week, unlike the previous year at Newton when their starters did all their scoring in the first three quarters before retiring to their rain gear to cheer on the Tiger cubs, Newton North waited until the fourth period to turn what started out as a good old defensive struggle into a rout, 25-6, scoring 19 unanswered points to close out the contest.

After the postgame single file hand shake with their players, I saw that my brother Joe had made his way down onto the field. He assured me, "It wasn't your fault. You didn't lose the game." My scowling gesture of retort was neither brotherly nor called for. Thank goodness our world back then had yet to perfect the means of memorializing for broadcast such extemporaneous vulgarity. The sheer wrongdoing of it scalds me to this day. (Oh, the memeworthy juxtaposing of coarse streetcorner obscenity with decorous cleated helmeted uniformity!) Joe was always my number one fan. He didn't deserve that. I'm glad neither of us have ever mentioned it again, nor his parting shot which I deserved very much indeed: "Fuck you! You did cost the game!"

It's interesting that the newspaper account of this particular game is mysteriously and conspicuously missing from the Dunn Family Scrapbook. I don't specifically recall dropping any big passes that day or committing any untimely fumbles, or missing key blocks, but the collective evidence, circumstantial though it might be (i.e., Newton exploding for 19 fourth period points after having mustered just two field goals over the previous three quarters; the fact that my mother chose to conveniently withhold from the scrapbook the details of this one game, and only this one game (out of a possible 30 over the course of three seasons), thereby creating a suspicious gap which smacks of Nixonian tampering; Joe's dubious post-game commentary) does seem to suggest a certain culpability on my part for the loss. I mean, let's face it.

Is it possible that I have just blocked it out all this time through stubborn long term denial? Then again, how the hell bad could the article have been? DUNN SHAMES SELF AND ENTIRE ANCESTRY?

Screw it, if I really want to know – and who says I do? – I can always just check with Joe. He'd definitely remember.

And one more thing (Heh!)... I'll never forget how during halftime of the Quincy game, a 0-0 tie to that point, our team physician Doctor John Lingos stitched a gash on the edge of Chuck's chin that he'd suffered being sacked on a helmet-to-chinstrap hit. I was next to them in the locker room for the whole procedure. Doc Lingos, an anesthesiologist by profession, flashed a pen light into each of our QB's eyes and got right down to stitching. No Novocaine or pain killer of any kind was dispensed; nor was the slightest wince evinced on the part of the patient. Old Chuck had grit, he took it like a champ. They threw some gauze on it, replaced his bloody chinstrap with a bulky padded one, and sent him right back out for the second half.

Oh, and yeah! For some strange reason – don't ask me – this one has always stuck with me... On the plush artificial turf of Parson's Field before the Brookline game, with players testing out the benefits of sneakers versus cleats, Mr. Colombo saw me stretching and asked which footwear I preferred. I nodded, "Cleats."

"Cleats are betterrrrrrrr!" he announced to everyone on the field. "Cleats are betterrrrrrrr!"

—

And that shall be the last of my game-specific remembrances of sophomore *temps perdu*. I promise.

Nevertheless! Between the second and third week of the season, with my future as a starting running back in real and well-deserved jeopardy, I was at my locker getting ready for practice when the lone bark of a midsize dog was heard coming from the coaches office.

The general locker room feedback was "—the fuck?"

"Maybe we got a new mascot," someone joked.

A dog's bark in the night puts a firm picture in your mind of its demeanor and size, and even its breed. Well this dog in the office being a Boxer made perfect sense to me.

The door to the coaches office opened a crack. "Is Greg Dunn out there?"

I got to my feet. "Yup!"

On my way there I passed a couple seniors who shouldered by me. The first sniped in my ear, "Here we go, party's over." His sidekick mimicked the ominous tolling of a bell: "Bonnnggggg... bonnngggg... Back to the burgers."

Ducking my head in the coaches office, there was no sign of Super Boxer Boy or his super bowls anywhere.

"Close the door, Greg," Mr. Colombo said. Then he reared back and yawped, *"RUFF!"*

"Bless you."

He blew his nose. "Thank you."

Unable to quite suppress a grin, I nodded.

"Greg, do you wear glasses?"

"Yuh," I kept nodding, grinless now.

"Contact lenses?"

"No."

The other coaches getting ready for practice caught my eye by the mere act of their returning to dressing after having taken in my response.

Mr. Colombo nodded at me for a while and when he opened his mouth to tell me something, he barked, *"RUFF!"*

We all blessed him and he called the meeting to an end with a simple, "Okay."

On my way out of the office, reverting to denial mode, I focused on my locker and did not deviate, acknowledging nothing and no one along the way, feeling the heat of a dozen pointed gazes. Although this day might turn out to be my last as a starting player, I was not about to reveal anything to any enemy, real or imagined, in that locker room.

As previously noted in these pages, good luck, timing, and chance are the makers and breakers of success. That same day, with zero ceremony or ado, I was removed from the punt return team and the kickoff return team, replaced in both roles by Matty Walsh (the best multi-talented football player I knew during my time at Brockton), but I brushed those demotions aside like so many arm tacklers because, much to my sure grin,* I was still being allowed to run with the first-string offense as one of its starting halfbacks.

By this point in the season, up-and-coming Owen O'Connor had simply taken as his own the other halfback spot. An overnight sensation on last year's freshman team, and now in just his second year of organized football, Owen was still learning the game but he had guts, and speed to burn. Thus, not only had two popular upperclassmen from the starting backfield recently been supplanted (at least for the time being), but in their steads were a couple of inexperienced sophomores.

Our similar situations brought me and Owen tightly together, on the field and off, to the point where we took to spending all of our free time together, either working out or hanging out at one or the other's house (e.g., that winter, the blizzard of '78 would hit while we were walking to his house after school, and would strand me at the O'Connors' for two days and nights). With fellow sophomore Chuck Colombo having emerged as starting quarterback, it made for a unique Boxer backfield indeed.

If our presence together in the huddle forged a stronger bond among the three of us, it also served to unite the seniors on the team against this new wave of what they took to be undeserving upstarts.

When it became apparent that predictions of my demise had been somewhat premature, the hitherto whispered and veiled Dunn-directed animosity came out to play for real. On Tuesdays during First-O vs First-D, I would take grinding knuckles to the ribs at the bottom of a pile as a matter of course, as well as raking handpads up under the face mask, and always with a spew of vitriol to boot. Doubtless emboldened by the sheer number of their fellow mutineers, the word *Vendetta* was actually growled during a number of scrums, I kid you not. (Ahhh... Where are the Ralph Abbruzzis of yesteryear?) And the funny thing is, most of the growling was being done by guys who were in real life some of the biggest pussies on the team!

* !

At home later, following that confab in the coaches office, my parents and I were talking at our dining room table after supper.

"And that's all Colombo said?"

"That was it. Then he just said 'Okay' and I went back out to my locker and got ready for practice."

"And it was a normal practice? You were going out for passes and everything?"

"Yeah."

"Alright. I don't know about contact lenses, though. Those things break. And if it's your good eye… Or might get knocked out during the game. How the hell much are they anyway? We hold off on those, they'll probably be cheaper than glasses in a couple years."

"They have the soft contacts now," my mother said.

"A guy I play handball with has those safety goggles he wears on the court, like Alcindor wears. He got poked in the eye playing in the Y handball tournament. Scratched his cornea."

"Prescription goggles?"

"Yeah, his regular prescription but on safety glasses. Gregga, who's that NFL kid now? Wears black glasses under his helmet? Big kid, running back."

I said, "Chuck Muncie?"

"Right."

Within a week my parents had secured me a pair of clear wraparound safety glasses with prescription lenses of thick scratch-resistant plastic. Dad had me bring my helmet and pads home to put the glasses through their paces out front as a litmus test.

"Shoulder pads too?"

"You need to get the true feel."

That evening after practice, outfitted in glasses, helmet and shoulder pads, we played a little catch on the lawn. He had me stand ten yards away with my back to him as he threw passes alternately over my right shoulder, left shoulder; left shoulder, right shoulder.

"How they feel?"

With the helmet pressing against their sides they were a little uncomfortable, but I figured that would pass.

"Good."

Even if the discomfort behind each ear developed into raw spots of soreness, it would be fine. Football is a game that lends itself well to a thorn in the flesh. Such irritations serve to keep one's attention rooted in the moment.

"They sliding around at all?"

"They're good." I shook my head around to be sure.

"Take off straight. I'll send some right over the top."

The vision was good, the firm fit good.

On our lawn stood a cluster of five white oak saplings, each of them eight inches or so in diameter.

"Now run weaves through these trees a few times carrying the ball as fast as you can for thirty seconds." As I did, hunching my helmet forward to avoid the few low hanging limbs, I cut the tightest angles I could. Here and there my shoulder pads skimmed against the thin bark of the trees. Dad would call out "Change hands" or "Reverse field" at odd intervals.

When I was all done, he said, "That's an excellent drill. They feel alright?"

"Good," I nodded, catching my breath.

"Whenever you run a drill, have a ball in your hands. Otherwise it's just exercise. They fogging up?"

I shook my head no. Our litmus test had been a success.

Unfortunately, warming up at the beginning of practice the next day during three-to-a-line fly patterns, the lenses almost immediately fogged up. When I tried to wipe them off they just smeared so I had to do without them.

"Probably because the weather was cooler today than the other day," Dad surmised later. "It's good we found out right off the bat. Glasses are one piece of equipment that's got to work a hundred percent of the time every time."

"Yeah."

"Don't shitcan them, though. You can still use them at the Y. For racquetball or handball."

"Baseball too, maybe."

"We'll figure out something else for you, though. Don't worry." (Sincere respect and kudos to teammate Champagne Charlie Lima for toughing out his set of identical eyewear, somehow making them work for years!)

Within another week, my parents had me fitted with a pair of Bausch + Lomb soft contact lenses which I wore in practice and games from there on out.

—

In the parking lot after practice one evening, my father was fuming red. "You think I have all night to sit around out here? Waiting for you to stroll out of the locker room whenever you feel like it?"

"No, but—"

"I hustle from work to get here, and you're the last one on the whole team to come out the door? Not 'one of the last' – the *last!* I watched every guy on your team come through here. Look at this parking lot. You see any other assholes still waiting? Everybody's been gone twenty minutes ago. They're all at home having supper now. They're— what's the matter?"

It was all I could do not to burst into tears. That day's acts of aggression had unexpectedly spilled over into the locker room. Although my words sounded stupid in my mind, I didn't know any way of putting it better. "They don't like me…"

"Who?"

"The seniors…"

"What do you mean they don't like you?"

All I could do was shake my head.

My father being a Dorchester Irish fuck-'em-all kind of guy, he scoffed, "I wouldn't blame what's-his-name for not liking you. You're cutting in on his playing time. You're cutting *out* his playing time. But those other shitheads…? The hell with them." When I didn't

165

respond, he said, "If they don't like you it's because they know you're not a quitter."

Dad put the car in gear and started backing up, collecting his thoughts. "Well," he said. "You know who does like you? Colombo. And he's the only one that counts."

We were quiet the whole way home.

Pulling up in front of our house, Dad gave my head a reassuring tousle the way he used to when I was a kid. "Take a second. Get yourself together," he said. "Everybody's waiting for us. There's a nice picture of you in today's *Enterprise*, scoring your touchdown. First one ever so Ma wants you to get a look before it goes in the scrapbook."

"Yuh?"

"First of many. We're getting Christo's"

"Okay."

"Listen to me. Hey. Listen: The seniors can go screw. Colombo's the only one that matters, and he believes in you. Or he wouldn't be putting you on the field. That's what burns their ass." I felt myself nodding. "But you know what's funny? Now watch: down the road these same assholes will be telling lies in the barroom to anyone who'll listen about how you and them are all old friends."

"Fuck that."

My father laughed, "Mark my words."

Dad had those seniors pegged cold. There were a few here and there who were alright guys, I thought: Chris Disangro for one, Sullivan, Frenette, Frank Cooney – albeit not to the extent that they disavowed their class allegiance by coming to my defense. Then again, who the hell could blame them for that, right?

"All set?"

"Yuh…" I nodded. "Sorry."

He tousled my hair again. "Nothing to be sorry about."

I started to get out of the car but needed another moment.

"Gregga. Hey. It's alright, let's go."

I took in a couple long breaths and let them out.

"It's like I tell you guys, a lot of people in the world are just shitheads. Most people. They don't like anyone who's got something good going. You're going to see this happen to people over and over in life, over and over again. The world's full of miserable seniors with nothing better to do. They can't even get in the game. So they gang up on one of the good guys whenever they get the chance. Makes them feel better about their sucky lives."

I understood.

"It's a good thing you're finding out early. It'll never hurt you like this again, because now you know."

"Thanks, Dad," I nodded and took in one more big breath of air. "…Christo's?"

"Yup."

Walking up the driveway, he said, "A lot of guys don't learn this shit till they're grown men."

"Really?"

"And it feels a hell of a lot worse for them then, believe me."

"Really?"

"Hell of a lot worse."

"Wow."

"Bet your ass."

My dear old Dad was right, of course, and that day's events turned out to be a developmental watershed for me. Up until then I had regarded on-field malevolence as nothing more than spirited chicanery, a pain in the ass maybe but nevertheless par for the course and wholly tolerable – for, all's fair between the sidelines. Once you're buckled up out there, play as tough as you want and as rough as you will because, as anyone who really knows the sport will tell you, it is a physical impossibility in football to be too rough in between the lines. Hence, only those actors ignorant of this will waste their hour on the field strutting and fretting in the name of intimidation; but bringing it into the locker room changes the game. Do that and you're making it personal.

But… I don't know. These seniors might have undergone a similar initiation in their turn and now dumbly regarded their antagonism toward me as carrying on a longstanding tradition, assholish though it might be. However, I really hoped this wasn't the case, because I felt a great innate respect for the legendary Boxer alumni who came before, and I didn't like the idea of them ever having stooped to bullshit like this, even if it suggested that this year's aggression toward me wasn't necessarily personal.

—

There's no doubt about it, 1977 was setting up to be a year of sea change transition all the way around. The new wave of Britain's punk scene brought with it debut albums by The Clash and Elvis Costello. Our own Talking Heads had just come out with their first record too. At home, Joe was in his glory. "It doesn't take an oracle," he would say, shaking his head. "Greg, come here. Check this out."

On the team, unexpected but nonetheless unavoidable change was in the air too. For some reason, partway through the season we were all issued new game jerseys of an entirely different fabric. Waiting my turn in line, the song coming from the seniors' corner of lockers was something by Emerson, Lake & Palmer...

I sang to myself, "I hate people when they're not polite."

Linxy, the gruff equipment manager, handed me my replacement '48' and made a mark on his list.

"Mr. Lanzetta?"

The bow of one eyebrow flattened out as he looked up from the clipboard. "Yeah?"

"Is forty-five available?"

I figured the closer I moved toward '43' the more progress I was making. (What can I say? It made sense to me.)

He squinted at me, and I got the feeling that somehow he understood my way of thinking. "Yeah, alright."

Walking away with my new number, I heard his barker call, "Any other requests? Who's next! No reasonable offer refused! Forty-eight's up for grabs, what am I bid?"

"I'll try forty-eight," someone offered.

"No you won't! Here – that's you! Next!"

Subsequently, when I would watch game films or see photos of me sporting my new number, I could tell I had been right; somehow '45' was less wrong.

Believe it or not, that bittersweet sophomore season ended on a high note, for me at least. (A tree grows in Brockton!) The ups and downs of a very down year claimed as one of its casualties all-around athlete Jimmy Direnzo. Our (barefoot!) punter, he was replaced of course by (shodfoot) Matty Walsh. It was too bad, though, because in addition to being an all-around athlete, Direnzo was an all-around good guy too, and the team needed every good guy it could find that year. Like all other roster changes, this one happened off stage, as it were, and since it took place outside the scope of my own private Boxiana, I didn't put four and three together until a couple days after the fact, by which time Jim Direnzo was officially gone.

In those days it was the BHS custom during the week-and-a-half leading up to a Thanksgiving home game to bring up select players from the sophomore team to practice with the varsity and then dress for the big game. It was a nice way to give those younger guys an early taste of what awaited them next season.

At practice that week, whenever a particular play had me positioned at wingback, blocking down on the defensive end, I found myself opposite one of the new guys, a sophomore named Rich Miano, younger brother of last year's tri-captain, Steve Goulding. Blocking was never my strong suit, but this kid was quietly exposing me to new depths of futility. Although we were about the same size, he was wiry strong, and quick. After just a few plays, I was asking myself where the hell this guy had been hiding. It was all I could do to maintain any kind of blocking contact throughout the play, and whenever I did so he would acknowledge it with an encouraging word or a pat on the helmet.

Miano would end up inheriting Jimmy Direnzo's vacated jersey assignment. By the time game uniforms were issued to the newcomers, I felt like I was on good enough terms with Rich Miano to invite him in on an illegal numbers game I had in mind.

"Rich, would you mind swapping jerseys for the game? I get your forty-three, and you get my forty-five."

"Yeah? Why?"

"Well my family number is forty-three, and—"

"Oh, of course. No problem."

With that, my short-lived stint as Boxer #45 had come to an undistinguished end.

It was with true pride that I sported '43' for the first time that Thanksgiving Day, and I knew that uncles Jimmy and Kevin in the stands along with Dad would have gotten a kick out of the surprise unveiling too. Marciano Stadium's dramatic PA announcer, Mr. Tom Hughes, repeatedly declaring throughout the game, *"Direnzo on the carry..."* fazed me not one whit, nor did the nice photo of 'Brockton's Jim Direnzo...' in the *Enterprise* the next day.

—

A couple days after Thanksgiving, my father took me and John Millett, whom I had become friends with over the last two football seasons, into Boston Garden to see Marvin Hagler's fight against Mike Colbert. With both boxers undefeated, and Colbert ranked as the middleweight number one contender, it was a much anticipated bout around here since Hagler fought out of a gym in Brockton. A victory over Colbert would presumably put him next in line for a title shot.

In addition to local hero Hagler, Brockton welterweight Jimmy Corkum also fought that night. Appearing on the undercard, he won something like his 25th consecutive bout in a dominant unanimous decision to remain undefeated as a professional. The things I remember about that fight are my Dad pointing out that Corkum was still a teenager – I mean, *I* was a teenager, and here's this kid fighting as a pro at the Garden! – and Corkum repeatedly knocking the other guy's mouthpiece out. (Unfortunately, his winning streak would come to an end just a few weeks later in a return to the Garden at the hands of yet another Brocktonian, Tony Petronelli; and Jimmy Corkum would eventually retire at the ripe old age of twenty-one in the wake of a loss to Dorchester-cum-Ireland fighter Sean Mannion, abandoning boxing for good to try his hand at med school and the rough-and-tumble game of gastroenterology.)

Apparently, the level of anticipation for Hagler-Colbert had been greatly exaggerated; that, or the stormy freezing rain, snow, and wind in the forecast kept fight fans at home. I've attended all manner of Causeway Street cultural events over the years (Ringling Brothers and Barnum & Bailey extravaganzas, Ice Capades, Celtics games, Bruins, Harlem Globetrotters, rock & roll in concert), but never had the Garden seemed so cavernous. The place couldn't have been more than a quarter full. Honestly, I've seen bigger crowds for the Beanpot, and considering the boxing ring's comparatively small floor space, the sparsity of sports fans that night was magnified even more. Although we had balcony seats, there was no doubt that our fanly cries of advice and support were reaching the ears of our hometown battlers. In fact, our section (which included Brockton Football assistant coach Tony Woods and his buddies seated directly in front of us by one row) cheered first, longest and loudest.

It turns out that the most excitement missed by anyone who stayed home that night probably occurred on the icy Southeast Expressway after the fight. Mike Colbert didn't look like any council or association (or federation or organization for that matter) number one ranked anything, unless it was for riding a unicycle backwards for ten straight rounds. When Hagler finally caught him, the fight was over. Those not in attendance didn't miss a thing.

Outside, Dad caught me with a rabbit punch when he tossed me the keys.

"*What?*"

"You're up."

The drive home was a trial-by-fire test of my learner's permit skills. Checking the rearview once, I caught Johnny Millett's face expressing something never before seen in all our days on the football field – maniacal fear. I almost cracked up thinking it a silly intentional caricature. It wasn't.

With the heyday of the singer-songwriter still very much visible in the rearview, modern music's hands-down head-and-shoulders greatest musical decade continued to add unexpected mountains to the horizon, ranging from the heaviest, hardest, glammest of Rock to the heart of the Blues and soul of Funk, to Reggae, to the incipient protean forces of Punk, New Wave, and, yes – credit where it's due – Disco.

That sophomore year, during free periods at school sometimes, or cutting short our lunches, Chuck and I would go to the Green Building IRC and, instead of borrowing books, we would check out from their library a record album along with headphones for half-hour intervals. Plugging in at one of the carrels, we'd listened to Dylan's greatest hits or the bottomless Beatles repertoire, or *Let it Bleed* or the Kinks or *Transformer*, or something else we liked from the Green Information Resource Center's limited but surprisingly high quality collection.

We were at that age when music was becoming important to us. Whenever we'd find ourselves in a department store, for instance, we'd always be sure to spend some time browsing the album section, making a point of stopping to reconsider Roxy Music's cover art, and *Mom's Apple Pie,* and *Electric Ladyland.*

I remember well, on one prearranged day off from school in early spring of 1978, we went to Westgate Cinema with Matty and Bob Burchard and John Berksza to see Martin Scorsese's eye-opening *The Last Waltz*.

By the way, I have previously identified Matt Walsh as the best multi-talented athlete I ever played with at Brockton, and that statement is true as North. Well, John Berksza is the best multi-talented athlete of my contemporaries I *never* played with at Brockton. A six handicap golfer; Suburban League all-star in the sport that best measures athleticism – basketball; hitting fourth in the varsity baseball batting order; he was a true all-around athlete, perhaps best equipped for a decathlon. At 6'2", 190, he had size, excellent foot speed, great hand to eye, and a howitzer for an arm.

Just one grade ahead of me in school, he and I played in the same summer leagues, and in the same sports at times during the school year, but had he elected to go to Cardinal Spellman as his dad once suggested, we would have ended up playing together on the very same number of school teams – exactly zero. It was the powerful hands of Timing and Chance that held us apart, oddly and unfortunately preventing our ever becoming actual teammates.

—

It was around this time that our garage, which had some time ago been converted into a playroom, was reconverted into a wrestling room, complete with authentic Resilite hard foam matting which covered the entire floor, wall to wall. It had become clear that my brothers Rich and Steve possessed a special talent for the sport of wrestling. Their bedroom at the end of the hall was amassing age-group medals and trophies at a rate of two or three a week during the season from tournaments near and far. More often than not they both won their weight class, or if one of them didn't take first place, the other did. With Rich the more methodical of the two, relying on superb skill and finesse, and Steve competing in the next weight class up, equally skilled but more of a rough and tumble customer, it often came down to one or the other being named the tournament's outstanding wrestler.

I remember heading out in the middle of the night to tournaments as far away as Wilkes-Barre, Pennsylvania, piling the twins in the back seat to sleep and keeping my father company on the drive. We would listen to cassette tapes he had made of Eddie Andelman and *The Sports Huddle,* or old time radio shows like *Amos and Andy* and *Duffy's Tavern.*

—

Tryouts for varsity baseball that year once again coincided (not unintentionally) with my father's batting practice regimen having polished my swing to a robust shine (Thank you, Dad!). Tryouts also coincided with what my brother Joe immediately identified as "the writing on the wall."

I had told him that I'd been crushing balls to dead center field that day.

"That's where you drive them when you're in the zone."

"Yup. Rick Carbonara was grooving me BP melons, just one right after another."

"You hit any out?"

"Huh? No. We were at West Junior High, so…"

"West? Why West?"

"They sent half of us to West. The rest stayed at the high school."

"And you were one of the ones that went to West?"

Besides his annoyingly singsong word choice, I didn't like what I was hearing in Joe's voice. I replied, "Yeah…"

"Where was Pileski?"

"…The high school."

Joe let out a bitter chuckle.

I said, "Well, they sent Doc Kostka to run things at West."

"Oh, okay. Doc saw you at bat, you're all set."

"Ah… Well, he hadn't gotten there yet."

"*He wh—?* So why'd you even get up?"

"I…"

"Greg! *I can't believe y—* So nobody even saw you get up to hit? Except Ricky? Nobody got to see your, ah… 'fine sheen?'"

"You mean robust shine?"

"You should've just called it 'fine shine' and left it at that."

"Eh," I winced. "Too rhymey."

"Yeah. In other words, nobody who mattered saw you hit shit today."

Joe used to say I was the dumbest smart guy he ever knew. It was times like this that I heard where he was coming from.

He took a couple aborted breaths, but the rest of our unpleasant conversation went unsaid. Finally he turned away and left our room. I saw him shaking his head on the way out the door, and heard him muttering to himself, "Believe this shit...?"

—

I have a nice photo taken by my mother of a very youthful me and an equally youthful Chuck standing side by side on the steps of Saint Margaret's Church in our red robes the night of our Confirmation.

Earlier in the day, I had played a JV baseball game at Newton North; for, alas: my brother Joe had correctly interpreted the illest of omens written on the West Junior High wall during tryouts. (Chuck and Steve Tuite made the cut for varsity that year, rightfully so; whereas I, wrongfully, did not, even if I do say so myself.) When I was at the plate during pregame batting practice, I overheard Coach Fouracre mention to the Newton coach behind the backstop, "Our leadoff guy right there's our best hitter." That kind of thing is always nice to overhear.

At church I was seated in one of the pews up front, waiting for the proceedings to get under way, when Chuck sat down next to me.

"Let the sacraments begin," he whispered.

"And also with you."

"How'd it go at Newton today?"

"Victory was ours, 5-4."

Chuck tested the weight of the kneeler with his foot. "How'd you do?"

"Led off the game with a fucking bomb to dead center, thank you."

"Hit it out?"

"Yep."

"Dunna!" he punched my shoulder.

"Then next time up, the guy tried to take my head off with a high fastball that kept running in on me. I just twisted away and bailed, it was all I could do. Don't know how I got out of the way, actually. And trying to keep my balance I had to kind of run in a big semicircle away from the plate, and Frenchy thought I was going after the guy or something. He jumped up from the bench waving his arms yelling, "No no! No!"

"Pitchers refuse to forgive us our trespasses."

"Amen. So then when he walked me, he drilled me twice diving back to first on pick off throws. And that sniggering first baseman... faking like he was trying to get me out but letting the throws go through."

"Where'd they get you?"

"Both right here." I clapped the ribs under my right arm. "Newton..."

"Frig Newton."

Chuck's always been quick on the draw like that. I squinted hard, turning away to bow my head, wringing every bit of silent breath out of the laugh. "Then later," I went on, recovering, "the resident old-timer said he'd never seen a ball go that far out of dead center field."

"Heh! Resident old timer..."

———

In June at the end of sophomore year, I was formally introduced to Chuck's brother, Donny. He had joined in on a concert excursion with me, Chuck, and Mike Barry, to the Providence Civic Center to see the Kinks, and it must be said that he made a grand first impression.

Right off the bat he offered to handle the driving, immediately endearing himself by enabling us youngsters to be as wanton as we liked in our indulgence of canned beer on the ride to Providence – by which I mean that Chuck and Mike and I could each revel with reckless abandon in our more than adequate allotment of three Schlitzes apiece. At the wheel, Donny nursed his same beer for the duration of the ride.

While we all made small talk, Mike and I joshed with each other in the back seat, calling attention to the jampacked musculature in our t-shirted driver's shoulders and back by elbowing and jostling one another. On the stereo, a Kinks cassette was extolling the simple virtues of fair weather laziness, and fashionable dedication.

"I hope they play 'Lola' first," I declared.

"Dunna's going to this concert to hear one song."

Donny said, "I hope that's not true."

It wasn't, but this would be my first concert ever (Mike's too) and I was kind of jazzed about all things Kinks and didn't care who knew it. I posed a question to the tape deck, "You claim you're not dumb – but you can't understand why Lola walks like a woman but talks like a man? Really? Let me tell you something, buddy—"

Mike finished my thought, "You *are* dumb!"

"Xactly!"

He elbowed me and nodded toward the front seat. After having seen Don Colombo play linebacker at Marciano Stadium for years, and having watched so many of his wrestling matches, including the state finals in '75, it was kind of weird reconciling that larger than life figure with Chuck's laconic big brother sitting so casually behind the wheel. The thick triceps of his right arm adjusted in subtle visible flexes as he steered. Mike and Chuck were wearing t-shirts, too; their tri's didn't do that, and neither did mine.

Of all the Colombo brothers, Donny would turn out to be the least accessible. Although each of them had played on the football team, he alone ventured into the ascetic world of wrestling. After graduation he matriculated at Brown, of all places, following his own lead again, and in so doing shoved aside the bookcase at the entrance of the Ivy League's secret passageway which had loomed so formidably in the Brockton psyche, as it did most everywhere – not so much as an obstacle but as personification of a pie-in-the-sky notion, the like of which should not even be entertained in jest by lowly commoners such as us. This newfound ability to gaze through that open doorway and peek around in there served to embolden the next generation of blue collar Boxer athletes to toss their own hats across the threshold, which in turn encouraged the group behind them to do the same, and likewise the next group, and so on.

In fact, you know what? Cheers right now to Don Colombo. He had a big hand in helping to get that local groundswell going.

Toward the end of the trip, Mike proclaimed in mock childish anticipation that was only semi-mock, "Welcome to Rhode Island!"

Then, to contribute something topical to the proceedings, and for lack of anything better, I came up with, "So who's going to win the Belmont?"

"Is that today?"

"Ah... *next* Saturday."

"Gotta go with Affirmed, right?"

"I was talking to my brother Joe—"

"How is Austin," Donny said, checking with my reflection in the rearview.

"He's good."

"Whereabouts they station him?"

"Pensacola, Florida," I informed him, which he acknowledged with a thoughtful nod at the traffic. "So Joe says Alydar all the way. He says if the Preakness was twenty yards longer, Alydar would have took it."

Chuck supplied, "And the Belmont's the longest one."

"Right. And he makes another good point: No way there's back-to-back Triple Crowns."

"Austin... always ahead of the curve," said Donny.

Even back then, Chuck was showing a predisposition to advocate on behalf of the devilish. "There's many key factors, though," he stated. "Quality of bloodline. Jockey. Track conditions on the day."

"Joe says throw all that shit out the window."

"Heh!"

Mike Barry weighed in, "I don't really know Joe, but I'm with him."

"Greg, next time you two talk, give him my best, please."

"I sure will."

"Appreciate it," Donny nodded in the mirror.

After a while Mike proclaimed, "Entering Providence!"

"Is that the Civic Center right there?"

"That's it."

I was looking around. "Where's Brown from here, Don?"

The evening sky was sunny and clear. "Due east about a mile. See it up over there?"

When we got off the highway, someone (most likely Donny) made the excellent suggestion that we stock up on beer for the ride home later.

Full Disclosure: I am not now, nor have I ever been, related by blood or affiliation to Roger Williams or Moses Brown, nor to any of their revered descendants. For that matter, I've never been considered a "friend" of a Patriarca patriarch, nor a buddy of any Cianci. Nevertheless, the city of Providence, RI, is A-Okay in my book; always has been, always will be.

In the busy package store, Mike and I sought out a more suitable brand of beer – something famed for its taste, smoothness and drinkability, perhaps; or a refreshing malt beverage effervescent enough to put us back in the high life again – in order to cleanse our palates of that Schlitzy aftertaste. We broke off from Donny and Chuck in search of same.

"Here we go," Mike said. He slid open one of the doors to the refrigerated shelves along the back wall of the store, grabbing us a six-pack of cold Miller cans.

"Good call," I agreed, adding by way of unpremeditated whim, "I'll block."

Without another word or look, we lightfooted it to the exit.

Bear in mind, at that point in time I had only recently, yet without a doubt permanently, left the life of the teetotalist behind me. You could count on one hand and both feet the number of times I'd ever been intoxicated. I mention this by way of alibi, flimsy though it might be, and in the spirit of mitigating circumstance, because... Was shoplifting a common practice for Mike Barry and me? Certainly not. Were we closet kleptos fulfilling our secret mania? Hardly. In fact, if it please the Court, I would like to file an objection. We were kids! Come *on*... Right? What it boils down to is this, your honor: Should the slightest bit of mercy exist in your jurisprudent soul, I hereby throw myself upon it.

Of course, my game cohort and I hadn't mapped out any sort of plan beforehand, let alone an exit strategy, but we would have been hard pressed to convince eyewitnesses of that. To them we must have looked like a reunited dance team from the Burglars Ball the way we so effortlessly fell into step with one another and glided out the door in our illicit minuet.

Oh, by the way, my friend Mike Barry might have missed his calling. As soon as we hit the sidewalk he tucked the six-pack and *bolted* with the untamed hurtling gait of a man on fire. Although I'd inherited the natural footspeed which had blessed uncles of mine from both branches of the immediate family tree (the Irish Dunn/Ashe branch, along with the Cascia/Ciaccialo branch of Sicily and Italy), and despite Mike's unwieldy added weight allowance of six full cans of beer, he kept right up with me.

It's funny how quickly one's innate ~~criminal~~ survival instinct kicks in when thrust into flight mode. As if choreographed down to iotal detail and rehearsed and rehearsed by heart indoors, we executed a synchronized deke into the first available alley, which opened onto an empty fenced parking lot of tar, worn gray and pitted with age.

Nineteenth century brick buildings flanked us on both sides. Across the chain link fence lay a similar lot, at the far end of which ran another alleyway. Veins of grass had sprouted up through pavement cracks here and there. The longest vein followed a varicose path from the middle of our lot to the middle of the other one, squiggling under the fence along the way – a subtle reminder of nature's disregard for silly things like property lines. Not to get all Speakers Corner coffee house on you, but it occurred to me that the presumptuous, not to mention arrogant, notions of terrestrial property division and deeds of so-called entitlement are recognized by those most invested in promoting the delusion that such things actually exist, namely the perpetually current generation of land "owners."*

*[Musicological and Philosophical Aside: I had recently happened upon David Bowie's 1970 *The Man Who Sold the World* album while searching the Green IRC's record catalogue in vain for Bowie's essential *ChangesOne* album which was nowhere to be found. The best thing about this uneven pre-glam record was the title song, of course, which smote li'l ol' me like satori in Paris. That song opened my eyes. Oh, let me get my hands on the charlatan who sold our fucking world, not to mention that solipsistic asshole who bought it! You can't *sell* the ocean, man – it's not yours, it's all of ours – any more than you can divide the sky into parcels and sell those off; and you cannot sell the Earth either. You might *think* you can. You might've been whistling that very tune every day while working through the heavy-lifting years of early adulthood, looking forward to the comfort and security of entitlement one day like it was your birthright. Maybe you even had a legal looking "bill of sale" drawn up to discourage future claims and supersede all prior transactions, proof that you'd paid, oh, $24 for the whole shebang, or sixty guilders, or a tentload of wampum and beads. The thing we need to ask ourselves is, where'd the guy who sold it to us get it from? And going further back, and further from there, and then further still, just where exactly does the provenance originate? And who the hell authorized it there in the first place? Spoiled victors and thieves, that's who. We all know that; because somewhere, sometime, way back when, this plot of prime real estate you're standing on belonged to the seasons and the wind, as it rightly should, not to some grasping little biped looking for a leg up. The world was vast and pure. The fields were vast and shared – and some guy strolled up and snatched them, broad daylight, just like that; commandeered them, took ownership, lock, stock & barrel; and – like it or not – that guy's *with us!* (which is why we never bring it up anymore, or even care).

Let me be clear, I'm not against the concept of territory and personal acreage, per se, but I am very much opposed to the oh-so hypocritical yet universally condoned practice of Takers-Keepers! It's-Mine-Now! Catch-Me-if-You-Can-Suckers!

By the way, the *second* best thing about *The Man Who Sold the World* is undoubtedly the album's cover photograph of Bowie lolling on a daybed in a kimono and knee high boots, looking like a slightly homelier, slightly worse for wear sister of Stevie Nicks, or a considerably cuter kid sis of Janis Joplin's. No shame on Pearl for that one, though. David Bowie's prettier than a pail of southern peaches.]

Catching our "Now what?" breath at the fence, Mike and I both said, "Hah!"

A car too big for the narrow alley came squealing in from the street, barreling through at some devil-may-care MPH. We had the little lot all to ourselves: me, Mike, and now the dark-skinned white dude at the wheel. Could his be a hot heeled get-away too, having just robbed the package store register? On the other hand, hadn't I grown up hearing stories of tough boroughs like Boston's North End where street crime was virtually nonexistent due to a well-earned reputation for self-policing? Was this guy a duly deputized member of the neighborhood watch, Federal Hill style?

Mike put down the beers. The gold coupe sped straight at us before shuddering to an angled halt that had us hemmed against the fence. Whatever this guy's problem was, it was us. The door flew open and he flew out.

I would liken the placid concentration that came over me in that parking lot to the serenity I sometimes felt during football games tracking the soar of a punt as it topped out in its tantalizing pre-plummet hover above me.

[Author's Note: Writing this, I made a spur-of-the-moment yet nonetheless binding pact with myself, a verbal contract if you will, to refrain from using the word 'apogee' in that last sentence. I am not John Fucking Updike. He gets to use that word. I don't. Besides, if I used apogee just then, although it is irrefutably *mot juste* in this case, I would never be able to employ it again anywhere else in my writing. As with 'cunt', you shouldn't use the word apogee just because you can. It sticks in people's craw, and they rarely forget the circumstances surrounding its employment, specifically the famous five W's, with an emphasis on the Who and the Why. Encountering it a second time from the same source, a reader could not but snort, "Fellow sure likes to throw apogee around, doesn't he? Probably thinks it makes him sound like a real author or something." Hence ergo forsooth, I'm saving apogee for later.]

In such moments I was allowed to indulge in pure detachment. The rules of our sport bestowed an immunity on me akin to that of an untouchable made man. Our Bill of Rights, so to speak, empowered me to stand apart, staring straight up to the heavens, focusing on the one single thing that mattered in our universe, completely blind to, and completely disregarding of, the irrelevant entirety of every*thing* else and every*one* else whirling around me.

The main difference between the playing field and the parking lot, of course, was that in one the protective rules stood guard around me and in the other I wasn't even sure there were rules in play at all – which makes the sangfroid of the latter all the more puzzling; but there it was.

Within those few tranquil seconds in front of the fence, I couldn't help noticing that this two-door ark was as wide as Rhode Island Sound. It bore an Ocean State license plate and a small coat of arms above the grill which I could not readily identify. The tires had a narrow white wall stripe, and although the vehicle didn't appear to be new it was obviously being carefully maintained. Its cream hardtop went nicely with the dark gold of the body. Just to the rear of the backseat side window, in silver metallic script of almost self-deprecatingly inconspicuous font size, "Electra 225" was inscribed.

"Think you going!"

Mike and/or I would have called out any number of our friends if they'd come at us with such questionable diction but we chose to overlook it since we hadn't even known this guy for five full seconds yet. His billowing shirt tails of greenish synthetic paisley, worn unbuttoned over a tucked-in sleeveless t-shirt, as was the fashion in certain urban wards, might have drawn a quip or two too. With my back against the fence, it was impossible to confirm the exact color of his dark, probably pleated, slacks due to the raging glow of the lit cigarette he was holding inches away from my eyeball throughout the interrogation. I was hoping Mike didn't move a muscle in my defense or do anything that might jounce the temperamental fellow's hand.

"Huh!" he barked.

The acoustical properties of the open air brick walls produced a resounding echo, the type of cinematic echo effect you overhear inside matinee theaters as you're nearing the heavy closed doors of the theater proper because you're showing up late and the picture's already playing inside.

"Nowhere—" "Took a wrong turn…"

"What you doing!" Again, despite the awkward phrasing, his clarion message rang true.

"*Nothing—*" "Not from around here…"

Fortunately, he had chosen my left eye above which to dangle his burning sword of nicotine. Thus, it was with the clearer vision of my right, i.e. good, eye that I caught a glimpse over his shoulder of Chuck skedaddling past the alley, followed by Donny with a case of beer in his arms.

Donny glanced our way as he ran by, but a second later he was gone. I hereby attest that true and full fledged heartbreak can most certainly take place within the span of just one passing second. The same is true of salvation, for Donny then reappeared like a knight in backpedaling armor, with Chuck in tow.

Our natty vigilante might have detected some change in my countenance because he turned around and, at the sight of Don Colombo closing at a trot, he spiked his cigarette into sparks on the gnarled pavement. It wasn't a gesture of gauntlet throwing so much as an acknowledgement of nonsense coming to an end with the arrival of a fellow grown man. If he and Donny communicated directly at all, they did so in the manner of those like beings we've heard tell of who instantly, unfailingly, via otherwise imperceptible signs and characteristics, and with an enviable economy of to-do, recognize their tacit kinship when encountering another of their kind somewhere out in the world.

Approaching, Donny's eyebrows rose like two dark angels. "Everything alright? Where'd you guys go?"

We feigned, "Got turned around," or some such.

The dignity of his neighborhood apparently restored, the watchman (charcoal slacks, black shoes) got back in the Electra and whipped it around for a speedy but squeal-free departure.

"What the hell was that about?"

"Who knows? Guy just came at us out of nowhere, bombing down the alley."

"No, why'd you try to steal beer? We had money."

"So did we," I said laughing. "I don't know."

Back on the sidewalk, we were immediately collared by Providence PD.

"That's them," the liquor store proprietor told the cops. Then he said to Donny, "I thought you said you didn't know them."

"We don't."

The six purloined champagnes of beer were reappropriated and my trusty accomplice and I were put in the back of the cruiser. The officers took our information: who we were, where we were from, what we were doing in town. One said to the other, "Brockton assholes."

"Figures."

"Let's see your tickets."

We showed them.

"The Kinks," one said.

"Figures."

I resented that more than the aspersion on our hometown.

"How are the Marcianos doing?"

"They're good." I almost added, "Rocky's sister is those other guys' mother," but then I remembered it would've queered their alibi.

With the world-weary sighs of swamped bureaucrats, the patrolmen got back out of the car to confer with the storekeeper down the sidewalk while Mike and I awaited our fate.

"That was fairly dumb," I apologized.

"Fairly fun, though."

After five oddly tranquil minutes, the policemen got back in the car.

"You're lucky. He's not pressing charges. Better get the hell out of here. And don't none of you ever show your face in Providence again."

"We can't go to the concert?"

"After the concert!" the officer at the wheel snapped. "Assholes..."

You know what? A tip of the hat to the Providence Police Department: To protect and serve. They get it.

Mike and I groveled, "Thank you."

"Don't thank us, thank him."

When they let us out of the cruiser we said, "Thank you, sir."

"What!" barked the proprietor, checking his swing on a backhand bitch slap. "—the fuck out of here... Lucky these guys caught you." He spit on the sidewalk. "Telling me 'Thank you...'"

We met up with Chuck and Don around the corner at the car.

"Don-ny, *bomaye!* Don-ny, *bomaye!*"

"Would've thought you two knew better than that," he smiled. "Shoplifting?"

Chuck was shaking his head. "I know. That's something Matty would do." Then he clarified, "Except Matty wouldn't have got caught."

Mike said, "I have an idea! Let's pound a couple beers and get to the Kinks concert!"

Once inside the Civic Center, I wondered aloud, "Are they going to sing it, 'tastes just like Coca-Cola' or 'tastes just like *cherry* cola'?"

"You sure you didn't come to hear just that one song, Greg?"

"Long as I'm not hearing it from a holding cell."

On 95-North on the drive home later after the show, Donny said, "Anybody up for some empty calories and greasy carbs and fat when we hit Brockton?"

"Cheeburguh! Cheeburguh! Cheeburguh! Cheeburguh!"

—

As if the cold shoulder disdain of our varsity baseball team that year (to wit, its banishment of an impressionable young competitor during tryouts to the Tasmanian island of also-rans known as West Junior High) wasn't portentous enough for me to at least rethink my baseballian future, the nasty midseason slump which soon followed pretty much shucked the clam as far as I was concerned.

Was this latest crash as catastrophic as its predecessor, the Great Collapse of '77? Hell no – to top that one for sheer concavity you'd have to go all the way back to the earth-shattering crater left by the dinosaur death star, but the impact of this one was deep too, don't get me wrong – a definite game changer.

And to think, not much more than one year earlier the term "batting slump" had practically no meaning for me. All the baseball seasons I had played to that point represented an accumulation of individual games, each with its own discrete set of plays and at-bats, which took place in the vacuum of one particular day. Just as the runs tallied in a double-header's matinée will never be credited to the score of the second game, so too were plate performances from yesterday's game, good and bad, entirely without relevance to those of today.

Sophomore year's JV baseball season which had started so well petered out like an okay song the writer can't figure how to end so he just keeps dialing down the volume till it fades out completely in shades of mediocrity. Coach Fouracre's "best hitter" shortstop went from leading off with home runs to scraping for fielder's choices in the bottom of the order while adjusting to the isolation of playing *right field*. Alas, the infection of my sophomore slump had in due course spread from the barrel of my bat to my Wilson A2000 to my already sporadic throwing arm.

Lacking the necessary wherewithal to overcome a slump – regardless of season length – is to be possessed of a cardinal character flaw worthy of a scarlet **S** on one's chest (and not the good kind). So, the ending of that season represents the true beginning of my break up with baseball, or, to put it more accurately, baseball's break up with me.

At the time, when many players of my age group and skill level were foregoing their second year of Colt League eligibility in favor of playing Legion ball that summer for Post-35 or the newly established Spartan A.C., I elected to remain in Colt League, playing out my baseball string, like going through the motions in a defunct relationship despite there obviously being no future in it; and although that redundant season of lower league limbo scored no runs for novelty, and lacked the fulfillment and exciting uncertainty of ascension, it nonetheless shines in my memory to this day thanks to two late-season games in particular.

My Colt League coach, Billy Burchard (who had played tight end on that great 1973 Boxer Super Bowl team), was a high quality dude and a lot of fun to be around. He made a point of changing all the coaching signs every game lest a devious opponent's scout crack our sophisticated coding system...

It was the last game of the regular season, an overcast evening as I recall. A win would qualify us for the playoffs. Early in the game, having reached first, I saw that third base coach Burchard was giving me the steal sign. I liked his style; make things happen right away. I took off on the first pitch and slid in safe at second. Dusting myself off, I saw him clap and shout encouragement to the batter and then casually slip both hands into his back pockets, signaling for another steal. Next pitch I took off and was safe on a close play at third. I stood up with one foot on the base, swiping dirt off my knee.

Billy came in close to confer, sotto voce, tête-à-tête.

"What the hell are you doing?"

"You gave me the steal."

"Oh, shit!"

"You didn't know?"

Later in the game, I was on deck in the last inning. We were down by one with a man on first. The batter ahead of me popped up for the second out. The other team brought in Jay DiBari to face me. He was a good lefty whom I hadn't faced since Little League in the City Series.

While he was warming up, Billy hustled over from the third base coach's box and put his arm around my shoulder.

He said, "These guys are stalling. Game's going to get called for darkness any minute now. Dunna, I've never said this to anybody before. You gotta hit it out."

I drove a fastball on the outer edge to deep right-center. Mike Piccanzo caught it at the fence. Ten more feet toward the right field line, it would've been out.

Years later, I told Billy's brother Bob this story. The next time I saw him, he said he'd brought it up to Billy.

Bob laughed, "I asked my brother, 'Did you really tell Dunna to hit it out?' He said, 'Yeah, and he did!'"

Bill Burchard was the best.

The other game that sticks out from that year took place several weeks later at the New England Colt League All-Star Tournament, and I couldn't forget it if I tried.

The night before the memorable game there had been a parents-away-for-the-weekend party at Mike Barry's house. Once the festivities wound down, he and I talked the night away in the basement, drinking beer and playing tunes on his stereo.

Finally, I said, "Aw, shit! Is that the sun?"

"How does this keep happening to us?"

"Shit, I gotta hit the road, Mike."

He said, "Drive home? Now?" Curling one eyebrow, he considered me askance. "Pardon the expression, but… aren't you drunker than a shit house rat?"

"Maybe so, but I–"

"Maybe?"

"Alright, granted. But still–"

"No no no. You're bivouacking here, soldier."

Great guy, Mike Barry. Nevertheless I pressed, "Can't be done, brother. I'm being picked up in a couple hours at my house. Gotta go try to catch a few zeez first. If I can. Beforehand."

"Picked up for what?"

"Colt League all-star tournament."

Mike Barry then executed a perfect spontaneous spraying spit take, the best ever seen in real life. "You got a game today!" he spluttered. "Get home!"

We were both cracking each other up by laughing so much. On my way up the stairs, I said, choking on a laugh, "Should have listened to you and gone out for Legion!"

"Oh, man… Where's the tournament?"

"Rhode Island."

"Not Providence!"

"Hah! Pawtucket I think."

"Get your butt home, get a little sleep, you'll be fine," he tried to assure me but couldn't keep his face straight. Then he blurted, "You should have played Legion!"

"Yeah, thanks a lot, Mike."

"Sorry, Gregga."

"Yeah, yeah…"

In the cool of the morning, as I started to pull away, he called out from his front steps, "Hit me a homer, Greggy!"

Evidently I made it to my house safe, got my gear together, and sat down in my father's chair to close my eyes for a minute.

In a dream a far off song drew more and more near as it turned by beats from a song to the bleats of a car horn's blare.

"Nngu! Whuh?"

I scrambled out the door with my stuff, leg heavy but a little less drunk, with the stale taste of nausea hanging all over me.

"Thanks a lot, Mr. Martel," I said. "Good morning."

"Morning, Greg. Ready for some baseball?"

"Oh, yuh." I opened the back window an inch for the benefit of all, not knowing if I'd brushed when I got home, but knowing I probably reeked of beer.

From shotgun, my teammate Dave cracked a smile. "How you doing?"

I mouthed, "You guys waiting long?"

He shook me off with a frown. "Just got here."

Although it was rude, I had no choice: "I'm going to close my eyes for a few minutes if that's okay."

I pulled my baseball hat down past my eyebrows, folded my arms, and nestled in the nook of the backseat with my head by the window's soothing shaft of breeze.

That inopportune all-nighter marked just the second time I'd ever stayed out long enough to see the sun come up. The only other time had been recently at the tail end of another parentless get-together. While Mr. and Mrs. Colombo were spending a week down the Cape, Chuck had invited a few of us over. It was good having a safe place to hang with no fear of confiscation minded cops rolling up to take our beers. Coincidentally, the wee hours found me and Mike Barry repairing to the cellar after the other guys had gone home or crashed on couches so we could keep talking our heads off and digging tunes. The first light of Genesis couldn't have been more astonishing than the one we witnessed that morning.

"You know what? This is something I bet neither one of us ever forgets."

"Of course – first sunrise ever."

"You too?"

"Yup!"

With the breaking of morning, Mike and I had tacitly agreed that the music portion of the show was officially concluded. We kept up the conversation, though, as well as the consumption, for at least a couple more hours.

Bright and early, Chuck, ever the early riser, called down to us, "We're going to breakfast, boys. You coming?"

"They got beer?"

"Heh! We'll be back. Hold the fort."

Left to our own devices, I surveyed the cellar. "Seriously, is that it for beer?"

"Last one," Mike confirmed. "Mission accomplished."

"Somehow this accomplishment tastes way more bitter than sweet."

"I'll take a look upstairs."

The sound of the kitchen door opening stopped us. We heard a woman humming to herself.

We both mouthed, "Who's that?"

The kitchen must have looked like a redemption center on St. Paddy's morning-after. We gritted our teeth and listened hard. The Colombos wouldn't be home yet, would they?

Whoever it was, she started cleaning up.

Without a false step or so much as a single creaky tread, I sloth-crawled halfway up the cellar stairs on all fours to a point where I could see through the horizontal half-inch gap at the bottom of the closed door. If I hadn't known better, I would have said the plump nylon-stockinged feet padding around the kitchen were my Italian grandmother's, but I had known better.

After masterfully descending the stairs, I whispered, "Chuck's grandmother," in Mike's ear.

The last thing we'd want to do is frighten Mrs. Marciano.

"What if she comes down?"

We shushed each other with a helpless grimace.

Quiet as we could, we moved out of view and kept very still. If the signora did decide to do a load of laundry or something, at least we could warn her by announcing our presence with a friendly "yoohoo" from the wings.

A half hour passed and the sounds of tidying up eventually quieted down, replaced by the distant murmur of a television. It would have been quite convenient and much appreciated were Chuck and the guys to return right about then.

I slithered halfway up the stairs and then waved Mike over. "No more feet going by," I whispered. "Must be in the living room."

"Make our move?"

"I'll block!"

Under the comical cover fire of Abbott and Costello, we secured the (spotless) kitchen beachhead. Quiet as kittens, our stealthy objective thus achieved, we were yet betrayed at the very last by a squeaky kitchen door.

"Eh?" came from the living room. "Who's there?"

"Ah…"

"Oh, hello Mrs. Marciano. Nice to see you."

"Yes!" The enthusiasm in her greeting belied the single word's deceptive versatility. At once she had reciprocated and welcomed and put us at our ease. Then again, her whole face beaming her great natural smile might have charged her reply, economically unsurpassable though it indeed was from a syntax perspective, with a warmth of generosity perhaps otherwise absent.

"Is Chuck home?" we white lied.

The charming lady told us in her sweet Italian accent that Chuck was not in at present but we were nonetheless welcome to stay a while to await his return – not in so many words.

"Oh, no, no, we won't distur–"

"Yes!" she insisted, and how could we refuse?

In the spirit of old-world hospitality which was nothing new to her and which would benefit us all to resurrect, Mrs. Marciano fixed for me and Mike each a nice cheese sandwich with tomato and pepper. It would have been inconvenient, or at least a tad awkward, were Chuck and the guys to crash our little *prima colazione* right about then.

That fond memory came to mind as we drove along Route 128-South toward the Rhode Island tournament. Meanwhile I was trying to nestle myself deeper into the blackness of the backseat nook of Dave Martel's dad's car, striving for merciful surcease of consciousness, but all was not well in the deepest regions of my gut. A saturation point had been reached and water levels were definitely on the rise. I opened my eyes to stare them down, and they instantly subsided, allowing me a grateful controlled exhale of breath. Come to think of it, no, I had not brushed my teeth earlier.

The telltale ebbing and flowing was precursor to an imminent (i.e., all but inevitable) surge which was even then lapping at my larynx. I took in a hard deliberate swallow of water at my jowls, at once sour and bitter.

"Mr. Martel? I'm not feeling so good, would you mind pulling over for a minute?"

"Right this minute?"

"Yes, please."

Dave Martel is alright in my book, and so's his dad. Not a bit of adult scolding or beleaguered harrumphing ensued, nor the mockery of the sage. No metamessages were sent out masquerading as innocent sighs. We simply pulled right over on the highway and I dove from the car. Clutching the guard rail, I gave in to the sour rising tide and the bitter dredged up bile.

"Phew," I said, ensconced in my nook again. "Thank you."

"Feel better?"

"Yah. I do. Whew…"

To show there were no hard feelings, Mr. Martel generously provided me an out: "Car sick?" (Not a droplet of sarcasm detected.)

"Ah…" I kind of moaned. "Don't know."

"Well if we need to pull over you just let me know."

We sure did, and I sure did, once more.

By the time the Brockton Colt League All-Stars took the field in Pawtucket, skies were partly cloudy and so was my vision. I jotted a mental note: Hangovers and sports don't mix.

During infield I took off my hat to make sure I hadn't grabbed a teammate's hat by mistake. The temporal throbbing remained barely bearable as long as I stood a certain way and didn't move around too much and didn't hold my head too high. A wave of sudden heat escaped my whole body by force, forming a clingy all-over perspiration which immediately evaporated. I checked my hat again for size. Hangover Note: If worse comes to worst, call time-out! The dirt between second and third is not for the covering up of carsick shortstop puke!

Mike Barry had asked me to hit him a home run. I'd be lucky to even get a hit, the way I was going. For that matter, I'd be lucky to *get* hit.

Our opposing pitcher's motion was a low smooth deceptively slow whip, à la Bob Feller, practically sidearm. Like Feller this guy delivered extraordinary heat. As soon as we saw him warming up, other lofty comparisons were made.

"Vida Blue!"

"Walter Johnson!"

"You never saw Walter Johnson play."

"The Big Train!"

"Who'd he play for?"

"Fuck you."

"Fuck YOU!"

Sticklers aside, we were united under the same bright idea as it dawned on all of us: We gotta work the count!

When my turn at bat came, I dutifully took the first pitch which blew by me like a JUGS tennis ball. I then tried to push a bunt for a hit that rolled foul halfway up the first base line; strike two. Next pitch, Nolan Ryan, Jr., (apt comparability, we all agreed) ran a fastball in that drilled me on the baby finger. I leapt and hopped from the batter's box, cavorting in pain toward first, trying to resist squeezing my hand in my armpit or between my thighs, but the umpire interpreted the *twank* of the ball on the aluminum bat-knob as a foul.

"That was my finger too!" I protested.

He swiped the palms of his hands together twice for all the crowd to see what he thought of such shenanigans.

My whole finger was vibrating. I cried, "Really? Fuck Ryan out loud…!"

It was not shaping up to be my day. On the bright side, at least this new pain took my mind off those thudding headache throbs.

I couldn't wrap my swollen knuckle around the bat handle so I had to tuck my pinky under the knob. One of Dad's homespun recipes for staying loose in the heat of battle was simply to let out a calm controlled breath at the critical moment. He said, "Relaxation concentration. Your muscles can't tense up when you're exhaling." That made sense to me, and it sure enough worked. I had employed this trick with my drives on the first tee, with shooting foul shots, fielding punts, and yes, sometimes behind in the count 0-and-2.

You don't have to mace me, I usually catch on after a while. Their flamethrower hadn't so much as shaken off his catcher even once yet, so I was sitting dead-red. I stroked a low liner off the end of the bat over the shortstop's head toward the gap in left-center. The ball bounded more than bounced, somehow gaining momentum as it landed – a hare darting headlong for cover – which flummoxed the converging outfielders, I guess, because they both left their feet, laying themselves out in collision course mirror image dives. Unfortunately (for me) this routine hit, a harmless single most any other day, had threaded that thinnest of needles and was rolling along hippity hoppity all the way to the fucking fence.

I would have been fine with a double, believe me, or a stand-up triple, but our third base coach was pointing toward the plate and furiously windmilling his other arm.

My little comedy of geometry reminded me of the home run I was generously credited with in that game against Mike Barry and the BHS freshmen a couple years prior. It also reminded me of him calling for a homer as I pulled out of his driveway earlier; but it mostly reminded me of puking up colorful undigested lo mein during the team jog at my first captains practice.

Hangover Note: Strike out swinging, kid, and nobody's the wiser.

Mike Barry called my house the next day, laughing with admiration, when he read the account of the game in the paper.

"Are you kidding me!"

"Heh! Yup." I was laughing too. "I mean nope."

We had defeated Manchester, NH, Woonsocket, RI, and host team Pawtucket to win the New England championship. I suppose it never occurred to Mike to press for details of my unlikely heroics, assuming that the description in *The Enterprise*, which reported simply that I had "homered", implied some form of deep arcing ballpark departing smash – and far be it from me to ground the heady flights of a good pal's fancy.

So, with that, my beloved baseball was, as they say, a thing of the past.

And let me tell you this: When your first love turns into your tormentor and then simply leaves you for dead, it does so with an indifference that takes your breath away. The *absurdity* of being abandoned by Earth's only other inhabitant, and the realization that all you can do now is watch from the beach while Love itself slowly swims away... is breathtaking.

———

Now that baseball was over with, for the time being at least and once and for all at most, the remainder of my summer became focused solely on preparation for the upcoming football season. With last year's difficult yet invaluable season of sophomore experience under our belts, Owen and Chuck and I were ready to restore the vaunted Boxer Wishbone to its once and future dominance, or – like last year – fail trying.

Although our offense had lost to graduation big Rod Heger, a three-year starter at fullback and two-time Suburban League All-Star, there was unanimous optimism surrounding his replacement, senior Don Barlow. A beast in the weight room and all-around good guy to boot, he brought brute strength, athleticism, and footspeed to the pivotal fullback position, as well as a single-mindedness of purpose that had been sorely missing among upperclassmen in recent years. A team player and natural leader, it was a foregone conclusion that he would be one of our captains.

Donny Barlow was also a perfect example of the depth of talent waiting in the wings at Brockton, up and down the roster. Whenever an understudy was called upon to fill the role of a featured player, Marciano Stadium's home side audience would as often as not come away raving over the back-up's performance, as with witnessing the coming of a newborn star.

Until captains practice started up again in August, Chuck and I were glad to resume the off-season weightlifting regimen that we'd shelved during baseball. All through the previous winter, and now again, we worked out at the downtown Y, focusing on chest and arms on Monday/Wednesday/Friday, and then shoulders and back on Tuesday/Thursday/Saturday. Our identical measurements in the key data points of height and weight (and age, too) made us ideal workout partners. We were always at the same stage of development, progressing at the same pace, which worked great because unlike golf, where partnering with your betters serves to improve your game, weight room mismatches are kind of a drag on both ends.

Also, we understood how important it was for guys like us to add a few pounds of muscle wherever possible because although our builds were considered smack dab textbook "average" as measured against the general population, we definitely came up short on the football field, not to mention several pounds light.

The facilities at the Old Colony YMCA were actually damn good, if not necessarily the most modern, and if in some cases just plain odd (an *astroturf* jogging track?). They provided us many and varied options for cardiocentric alternatives outside of the weight room, and when our lifting was done we partook of pretty much everything at one point or another (with the exception of the swimming pool) – multiple basketball courts, two indoor tracks, wrestling mats, racquetball courts, handball courts. The dearth of outdoor amenities might be considered our local Y's only real shortcoming, but being located in the geometric center of town it made sense that the surrounding real estate was occupied from curb to corner by shops, municipal buildings, and the evilest of city necessities, parking lots.

However, a resourceful problem solver in our Y's employ (perhaps an ambitious assistant with aspirations in city planning eager to prove his worth and show off his ingenuity), charted a two-hundred-yard roundtrip course along the perimeter of three adjacent parking lots out back. The roundtrip was by no means round, or even oblong. In fact, viewed from the altitude of the Young Men's Christian Association building's sixth floor, it resembled a gerrymandering map; but when jogging it, some of its straightaways were just long enough to help you forget about all the angular turning points.

Chuck liked a good jog, his brother Donny too from what I had heard. I think all the Colombos did. Although I was fleeter afoot over short distances, jogging was never my thing. I'd do it for conditioning when I had to, but that was about it. Once around our block in Southfield measured exactly one half-mile. Going for two miles at a jog was no problem, but I rarely did more than that – three, tops. I'd hear Chuck talk about "getting a run in" after dinner, and going for five miles, seven miles, *ten* miles. That made no sense to me. I just couldn't relate to it, the whole concept, on any level.

At the Y when we jogged outside, he'd be leaving me in the dust by the third or fourth straightaway. I was faster than he was so I'd speed up at first, but I wasn't able to keep up with the demands of that higher gear for very long. Meanwhile, there goes Chuck, cruising right along at an easy clip, no strain whatsoever. His default cruising pace would be lapping me in no time.

"It makes no sense," I was telling Joe later when he called from Pensacola.

"What's to make sense of? You're Valeriy Borzov, not Frank Shorter. Who cares about the marathon?"

"Yeah, but–"

"Hey, *Yeah butttt!*"

"Hah!"

"Greg, all I'm saying's 'Be what you is, not what you is not.'"

"Hah!"

"You're a man of spirited bursts, right? Face it. Embrace it."

I shrugged and nodded. "Yeah…"

"Something works for you, you embrace it."

Joe had done it again. He said, "Chuck's more a slow and steady guy. That works for him."

"You're right."

His point well made, I heard the crack of a brotherly smirk in his voice. "If you guys were characters in a book, this could be developed as a nice little metaphor."

"Alright, say goodnight, Mr. Wizard."

———

At home one evening, I sat lounging on the floor in the parlor, watching TV, using the hassock as a backrest. My mother was at the table teaching Rich chess.

When Steve walked by, I said, "Come here, let me see your eye. Wow, nice shiner. Looks like a cigarette commercial."

My father came home from work and said, "Oh, that's a beaut."

"Head butt," Steve explained. "We both shot at the same time."

"You should see the other guy," Rich grinned from the dining room, obviously none the worse for wear.

"You want a black eye, I can give you one right now," Steve warned.

Dad asked me how the first day of double sessions had gone.

"Good, but Donny Barlow's probably out for the season."

"What happened?"

"Knee. We were doing man-ball-man, and... I don't know."

"You said he was ready for a big year. That's too bad. Goes to show you."

As expected, despite his injury, Barlow was voted tri-captain by the players, along with Matty Walsh and Paul Capachione. As might also be expected, the next guy in line at fullback stepped right up to fill in serviceably to start the season. Senior Bernie Goodman, a South Boston transfer, was a big-boned bruiser. After he too went down with a nagging leg injury, legendary Little League prodigy Bob Stone took over. I had caught for Stoney when we played baseball together on Teamsters, so I'd seen first hand the lengths of superlative athleticism at his disposal, but he three got dinged up, opening the door for rough and ready sophomore Ron Byrnes to finish out the year.

I realized double sessions didn't change much from one year to the next. We sweated like hell on the field, as usual, and I felt the marrow of my shin bones petrify in the grip of our giant taping table coach again.

Although with every new season hope springs eternal, we knew we actually had a pretty good team that year, good athletes on both sides of the ball, and everybody fully expected a vast improvement over the previous year's 3-6 record.

Friday night before the first game, awaiting my bed-check phone call, I answered the ringing phone. It was Joe calling from Pensacola where he'd been stationed following his Air Force enlistment.

"Ready for tomorrow?"

"Yup, just waiting for bed check."

"Who's going to call you?"

"I don't know. Mr. Colombo? Mr. Marrow?"

"I'll be quick. Don't forget to utilize your speed out there tomorrow. You're going to be one of the fastest guys on the field so use that to your advantage. Sometimes you don't."

"Jay McGee's going to be playing."

"As a freshman? Wow."

"On kick return at least."

"As long as he's not chasing you, who cares? One of the only guys faster than you's on your own team. Good."

"Yup."

"Remember that time at halftime when we got in on that kill the man with the ball with those guys? That's how you have to run, just like that. Like you're running for your life."

"I will."

"I gotta go. Give 'em hell, Greg."

"Oh, I will."

Mr. Colombo called a few minutes later, reminding me to get to bed early and to eat well in the morning.

Having added a tenth contest to our 1978 regular season schedule, we opened with a non-league game at Dedham, a thitherto unknown entity. I felt great starting the season off with number 43. It was a beautiful sunny day. I felt strong, I felt fast.

Don't worry, I'm not about to break down every play of every game, but after kicking off to them, we (i.e., my buddy Steve Litchfield) intercepted their first pass attempt, giving us the ball at the Dedham 30-yard line. As fate would have it, our first offensive play of the season went to me, just as it had the year before, and compared to the previous year's first play versus Chicopee, which netted negative-four yards, the straight dive play we ran against Dedham was a rip-roaring success: 0.00 yards.

Our *second* play from scrimmage that year (I'm telling you, don't worry!), run from the seldom used I-Formation, was a sweep right that I took 29 yards down to the one. Chuck then scored with a cute quick-count QB sneak. On Dedham's next possession we sacked their quarterback for a safety and were off and running, 9-0.

I ended up leading all Boxer running backs that day with a total of 33 yards rushing. Okay, let me repeat that. It is not a typographical error. There should not be a 1 before or between or after that pair of 3s over there. I don't know how many yards Owen had, and I don't know how many yards our new fullback Bernie Goodman had, but I repeat: That day... I led the team... with 33... rushing yards... in a game we somehow went on to lose, I shit you not, 10-9.

I say 'somehow' because to this day it's hard to reconcile the blocked punt for a touchdown (plus two-point conversion) against us, the 4th-quarter safety against us, and the coup de grâce: With less than thirty seconds left in the game, on first and ten from the Dedham 25-yard line, Chuck lofted a TD pass in the corner of the end zone to Matty who was flagged for offensive pass interference. Okay, tough break, right? There was still plenty of time for another couple plays and/or a field goal attempt, right? *Right?*

WRONNNNG!

Not only was the touchdown negated, but such a penalty somehow carried with it a ruling of *touchback!* Translation: Loss of downs – plural! – and we had to kick the ball away to Dedham. Better translation: Game fucking over!

1977's shadow of futility was looming still, as yet another halftime lead was blown to bits.

Then, just for the hell of sticking one more splinter into the reddening swollen soreness of a – let's face it – *harsh* defeat, Chuck told me afterwards in the locker room that he'd seen my girlfriend riding around the night before with some other guy we knew.

"I didn't want to say anything to mess you up before the game," he explained. "But I had to tell you."

Already well aware that love was a many-splintered thing, I absorbed this latest prick and gave Chuck my heartfelt thanks. After all, not everybody does what they should.

—

Monday practices during the season were reserved for watching film of the game we'd played on Saturday. Everybody would crowd into the Armory's equipment room, coaches on folding chairs by the projector, players sitting where they could on the floor or laid out with footballs for pillows. An exhaustive, often tense, analysis of every down's execution would follow. Missed assignments, dumb penalties, blown coverages, and all manner of mental screw up would play out upon the collapsible home movie screen at a dreamy ¾ speed in rich cinematic black-and-white for all to see, backward and forward ad infinitum at Coach Colombo's discretion. The ticking of the 16mm film as it spooled through the projector only added to the room's dark, otherwise silent, drama.

Whenever a play happened to unfold without interruption it did so to the private relief of at least one or two scofflaws, for sure, who harbored the sneaking guilt of spared sinners (although in all honesty, if the coaches had pulled us over for every misdemeanor, we'd have been locked up in there till Tuesday).

The more obviously stupid miscues would be announced to one and all not by a tongue lashing but by Coach Donovan switching (per order of Mr. Colombo) the projector's "play" knob to "reverse" for a few seconds, then toggling forward again, then backward, and so on, pivoting on the fault point, until none of us would have required Dandy Don's jocular commentary to spot the blunder up there on the screen, nor the blunderer.

For particularly egregious transgressions, Mr. Colombo spat the offender's full name and snapped, "Have an idea!"

We learned a lot about humility on those Monday afternoons. Compliments were as scarce as sasquatch hooves, even following a win. "Films are for educating," Coach Bradshaw advised me on one such Monday, "not congratulating."

For this day's screening I dragged one of the tackling dummies to a place directly below the projector. It seemed best this particular Monday to be as up front as possible in the face of what was coming.

I couldn't have possibly envisioned for myself a worse opening day performance than the previous year's Chicopee debacle, but leave it to those notoriously thin-skinned gods of Fate to regard this measure of comparative confidence as some kind of hubris on my part, or provocation, or something, because in addition to limiting my yards rushed to a starting-job-jeopardizing pittance, they saw fit to channel Dedham's biggest scoring plays directly through me.

Firstly, on the blocked punt, I had taken my position as one of two backs set up behind our offensive line. My spot on the punt team was between guard and tackle on the right side, in a two-point stance, hands on thighs. It was the job of us backs to serve as the second line of defense to protect our punter, picking up anyone who might make it past our big guys up front. When I got set, I gave my fellow up-back a curt nod, just as I had been doing since the first day of double sessions. But lo! My fellow up-back failed to return the salute. Now I'm no great stickler for etiquette, I can be as informal as the next guy, but in this case the next guy was nowhere to be found.*

'Aha!' I immediately surmised. 'We only have ten men on the field!'

No problema. I made a lateral sidestep adjustment to my left. That way I could shoot over and pick off anybody managing to squeeze through on the left side of the line, or, just as easily stand pat to thwart penetration on my side; two birds, one stone. Problema resuelto.

Of course the fatal flaw of this brilliant stopgap measure lay in my ill-advised choice of conjunctions. An average blocker at best who just never quite got the hang of it, I could nonetheless be counted on to usually hinder, hamper, or otherwise impede an opponent's charge coming from the right side of the line *or* the left side, but from the right *and* left sides at the same time? Well...

Attempting to dissuade two opposing onrushers for the price of one, I was promptly knocked ass over teakettle and left rolling like a tumbleweed while one Marauder (apt name, that) burst past to block the punt and the other one picked it up and took it in for a touchdown.

*[No-Show Note: The AWOL teammate in question, a year my elder and an athlete my better, who never once treated me ill, shall remain nameless here.]

(We subsequently went offside during the PAT so Dedham figured, 'Why not take advantage of the penalty yardage and go for two?' Dedham figured right.)

Secondly, the cardinal sin of a safety scored against us was a classic making-the-worst-of-a-good-situation turn of fortunes. With Dedham on the verge of a go-ahead fourth quarter touchdown from the three-yard line, they coughed the ball up.

The next play – and that play alone – shot me to my feet three-and-a-half decades later right after Malcolm Butler's goal line interception in Super Bowl XLIX.

"No safety! No safety!"

I was by myself and beside myself in my living room, exhorting the Patriots' offense to be mindful of the immediate peril surrounding their good fortune.

"Come on, no safety!"

Our first play following the recovery of Dedham's fumble was, as I recall, a 36-Heavy. This running play called for the 3-back (i.e., left halfback) (i.e., me) to run through the 6-hole (i.e., off right tackle) behind a "heavy" blocking scheme. It was a generally solid play but given our field position it required my first several steps to take place in our own endzone as I ran parallel to the line of scrimmage before cutting off-tackle. The play itself felt like it took longer to develop than my explanation of it here has. When the ref blew the whistle, one of those witty Dedham players slapped the endzone turf and yelled, "Two points, takedown!"

We know as adults that the dread of anticipation often outweighs whatever pain is ultimately suffered when the dreadful thing actually comes to pass, but I think you can understand how little I was looking forward at the time to sitting through the film of that Dedham game.

The equipment room went dark. The projector's lamp came on, casting the top fifth of my head in shadow against the bottom fifth of the movie screen until I scooched a little farther down the tackling dummy so that I was now slouched against it staring straight ahead past my feet at the screen like I did at home on the parlor rug.

At Marciano Stadium, filming of our games took place from the windy roof of the press box high atop the home stands, so films of home games had a distant almost clinical remoteness. Away games, on the other hand, varied greatly depending on the size of the stadium and position of the film camera. Sometimes the films for our road games showed the players so much closer up that you could practically make out facial expressions on plays run toward the near sideline. I was sort of hoping Dedham's camera crew had been shooting from that propeller plane which kept circling the field on Saturday, towing a "GO DHS!" banner; no such luck, of course. There I was up there for all to see, 30% larger than I would have been at home, every misstep vividly exaggerated: Failing to score on my one good run, stepping aside as deliberately as you please to cover for our missing punt team guy (Why the hell hadn't I just called time out?), later being taken down in the endzone.

During review of the game's first quarter, Coach Donovan was kept busy replaying our gaffes, as usual, and Mr. Colombo took several players to task indeed. On the sideline at the game, he had already torn the absentee up-back, along with our special teams coach, a new anus apiece, so when the blocked punt play came on the screen the only culprits left to grill were the linemen responsible for the security breaches, and me. He said, "Let it run, Mike," as Mr. Donovan instinctively played my pre-snap sidestep in reverse, but he laid into those other guys with lather as they simultaneously got off the ball a fraction too late, made futile lunges, and fell to one knee over and over and over and over and over. When it came my turn, Mr. Colombo said from behind me, "Greg…"

"Call time out," I nodded at the screen.

I sensed he was nodding too. "Always."

That was it. When we got to the hideous fourth quarter, everybody just sat there in stunned silence, reliving the shock of the safety and that utterly flabbergasting touchback. I think world-weary Job himself would've taken his bootstraps in hand and set about enumerating blessings upon hearing the collective despair in our sighs and groans as we rose to leave the equipment room.

For all that, 1978 turned out to be a season of transition and rebirth for Brockton Football. Despite shooting ourselves in both feet and the face in our opener, and losing *ugly*, we went on to beat seven of our next eight opponents, including an especially tough and talented Newton North team. Our resurgence that year came about due to yet another stout unsung defense and a couple tweaks made to our offensive scheme.

I presume the coaches held a summit meeting of some kind behind closed doors, but that's just a guess. All I know for sure is, following the Dedham loss the Wishbone was out and the I-Formation was in. As I say, nobody consulted us players or even made mention of any kind of formal change but I can't help thinking that the switch was enacted at least in part to better feature Chuck Colombo's talents as a dropback passer. The result of this gambit was immediate and indisputable: 1978 became The Chuck and Matty Show.

Chuck led the whole state in touchdown passes that year, and Matt Walsh set the Boxers' all-time single season record for scoring, as well as for TD receptions.

You know what? Let me take this opportunity to retrospectfully salute Coach Armond Colombo. In one fell swoop he demonstrated the foresight and, more importantly, the guts to break away from Brockton's battle-tested signature style in favor of opening an untried door, a door which would ultimately lead the way to even greater success.

I'd always felt like tailback suited my skill set better than its halfback cousin anyway. My one season in the Hercules backfield we had run the I-Formation, and I liked it. Even last year as a Wishbone team we would throw in an occasional I-play here and there as a change of pace, and it always felt good back there. My speed merchant buddy Owen seemed to prefer "dotting the I" too, and why not? For one thing, the panoramic view of the whole defense which an upright two-point stance provides was invaluable. You were able to watch each defensive formation settle into its geometric shape right before your eyes, identifying vectors that would have otherwise been invisible from the obstructed arse-eye view of a halfback's three-point crouch. Also, for plays between the tackles, tailback gave you another couple yards' head of steam going before you hit the line. Of course whenever one of us was set out on the wing to block, a low three-point stance was best, sure, but other than that, O and I were about to be operating from the proverbial catbird seat back there, seven yards deep, masters of all we surveyed, licking our chops.

During our first full-contact practice post-Dedham, Mr. Colombo gave our offense a crash course in I-Formation operation. We were pitted the entire day against our first-string defense, running the same play full tilt again and again several times in succession until we blocked it right and ran it right. With no element of surprise to keep the defense on their heels for even the slightest bit of a trice, I made damn sure that by the time I hit the line I was already at maximum velocity, headlong and hurtling.

I remember we ran one play to me for five or six plays straight, the same play, 34-Crossfire if I'm not mistaken, each carry yielding incrementally diminishing yardage, of course, until finally the so-called yardage could've been counted as footage, or even inchage. Following that mess, Chuck hit Matty deep down the right sideline for a slick touchdown. Next play, Owen took a 49-Jet (sweep left) all the way for another long score.

In the huddle, I was still catching my crossfire breath. "My turn again already? Don't tell me – right up the gut." When nobody offered even a chuckle of sympathy, I said, "Man, fuck you guys."

Sitting in front of my locker after practice, I tore off three strips from a roll of white athletic tape and posted a block letter "H" above my locker to remind me, on the off chance that it ever slipped my mind, to *Hit the Hole Hard!*

At home that evening, I walked in to find my three younger brothers parked on the parlor couch. Dad was wrapping up a lesson on the basics of public presentation.

"See how Greg looks? He's not all dressed up, you don't have to wear a suit and tie every time you go out the door. But if he's going to be outside, he knows: when you're out in public you gotta look right." I vamped for a moment to make my brothers laugh. "Clean clothes," my dad continued. "Hair combed. Clean shave. We don't leave this house looking like slobs… like a bunch of goddamn stumblebums. That's not how it works. Not around here." He shook his head at the very idea of such a thing. "It's not done."

Steve had the temerity to point out that brother Joe hadn't always abided by this code.

"Bet your ass Joe's following that code now, I'll tell you that," Dad argued. "But he's a grown man in the Air Force. I'm not talking about what anybody outside this house does. I'm talking about what everybody in this house *should* do."

I went to put my books and gym stuff in my room, chuckling to myself, "It's not Dunn." I liked that. My dad came out with a good one every now and then.

Back in the parlor, he stopped me on my way to the fridge. "Hold on for a second. Gregga." Then he asked my brothers, "See what I mean?"

The joke was on me, I guessed, or the sartorial tutorial wasn't over. I said, "Ah… What?"

"See his bow legs. That's where he gets his balance."

"What bowed legs? I'm not bow-legged!"

"Stand right there for a second, facing me. Put your ankles together." I did so in the kitchen doorway and caught the lobbed Miller bottle. Dad said, "Your ankles are touching but your knees don't, right? Your legs angle apart–"

"Oh, slightly, there. Yuh."

"That's what I'm saying. That's where you get your balance. And with those long arms you'd be perfect for wrestling."

"I'm trying to pack on every pound I can for football. I don't want to turn around and suck weight in the winter."

"You don't have to suck weight. The Colombo who wrestled did both."

I remembered Joe's stories of Donny Colombo wearing a vinyl sweat suit while running the bleachers of the high school's indoor pool between classes, but I didn't want to argue about it. The prospect of my taking up wrestling, as all my brothers by then had, was one of my Dad's pet notions which he would bring up from time to time.

This time I parried, "Maybe if I was as strong and intense as Don Colombo, I could…"

"You are, you just don't know it. But I do, I've seen it."

After a while Dad got around to asking me how practice had gone that day, as if finally addressing the main point of interest on our agenda, and as if he'd fully expected wholesale changes of one kind or another to have taken place. Perhaps it was the potential downturn in my football fortunes that made him choose this particular evening to relaunch his wrestling campaign.

"Whew," I whistled. "No personnel moves…" To this he gave his familiar close-mouthed nod of the head which never failed to call to mind Bogart as Sam Spade, deliberately down once and deliberately back up. "But check this out, Dad…"

When I was through recounting the unusual day of practice, he said, "You've been rubbing that arm this whole time."

"Oh, yeah." I poked at a swelling on my upper forearm. "It's weird, look at this."

"Let me see."

"Is there such a thing as water on the elbow?" This was intended to be a joke.

"Yeah," my father explained. "But this starts way down here on your forearm. Can you straighten it?"

"Yup."

"Any pain when you bend it?"

"No, just a little burning. Right at the elbow."

Dad prodded the swelling here and there, again and again, watching the liquid displace and refill. "Any pain when I do that?"

"Nope."

"It's not a bruise, but you must have banged it. Probably at practice."

That made perfect sense. "This one too." I showed him my other arm which had a similar distended sack, but to a lesser extent, ranging from my forearm to just below my triceps.

"Let me see. Not as bad, but the same thing. You carry the ball in your left hand mostly, right?"

"Yup."

"Let's put some ice on it and see what happens."

Icing my elbows, leaning back against the hassock, I believe I was starting to doze off when Dad said, "I was talking to uncle Tony about that concert you guys are going to tomorrow…"

"Huh–"

"And he said seeing Bob Dylan in a live concert in person is a real happening."

—-

The next day, Mike Barry and John Berksza and Bobby Burchard met me, Chuck, and Matty in the Armory parking lot after practice and we left for the Boston Garden straight from there. I wasn't expecting this evening to be anywhere near as eventful as the Kinks concert that spring, but our giddy anticipation couldn't have been higher. Dylan was touring in support of his *Street Legal* album which was a pretty good one in my opinion – not on a par with its predecessors, *Blood on the Tracks* and *Desire*, but that's no slight; those two are as strong a pair of back-to-back albums as have ever been released by anyone.

I was glad to see that the Garden was packed. A full house adds so greatly to the overall atmosphere. The year before at the poorly attended Hagler fight, it kind of sucked being able to hear anytime a cornerman coughed.

Dylan played a bunch of my favorite songs that night although I would have preferred to hear them in their familiar form rather than the showy arrangements he decided to go with. Then again, who the hell am I to grouse? It was Bob Dylan for Christ's sake!
—

A few days after our next game, Joe called from Pensacola
"Austintatious!"
"Tell Ma thanks for the tapes," he said. "I listened to North Quincy last night."
"Oh, cool."
"You had a good game. Despite a couple fumbles."
"Dad said they ought to put a handle on the ball for me."
"I'm surprised he doesn't got you sleeping with it."
"That strategy has been advanced."
"Well you don't want too many more games like that one, fumblewise."
"It's those damn forearm pads. The ball slips around sometimes."
"Why the *hell* you wearing forearm pads," Joe snapped.
"My arms were getting banged up. So Doctor A.J. Dunn, Sr., prescribed–"
"Shit, I'll take bumps and bruises over fumbles any day."
"Right? But I got these like… fluid sacs protruding now, from my arms. It's weird."
"Water on the elbow?"
"I guess. Something like that."
"Maybe adhesive tape over the pads. It's kind of tacky, ball won't slip."
I said, "That's not bad."
"And it sounded like on both fumbles you were already through the line."
"Ah…"

"When you're making a cut, or bouncing off, or jumping through the line, your arms are going to flail out. But you can't run wild like it's kill-the-man-with-the-ball."

"Yeah…"

"Just adjust. Tight to the chest when you're making a break. Right to your heart, tight as tight."

That's why I love AJD.

"So according to the tapes you had nineteen carries."

"Did I?"

"Almost all the carries. What's the deal? Owen hurt?"

"That's the thing, Joe. No he's not."

"So you're the feature back?"

"I don't know. I guess."

"Beautiful!"

"Yeah…"

"What's Owen got to say about it?"

"We haven't actually discussed it."

"You guys are pretty tight, though, right?"

"Yeah, man."

"That's what I thought. I remember during the blizzard you stayed over his house for a couple days."

"Yup."

"And Ma sent me the North Quincy game day program. In the running backs picture, it's just you two together. In the team picture, you guys are standing shoulder to shoulder."

"Yup."

"Kind of sucks then, huh?"

"Yeah, man."

"Would you rather it was him getting the carries?"

"Course not. But he's my friend."

Joe changed the subject. "So, was Armond losing his mind over all the penalties?"

"Yeeup."

"Can't blame him. Me, I don't mind penalties – as long as they're not on one of your runs. That way you get to regain the same yardage twice. But I could've sworn I heard him down on the field, really *railing* at someone."

"Probably did."

"Maybe a ref..."

"Yeah."

"Maybe you."

"Not me," I assured him without a doubt. [Author's Note For the Record: In all our time together, Mr. Colombo never once trained a rail on me; this despite fuck-ups and failures aplenty.] [I never asked him why, so please don't ask me.]

"And I gotta say," Joe said. "Zibelli and Charlie Bergeron do a nice job calling the games. And it's cool, you can hear the band and everything, the crowd. Tom Hughes on the PA."

"Yes! That's right."

"I could picture it all. Nice Sunny day, right?"

"Yup."

"On one of your runs, Mr. Hughes was like, 'Greg Dunn on the carry... Greg Dunn... *Greg Dunn...!* Ladies and gentlemen... *Gregory Dunn!*'"

I laughed.

"What was going on on that one? Or do you not even hear the announcer?"

"Not really."

"Remember which run that was?"

"No."

"Oh—"

"Third-and-one from midfield. Dive play over left guard..."

"Heh! Heading which way?"

"Toward the scoreboard. I hit the hole hard and bounced it toward the visitors' sideline, straight-armed a backer at the hash which gave me a little room to work with. Then at the sideline I straight-armed another guy..."

"'*Greg Dunn!*'"

"Yup. Then when I got knocked out of bounds, that's when I heard, 'Ladies and gentlemen, Gregory Dunn!'"

"Nice pick up."

"Twenty-nine yarder."

"Ah! Matches your longest of the season then."

"Well the season's only two games old."

"Still…"

"And at least North Quincy didn't proceed to totally shut me down afterwards the way Dedham did."

"Dedham locked your ass up like old Lucas Jackson after he got the rabbit in him…"

"Yup."

"Lassoed you with a choke leash. Manhandled you… With manacles."

"Alright, easy…"

"But hey – first win of the season and your first TD. First of many."

"Right."

"And your first hundred-yard game. That's big. Power-I feature back."

"Thanks, Joe."

"You guys get Christo's?"

"Yup."

"Shit," he said ruefully. "Pizza down here sucks."

―

My fellow Americans! You should know me well enough by now to expect with a high degree of certainty the fulfillment of some if not all of my campaign promises regarding the strict limitation of a single season's game-by-game details. Still, allow me to allay any lingering concerns by reiterating that I do not intend to bore you all with a mishmash of 1978's Brockton Football minutiae. That's a (campaign) promise!

Nevertheless, there is one other game in particular that stands out whenever I'm reminded of that year on the team. Our Thanksgiving finale against Waltham serves, along with Dedham, as an apposite bookend to the season, being that both our first and last games were similarly strange and all-around ugly affairs.

We rolled into Waltham's muddy Leary Field that morning holding the clear inside track to a Suburban League championship. A win would put us at 8-0 in league play and give us the title outright, ahead of Waltham and Newton North, each of whom already had one league loss apiece. Coincidentally, Waltham's defeat had come at the hands of Newton, whose so-called Black Phantom Defense (2 TDs and 1 FG allowed all year; six shutouts) completely slammed the door on the Hawks and their All-Everything back John Giusti, 25-0; and Newton's lone league loss had come at the hands of us. When my brother Joe called home after listening (very closely, it seems) to the Newton cassettes, he declared it a "great" win.

"The better team lost."

"Hey…"

"That's not an insult, Greg. That's a good thing. You guys did what you had to do to beat a superior team. That bodes well for your success."

"No, but—"

"No – no buts. You know they had 600 yards total offense—?"

"Bull shit!"

"You gonna let me finish?"

"Oh. Yeah. Go head."

"Yuh?"

"Finish!"

"Newton North had 600 yards of offense, before giving 200 back on penalties."

"Oh, tsch… Shit. Come on."

"That still leaves 400 fucking yards offense. That's not nothing."

"And how many'd we have?"

"Less than two."

"You sure about that, bro," I argued, for strictly rhetorical reasons. I knew if it came down to it, Joe's numbers would line up with Mr. Fitzgibbons' clipboard totals to at least two decimal points.

"They pile up 400 yards and only score once," I pretend protested. "Is that even mathematically possible?"

"Every big play in the fourth quarter went Brockton's way," Joe explained. "On your only sustained drive of the day, you guys score, go for two, and make it."

"Barely."

"Yeah, that's what it said on the radio. Puts you up, 8-7. Then they're driving and Dwayne recovers a fumble…"

"Right," I remembered.

"They get the ball back. Three minutes left, they miss the winning field goal."

"Uh-huh."

"They get the ball back again. Then Mike Cooney strips their running back *and* recovers the fumble…"

"Great fucking play by Mike Cooney!"

"They get the ball back… *again.* Thirty seconds left, Bob Stone blocks the fucking field goal."

"Joe, that dude is so clutch."

"Who you telling? Without him, you guys lose. Without any one of those big plays, you lose."

I thought out loud, "Yeah, you're right. They were hard to kill."

"All you heard all day was, 'Greg Dunn on the carry. Dimartino on the tackle.' They had him keying on you as part of their whole scheme, obviously. To take you out of the equation."

"My very first carry he comes in leading their charge on a sweep for no gain."

Joe sang, "I been through the desert on a sweep for no gain."

"We're at the bottom of the pile, face mask to face mask, and he's screaming his head off, 'On you all day, you piece of shit! All fucking day!'"

"Whoa! What'd you say?"

"Nothing. What was I supposed to say? *'Says you!'*"

"Well he wasn't lying. Put his money where his mouth is. Kept you under a hundred."

Joe's been the voice of real for me since the beginning, which I've always appreciated and respected, but he doesn't have to moonlight as Devil's Advocate too. Give keeping that shit to yourself a try, will you brother?

"I counted twenty-five Dimartino-on-the-tackles," he pointed out.

"Damn. Probably all on me."

"Probably were. You had twenty-six carries."

"Hah! I was actually seeing green for a couple plays, and my head didn't stop aching until supper time on Sunday."

"Could've been a concussion."

"Yeah, I don't know. But on the bright side, those frigging water on the elbows got straightened out somehow."

"What!"

"I think Dimartino just beat them down."

"Totally gone? No telltale signs?"

"You can stretch the skin out real easy now, and it's kind of numb to the touch, but yeah."

"No more arm pads?"

"I'm going to keep one small elbow pad."

"Left elbow?"

"Yes sir."

"Well, all in all a great win for the good guys. Great win."

As noted elsewhere in these pages, the transitive properties of Math and/or so-called Science when applied to Suburban League football matchups not only don't necessarily hold true, but when it comes right down to it they don't mean Jackson fucking Squat. If they did, the universally logical equation If (A > B) and (B > C) then (A > C) would prove out thus, and everyone'd be happy all the way round because:

If Brockton (A) defeats (>) Newton (B) by the score 8-7
And Newton (B) defeats (>) Waltham (C) by the score 25-0
Then it would stand to bloody reason that…
Brockton (A) will trounce (>) Waltham (C) by the score 28-2 or so

Right, Math folks? Right?!

Well, hold onto your hypotenuses 'cause you ain't gonna believe this no how!

INGENUOUS DISAVOWAL: Insofar as the previous impressions concerning Newton North amount to something more akin to Monday morning quarterback debates the likes of which you'd overhear in any company breakroom than they do to a play-by-play analysis of an actual Brockton Football game, they thereby should not be considered in violation of those assurances, express or implied, contained within the preambles of previous vignettes which forswore the excessive use of in-game specifics from that 1978 Boxer season due to the inherent boringness thereof. Thank you.

In preparation for Giusti and Waltham, we used the extra time between our week nine opponent and the Thanksgiving Day finale (twelve days instead of the customary seven) to experiment a little bit more than we normally would.

On the defensive side, sophomore linebacker Bob Collett had been making a name for himself on the burgers, filling holes and stuffing plays against our first-string offense, showing extraordinary instinct and a rare nose for the ball, to the extent that Mr. Colombo was regularly calling out – nay, *roaring* out – our linemen, individually, Christian name plus surname, demanding an explanation as to why the *HELL* they were telling Bob Collett the plays. It was pretty clear that he'd be part of our game plan come Thanksgiving morning.

We tried a number of new offensive plays on for size, too.

I remember Coach Colombo calling out a pass formation that had me in the slot with Matt Walsh split out wide. "Greg, you know how to run a Z-Out?"

The naming of plays in football is an intentionally simple process for obvious reasons, often straightforward to the point of blatancy. Therefore, it is not a brag, as such, to brag that having never heard of such a thing in my whole life, I promptly cracked the Z-Out code.

I said, "Yeah!"

"Alright, let's try it – on one. Matty, deep post. Greg, Z-Out."

From the slot, I angled for the left sideline, broke right toward mid-field for a few strides, then cut back hard for the sideline again.

To this day, I think the gleam in Mr. Colombo's smile was equal parts amused pity and amused admiration. He admitted that this pass pattern's name was somewhat of a misnomer, that the Z was actually a sideways V. "We'll call your version the Greg Dunn Z-Out," he joked after I ran the real play properly.

Another new wrinkle we toyed with leading up to Thanksgiving was a variation on the UMaine "punch-ball" play, brainchild of coach Jack Bicknell whose Black Bears had pulled it off in a game against UNH a few weeks prior. Exploiting a loophole in the rules, their field goal holder took the snap and flipped the ball toward their kicker who punched it forward out of mid-air, producing what was technically a live fumble which Maine then recovered in the endzone for a touchdown. Since the ball had been batted forward instead of passed, rules covering illegal linemen downfield did not apply.

Such ingenious loopholes hardly ever survive the off-season Rules Committee meetings, so our forward-thinking leader figured if we were going to capitalize on such chicanery, it had damn well better be soon, to wit: This Waltham game.

However, despite our repeated efforts that day in practice, the stars refused to align for the BHS rendition of the punch-ball play. Again and again I set up as deep-back in the I, fielded Chuck's pitch, tucked the ball on a fake sweep right, and pulled up short to bat it over the heads of the defense toward our waiting linemen in the endzone; again and again each attempt yielded the same fruitless scattershot result.

Stubbornness can be a blessing indeed, almost as often as it is a curse, but there comes a point where even Armond Colombo will not keep whipping a horse that refuses to run. In the spirit of Simplest Common Denominator as regards playbook nomenclature, he had dubbed our doomed experiment the "Greg Dunn Bat". After my sixth or seventh crack at it proved no more effective than the first several had, Coach Colombo shot me a no-hard-feelings glance, bit ahold of his whistle, blew the play dead once and for all, and we moved on.

—

Being a longtime fan of football as entertainment, I would've loved to watch our hard-fought Waltham game with the objective eye of a reporter or a disinterested observer. After all, a league championship was at stake, and both teams featured potent offenses with bona fide star power, namely two of the top three scorers in Division-1: Matt Walsh on our side, and John Giusti on the other. Coming into the game, Matty already had 100 points under his belt, putting him ahead of Woburn's Andy Clivio (92) by a slim margin while affording him a comfortable lead over Giusti (85). If he could manage to hold on for one more game, he'd be adding Division-1 Scoring Champ to his superlative season's heap of unprecedented achievements, establishing another Brockton first.

There was a lot of slow slippery back-and-forth in the opening quarter on Thanksgiving but only one score, a twenty-five yard run by Giusti who made up some valuable ground in the Scoring race. We also got word that Clivio had notched a first half TD himself, bringing his season total to a hot-breath-on-neck 98 points.

Matty answered the challengers shortly thereafter, though, recouping six points plus one to grow on by outjumping the defense in the back of the endzone on a beautiful fourth-and-two alley-oop from the thirty, and converting the PAT, which put him at 107 points and the Boxers ahead 7-6 midway through the second quarter.

On their next possession, Big Play Bobby Stone – who else? – came up with an interception deep within Hawks territory. As I took the field, slapping him and the rest of our defense five, I saw my dad and uncle Jimmy watching from the fence behind the endzone. We had great field position but in a game that was starting to feel eerily similar to that tooth and nail defensive struggle against Newton, we soon found ourselves looking at fourth-and-long from inside the Waltham twenty.

Catching our breath during the time out, Ronny Byrnes and I were keeping an eye on Chuck and Mr. Colombo as they conferred on the sideline. I wouldn't have been surprised to see the field goal unit come out. From where we were standing, it would have been about a 35-yard attempt, but Matty had made them from that distance before in practice, and from longer.

Although "just a soph-o-more", as Keith Jackson might say, Byrnes had stepped in at fullback recently when Mr. Colombo correctly recognized that Stoney's freewheeling approach to all facets of the game was best suited to the defensive side of the ball. Also, we were by-and-large a two-platoon team so, barring very rare exceptions (Matty, e.g.), the Coach came at you with two discrete units, ensuring fresh offensive legs and maximally rested defenders; not to mention, Byrnsey was *good*. Possessed of old-fashioned rawboned horsepower, he was a combination smashmouth blocker and slashing-type runner. Laconic as a high plains drifter, the only thing he said on the field was a gruff nodding "thanks" when you cuffed him on the helmet for a good play, if he even uttered anything.

Waiting for the Armonds to conclude their sidebar, I repeatedly spat significant amounts of spittle into my mud-caking palms, the better for to grip and to wipe off lingering game-day nervous energy. From out there on the field, in the loiterous limbo of an essential-workers-only timeout, I couldn't tell what Chuck and his dad were saying to each other, or even hear the sound of their lowered voices, but it was apparent that we were intending to forgo Matt Walsh's talented leg in favor of rolling the fourth-and-long dice.

Mr. Colombo sent Chuck back onto the field, not with a clap on the shoulder pad or fatherly smack on the ass, but rather a nod as sharp as a dress whites salute. Despite being muffled by the capacity crowd noise and our intervening distance, his marching orders rang out to my mind like a general's clarion "Charge!"

"Greg Dunn Bat," I saw him say.

All I could think was, 'WHAT!'

Suddenly the fidgety nerves of a moment ago were as wistful childhood lullabies.

'The FUCK?'

Chuck took his place across from me at the opposite end of our conventionally football-shaped huddle, knelt on one knee – completely straight-faced, mind you – and recited the orders, nodding like his dad, making brief but definite eye contact with everyone, as all good quarterbacks will. "Let's do this now," he ordered. "Greg Dunn Bat on two. Greg Dunn Bat on two." My friends, please pardon the reiteration, but just to be clear: he does this *with a completely straight face.*

On his second hut, Chuck performed a neat reverse turn and pitched me the ball underhand. I received it as naturally as one of my dad's hut-hut parlor empties and tucked it, ranging to my right, feigning a sweep.

Speaking of Dad, this seems as good a place as any to mention that from time to time over the years my father has made a point of instilling in us, "You take the bad with the good and deal with it, right? That's Life. What the hell else you gonna do? Pack it in?"

The sloppy footing saw our secret weapon unfold at a somewhat slower pace than it might have under normal conditions. I wouldn't be surprised if the Hawks "D" thought a halfback option was being orchestrated rather than a sweep play. Either way, though, they must have smelled something rotten in Waltham because none of their guys put up a pass rush or applied any kind of pressure at all. They saw our whole interior line breaking downfield instead of blocking, so, being a well-coached group they obviously decided to exercise discretion as the better part of valor and stay at home rather than getting caught out over-committing with pursuit. Whatever their reasoning, the absence of blitzing monster backs or corners suited me just fine. The Greg Dunn Bat was already working out better than it ever had in practice.

With that in mind, though, it never hurts to remember that those good old Fates are a funny bunch. They have quite the sense of humor, actually. Sometimes just for fun they'll make a point of dusting and polishing every tchotchke on the shelf to a fine gleam before pulling the rug out from under.

Even so, seizing upon this unusual moment of calm on our side of the line of scrimmage, I decelerated to deliver the surprise punch, volleyball style. Of course in slowing down I skidded on some mud, heeling backwards. All I could do before I fell flat on my ass was serve up a high fly ball and hope for the best. The last I saw, it was hovering at its apogee, strangely vivid against the overcast sky.

Not until we watched game films did I see my slipshod serve come back down to Earth. In the endzone, our left tackle Jim Pouliopoulos became a rowdy thirsty Brockton High alum elbowing his way to the bar at last call on Thanksgiving Eve at George's Cafe. I daresay he parted the sea of red Waltham Hawks jerseys like Moses Malone boxing out, and made the fate-defying catch, injecting us with a much needed shot of momentum just before halftime. Matty's PAT put us ahead 14-6 and brought his division leading points total to 108.

When I got back on the sideline, Mr. Colombo's smile was borderline sly.

As for our ensuing kickoff, the less time spent on that the better. Suffice to say that those blasted Fates, in the form of Hurricane Giusti, swept through with the force of catastrophe, swinging the momentum right back in Waltham's favor while reminding one and all that the 3-Dog was still very much in the scoring race and hot on the hunt.*

I heard someone on our sideline say, "How come *he's* not slipping and sliding?"

"I know! Dude's scooting around like Jerboa Jump. Or Savoir Faire. Or–"

"Are you drunk?"

Then came the game's second half and, like a beer bottle breaking in the shower, it was upsetting on multiple levels.

We can't say we didn't have our share of opportunities. In the third quarter we tried a new hook-and-lateral play that had been working nicely in practice. From the wingback slot I would throw a check-block on the defensive end and circle out into the hook zone. Our tight end, having run a hook pattern over the middle, would catch Chuck's throw and in the same motion pop a two-handed basketball pass to me as I sped past. Tight end Barry Durocher had good footwork, good size, and most importantly good hands. He must have played some basketball, too, because his passes were like a center posting up and kicking the ball back up top. Unlike that problematic Greg Dunn Bat play, this one worked in practice every time we ran it. However, in the game the lateral to me was at my shoelaces and I failed to come up with it cleanly. Had I done so, it would have been an easy fifty- or sixty-yard touchdown because the only things between me and the endzone were some grass and mud and a bunch of horizontal yard lines; but I bobbled and dribbled the ball for a good ten yards before I had no choice but to fall on it for an extremely frustrating first down.

On top of that, we had two sustained drives late in the game that were stopped on turnovers deep in enemy territory. Opening the fourth quarter, our running game was finding its rhythm for the first time all day. Waltham must have been wondering, "Where the *fuck* did this Byrnes kid come from?" Unfortunately, on first-and-goal from the ten-yard line we were intercepted in the endzone.

It wasn't Game Over, but we were trailing and the clock was ticking. You could realistically count our remaining chances to mount a drive on the claws of a one-legged hawk.

When we got to the sideline, the tension and frustration got the best of me.

"We run it down their throats the whole way [ok, slight exaggeration]," I fumed, shaking my head at Mr. Colombo. "Then we're knocking on the door, and we *throw?*"

My fellow Brocktonians, the molten rage aroar in his eyes burned me mute and put me back in my foolish place. Like much of the communication between Armond Colombo, Sr., and myself, this memorandum from on high, albeit loud and perfectly clear, was left unsaid; and, mercifully, never mentioned again.

*[HISTORICAL POINTS: Although our stubborn and defiant defense stopped Giusti's 2-point conversion rush, protecting our 14-12 halftime lead, the Waltham Whirlwind leapfrogged Clivio and Matty later in the game by rushing for two more touchdowns. Following his third score, our defense shut down yet another of his 2-point conversion tries, but he succeeded in pushing through for 2 after his final TD, thereby accounting for all 26 of his team's points that day while making off with the Division-1 Scoring title, miraculously nipping Matty at the wire, 111-108.]

*[HYSTERICAL POINTS OF VIEW: Although our 1978 clash with Waltham was undoubtedly a full on defensive struggle (their offense had a mere three scoring drives all game; ours had two), I have since heard words like "blowout" and "dominated" used in reference to this game from those in attendance and even from somebody on our own bench that day (obviously this guy's opinion came from the skewed perspective of a non-participant whose unsullied Boxer uniform renders such judgment questionable at best, and ultimately moot). Needless to say, it is patently impossible for a game we were winning at halftime, and which thereafter saw just fourteen more points scored, to be characterized as a blowout.

But don't get me wrong: I *understand*. A game like this can be totally misconstrued in retrospect. Giusti's individual performance is writ so large in the collective memory as to overshadow and, yes, dominate lesser characters in the play – the turnovers, the punts, all the three-and-outs. It makes perfect sense, actually. In time ordinary humdrum facts fall from our memory like desiccated pine needles and are swept away, having no relevance whatsoever to that beautifully trimmed Christmas tree we all recall so fondly.

I realize that nobody who was at that game feels like our defense played as well as theirs, but it did. When thinking back on it, nobody gets the feeling that our offense played as well as theirs either – including me! – but we did.

On that fruitless hook-and-lateral play, our guy put the ball in a tricky spot for me. I've made harder grabs in games, though; I should have made that one. Yeah, I know, "could've/should've", but in the collective memory, a long touchdown run on that one single play would have served to offset Giusti's great kickoff return to an extent, and suddenly the whole game feels a lot closer – not based on the scoreboard, per se, but in our overall impression of the event.

Of course no such offset was forthcoming.]

You know how sometimes you'll hear, "The game wasn't as close as the score." Or, "It was actually *closer* than the score." Well, but for the failure of one single play, our game would be regarded to this day in the public's collective memory as the back and forth defensive dogfight it really was. This has been on my chest for a while: Our defense that year – hell, our defense most years – never got the respect they deserve.

As quoted previously in these pages, the three kinds of lies are said to be "Lies; Damned lies; Statistics." For further proof of this dictum: in our game on November 23, 1978, Waltham's John Giusti and I had more or less the same amount of carries, give or take a few. He ended up gaining 5.8 yards per attempt according to the *Globe*, and it turns out I averaged 6.3 per. This meaningless statistic contradicts everything I've ever felt about my ineffectual efforts on the ground that day. I remember mud. I remember hits. I remember losing. Like everybody else, I remember Giusti.

There has never been a game, going into or coming out of, that I looked at from a Me versus So-and-So perspective. It's always been Brockton versus this team or Brockton versus that team. On the football field, a team of players runs the same way a team of horses does. If one of us is not in sync, the team won't run right. It *can't* run right. That's why football's the best game.

With that being said for the record, and in the spirit of friendly disclosure... John Giusti edged me out that day 1-0 in the crucial all-important Win column. Furthermore, he beat my everloving ass 26-to-zip in Points Scored, the only other stat worth a good goddamn, but the thing is: It wasn't a fucking blowout.

—

1978 BOXER FOOTBALL TAKEAWAYS

Despite the oddity of close friend and backfield mate Owen O'Connor's absence from our huddles, which cast a pall over the whole season for me personally, it did feel good to be part of such a fine team. It was a definite relief, too, to see that the 1977 aberration was more a one-off setback than a sign of downwardly spiraling things to come.

Matt Walsh was well-deservedly named to the All-Scholastic team. However, as if to illustrate how funny and ultimately flawed postseason awards really are, Chuck, who led the entire state of

Massachusetts in touchdown passes – who'd had a truly *great* season at quarterback – was not named. Fortunately, outside opinion has never carried much weight with Chuck. He knows what's what, and that's plenty good enough for him. You don't need a Gallup Poll to know who won the horse race.

Accolades are fun, though. There hadn't been a Boxer on the All-Scholastic team in years, and seeing one of our own up there was nice, but Matty's most eye-opening accomplishment that season was the way he shot from out of nowhere to the top of the scoring heap. I didn't even know they kept track of that stuff. It wasn't something we discussed, or even thought about, probably because none of our guys had ever been in the conversation until he got his foot in the door; and when Matty barged in he didn't just crash the party – he tore the damn door off its hinges and threw it in the fire, and the Brocktonians came marching in.

In fact, during the subsequent "Boxer's Decade" (1979 - 1990), a Brockton player was crowned Division-1 Scoring Champ seven times; to say nothing of the three years we took second place. Unlike being voted All-Scholastic, or Player-of-the-Year (as several of those top scorers ultimately were), there's nothing subjective about coming in first; it leaves no room for interpretation. Needless to say, that high flying era was something to behold in the old Shoe City, harkening back to the early seventies glory days of Alky Tsitsos & Ken MacAfee, and readying for the emergence in the nineties of Peter Harris (Players-of-the-Year all, by the way, and all under the tutelage of coach for the ages, Armond Colombo).

One of our litany of Player-of-the-Year recipients once explained, with no apparent irony, "It wasn't that I had such a great year. It's just nobody had a better one."

Was Chuck's outstanding '78 season overlooked by the All-Scholastic committee? Hell yes, absolutely. Maybe they didn't think that the recognition of both halves of any single team's quarterback/receiver combo was fair. Maybe they figured Chuck was just a junior and would be a shoo-in next year. Maybe, because subjectivity is the bane of competitive sport, they couldn't see the forest for the trees. I don't know. If you ask me, though, my pal was simply a casualty of that almighty and most arbitrary force, Timing (aka Shit Luck), because back in those days the All-Scholastic Football Team featured but 1 quarterback. On an offense consisting of 12 players maximum, there'd be your standard 5 interior linemen, 3 running backs, a tight end, a split end, and one extra player – usually another lineman or receiver. (Compare that era's team with Peter Harris's 1996 roster which carried five QBs and no less than twenty RBs.) But, hey – it couldn't have happened to a better guy because Chuck was strong enough and smart and self assured enough to take a stellar season for what it was. I think the snub has bothered me more over the years than it has him. He's always known: Unbestowed laurels won't suddenly change your fine silk purse into a sow's ear, nor will the pleasure of postgame adulation ever nullify a loss.

———

At home later after our Thanksgiving game, the Cowboys and Redskins were on TV. My angled neck and back, hip flexor and knees, left shin and ankles, doubtless acting on the circadian hunch that their day's toil was done, started to stiffen pleasantly into place as I became one with the hassock and rug.

Dinner was almost ready. In the meantime, Ma's annual holiday hors d'oeuvre, a roundly anticipated presentation in the Dunn house resulting from the painstaking application of a hundred brightly colored toothpicks, each skewering an array of pimento olives, cheese cubes, and folded pepperoni slices, and arranged in close-knit quills to cover a pineapple's plump hide like the edible feathers of a miniature turkey, was being made short work of on the coffee table. My mother had procured little hand-painted wooden attachments – an S-shaped turkey head, and a fan of tail feathers – to complete the landfowl effect. With every passing brother of mine another delectable feather was plucked. Little Julie alone abstained.

"Can you grab me one of those," I said. "Before that tiny turkey's completely naked? Thank you, Richeroo!"

"Want one, Dad?"

"Sure."

Ma's gravy and stuffing and potatoes and pies were warming the house with Thanksgiving aromas, savory with inklings of sweet.

"How many yards you end up with," Dad asked me. "One-twenty-something? Somewhere in there?"

I'd have been able to ballpark it anyway, but Mr. Fitzgibbons made a point of showing me my total on the clipboard after every game.

"120 on the dot."

"Good," Dad said. "Good tough game. Proud of you."

I nodded at the TV despite my neck. "Thanks."

"Not because of how you played. I'm proud of how you showed up." My father has a way of expressing himself with a certain ambiguity that lends his words – sometimes intentionally, I'm guessing, other times not – added depth. "That's what I like about all you guys. You show up."

"Thank you, Dad." I turned toward him and nodded.

"You sore?"

Returning to my angular slouch, "Yeah…"

"Well, plenty of time to rest up now."

"Yup."

We watched the football game for a while.

"Real good season," Dad summed up. "Next year'll be even better."

I nodded again. "Depending on the line."

"Of course." I knew he was nodding too.

"Tom Thibeault's going to leave big shoes to fill," I said. "Capachione. Those guys…"

"Both keys for you."

"Yup."

"Both tough. That whole line this year did right by you."

"Yeah they did."

"Ma," my father blurted. "Call the Globe. Find out dates for the rest of the Patriots' home games."

My mom went to the kitchen phone. "Is anybody even going to be there on Thanksgiving?"

"They're there. They're always there." Then, referring to the game on TV, Dad reminded me, "See? That's why I always tell you not to mill around the outskirts of a pile."

My mother took notes during the call with the *Globe* and spent a minute after hanging up to review and approve all her slanting cursive loops, and confirm every cross and dot. "Both of the next two games are away," she told us. "Then they play Buffalo Bills at home. Then the last one's away at the Dolphins."

"Alright, so three weeks till Buffalo..." Dad said.

"Two-and-a-half weeks."

"Two-and-a-half weeks..."

Dad's idea, a good one and generous as hell, was perfect. We (he) would treat the Boxers starting O-line to a Pats game at Schaefer Stadium in recognition of a job well done.

"Think the guys would like that, if we took them all to a game?"

"They'd love it," I laughed.

"What about a playoff game?"

"Hah!"

Never let it be said that my father balks at the prospect of improving upon perfection.

"So we gotta win two out of our last four to make it to the playoffs, right," he asked rhetorically. "Baltimore stinks, they're up next. Then who?"

My mother said, "Dallas Cowboys."

"Good tough team. Then the Bills... They stink too..."

"Then Miami," my dad's Girl Friday supplied.

"Another tough one. Alright... How's this: we hold off on the tickets at least till after the Colts this Sunday. Patriots lose, we go to the Buffalo game. Patriots win—"

"We let it ride!"

Instead of committing the funds right away to the Buffalo tickets, it was unanimously agreed that, for the time being at least, it was worth our while to let it ride.

For those next few Sundays at our house, we were caught up in full-fledged Playoff Mania, carried away by that addictive heady optimism which gamblers know and love: *action*. It was an atmosphere of anticipation and electrified excitement perhaps not equalled since the hippodromes of ancient Greece, or at least since the twelfth race at Raynham.

As expected, the Pats went on to beat Baltimore and, as expected, they lost to the Cowboys.

When Joe called from Pensacola before the Bills game, he said, "The Pats are fine, don't worry. They're about to break the single-season team rushing record. They're a team of destiny."

"And Buffalo sucks."

"And Buffalo sucks."

"Who holds the rushing record now?"

Joe said, "Buffalo."

"Hah!"

"OJ's '73 'Juice is Loose' team."

"Ah, alright. Makes sense."

"The weirdest thing about life, Greg? It makes perfect fucking sense."

The Patriots won their game, a squeaker against the Bills, thus clinching a playoff spot. Our (my father's) gamble had paid off. "I was just playing the percentages," he ho-hummed.

On New Year's Eve day, Dad and I, along with our Boxer center, guards, and tackles, caravaned in two cars to Foxboro for the playoff game against the Houston Oilers. The guys in our car exchanged furtive sidelong glances, envying the other guys their freedom to slam a couple or three beers on the way.

Unfortunately, Houston wrapped up the year for us once and for all. From a Brockton Football standpoint, I couldn't be too displeased with 1978. We had made important strides toward being a better team all the way around. As for the Pats, they put themselves in a hole early that day and it wasn't much of a game. Although I was certainly digging this very rare treat of watching Earl Campbell* at work, live and in person, I sensed in some of my huddlemates an antsy itch to exit early; and said itch turned out to be quite contagious, I must say. After all, wasn't there a whole bunch of New Year's Eve partying to attend to elsewhere, posthaste and forthwith?

*[Author's Note: Obviously I had never met Campbell but in addition to the great admiration I had for his ability as a ball carrier, I *liked* him. Through that curious process of transference which automatically places new acquaintances, or complete strangers as with Campbell, in high regard due to nothing more than their resemblance in countenance or demeanor to a fellow of whom we are already fond, the bruising Oilers tailback was alright with me; he was Jay McGee, writ large.]
—

When viewed forty years hence through memory's compression lens, high school off-seasons register like lulls in the dugout between innings, or the countless unvarying commutes to and from your job every day, which is to say hardly at all. The passage of time keeps boiling down these between-sports dormancies into miniature memory meatballs, one barely distinguishable from all the others in the pot.

So there's not much that stands out in my mind from that off-season winter. Of course Chuck and I resumed our weight lifting regimen at the Y, Mondays through Saturdays. (It sounds silly to say now, but in those days nobody lifted weights during football season.) (Sillier still, baseball players were actually discouraged from lifting, lest they become "muscle bound" and unable to properly swing the bat...) He and I had the usual weight room rivalry that everyone has with his lifting partner, a friendly but very real motivator.

Every so often, to kill time on a weeknight, a few times a month, Chuck would pick me up in his brother's car and we'd go to the movies at the Westgate Cinema with a six-pack of Miller's for us to split. On one such excursion, I remember Chuck saying, "Great directions!" as soon as I got in the car. (Somehow I had procured our beers the night before and stashed them in the woods on East Street.

During school earlier that day I had passed Chuck the goofy buried treasure directions, complete with landmarks, numbered paces, and a big **X** marks the spot.)

Sometimes too, if the marquee at the Skyview Drive-In Theatre showed a "Deadly Weapons" double feature or some such, we'd park on the side of the road off Hayward Ave. to sneak in through the woods out back and commando-crawl from the tree line with our beers to the rearmost tiers of moguls, giggling like fools at our artifice and the inane dialogue. Usually after an hour or so, with no more beer to combat the cold, one of us would curse, "Bas*tard!*" and we'd retreat through the woods and call it a night.

That whole winter was a season of workouts and recreation for us, during which the bond we had as friends (rather than simply school or sports chums) began to assume the permanence in our lives that it now knows. When we went "to the show", as my Dorchester-born-and-bred parents would say, it was just the two of us most of the time, although I remember a couple times when his brother Donny, home from college, would join us. Once in particular, a sunny weekend day, we caught the matinee screening of *The Deer Hunter* at Westgate. It was one of those unexpected moviegoing occasions that found us the only three paying customers in the whole place. Naturally we fanned out, migrating toward the frontmost rows, settling into seats as we each saw fit, the triangular points of an oblique constellation, lounging with feet up on forward seats like a trio of General Cinema board members.

Before the coming attractions, I heard Chuck whisper, "Dunna," from a few seats behind me as if the intervening rows were pews in church. I turned around. He whispered, "Want a popcorn?"

I shook my head no.

"Donny?"

"Chucky," his brother answered in a whisper from off to the side and further back. "Why are we whispering?"

Outside afterwards in the squinting glare, on our way to the car, processing the poignant experience we had just shared, Don Colombo, master of aperçu, gesturing with an imaginary rifle shell, summed things up: "This is this. This ain't something else. *This* is this."

Fast on the draw, Chuck crooned in reply, "You're just too good to be truuue... Can't take my eyes off of youuu..."

———

If winter off-season represented down time for me, it had long since meant go-time in our house for my brothers, wrestlers all. Rich and Steve in particular had taken to the sport. Strong, tough, and quick as cats, they'd each collected armloads of AAU age-group championships by this time. Though just seventh-graders, their reputations were preceding them. The high school's coaches already were looking to them as future Boxer linchpins.

One evening at home in the parlor that winter, with the pungent aroma of burnt wood emanating from Dad in his work clothes, he commented on the fatal drunk driving accident on the news.

"See, that's why I always tell you," he reminded me. "Out with your friends some night, the guy driving's half in the bag — just tell him to pull over, you're getting out. Call me, I'll come get you no matter where it is. Middle of nowhere? Out on the highway? Another state? I'll never get mad. I don't care, you call me."

"Yup."

"Your friends give you shit, screw 'em. If you ever think you're in danger in a car, make him pull over, right then and there. I don't care if it's four in the morning, you call me. If I'm at work, call the firehouse, we'll send a truck out to get you."

I nodded. I knew the drill.

My father surprised me by saying he was going to go lay down for a while.

"Hard fires last night, Dad?"

"Fair to middling," he said. "Not too bad. One working fire. But we're going to Pennsylvania tonight."

"Oh," I remembered. "What time?"

"Three."

"Ma, too?"

"Ma has work."

"Want some company?"

I rode shotgun through the night to one of those far flung wrestling tournaments, listening with Dad to his old cassettes of *The Sports Huddle* and of *Duffy's Tavern* and *Amos & Andy* while Steve and Rich slept in the back seat. My father very much enjoyed the fact that I enjoyed the radio broadcasts from his day. He never laughed with such pure hilarity as he did at those clever old shows.

Toward the end of the ride I was patting myself on the back for having stayed awake and alert the whole time, keeping Dad company, until my brothers nudging me brought me back to life.

"Look at the cool sky, Greg! Wake up!"

—

Joe called home from Florida one night, and after going through the usual weekly pleasantries, and comparison of notes on the upcoming Red Sox season, he said, "So you're not going out for baseball this year, are you?"

Hah! That's why my brother Joe's the best.

I had all but resigned myself to the prospect of a baseball-free future for Yours Truly, although I had yet to discuss this axis-tilting decision with anyone. Still, confronted so unexpectedly with Joe's overt challenge, I felt a knee-jerk compulsion to stand my ground.

"What do you mean," I said. "Why wouldn't I?"

"I can't believe you really haven't noticed, but – you're Greg Dunn now."

"Uh-huh. Greg Dunn: Ball player extraordinaire."

"That might be how you see yourself…"

"Uh-huh."

"But you and baseball are through." There it was. "Or haven't you been keeping up with the writing on the wall? Ought to check it out some time. Makes for good reading."

"Oh, yuh?"

"Know what it says up there, big as life? Says, baseballwise, you're all done."

I laughed. "I might be Dunn. But I'm not through…"

"Tell you what," said Joe. "Instead of going out for baseball this year, do yourself a favor. Go find a sharp corner somewhere and punch it hard as you can. You'll end up having much better luck, and a lot less hassle. Not to mention wear and tear on your confidence."

"Excuse me…"

"Anywhere you look there's walls. And they all have nice hard corners just ripe for the punching."

"So am I supposed to be reading these walls now," I quipped. "Or punching them?"

"Then again you could just go count dust."

"Joe…"

I've never been 100% sure my brother coined these homey little idioms himself but, knowing him as I do, I've just always assumed they're his own.

He said, "What I'm saying is, you can't go from being Greg Dunn, football star, in the fall–"

"I'm not a star."

"Cut the shit. And then come springtime, you're an underachieving junior on some joke JV team…"

"Joke?"

"…playing games on that wind-blown pebble-filled field, literally in the shadow of Marciano Stadium."

He was laying it on a little thick, I thought, so I finished his figurative portrait for him: "Site of recent gridiron glory?"

"Exactly."

"You're making a big leap, aren't you, taking it for granted I won't make varsity this year."

"Listen–"

"You listen. There's not eighteen players in that school better than me, Joe."

"Well every team needs five pitchers, right off the bat, so…"

"There aren't thirteen guys better!"

"Greg, there aren't ten. That's not what I'm talking about."

I think silence bespoke my resistance more eloquently than words could've.

Ever alert to cues, blatant and/or otherwise, Joe said, "Remember last year? Dana Kerr didn't make the team?"

"I know, that was just–"

"*Mike Barry* didn't make it! Those guys were in the top *five* baseball players in the whole school."

I couldn't agree more. "You're right. What the hell happened there?"

"What happened is... there was something about those guys... that rubbed Pileski the wrong way, pure and simple. It wasn't based on sheer talent, I know that much."

"Hmmm..."

My brother was trying to spoon feed me this bitter dose, using as much sugar as he could. "You're a lot like those guys," he said.

"Really...?"

Then I guess he had to just shove it down my throat. "You know how you said Armond saw something in you that you yourself didn't know was there?"

With the phone at my ear I silently nodded.

"Well, with Pileski, he *doesn't* see what you *do* know is there. Different side of the same shit luck coin flip."

I felt myself nodding again in tacit agreement.

"Hey, it happens," Joe said. "More often than not. Lucky for you, you got football. Because this is the kind of thing that fucks people up down the line."

I felt it fucking me up already.

I said, "Where the hell was all this perspective last year?"

"The writing wasn't on the wall last year. And you weren't Greg Dunn yet."

"Oh yeah? Who was I?"

"You were one of a group of newcomers trying to get on the field and stay there. Now you're in a class by yourself."

"Come on, man. That's just—"

"Greg: You're Colombo's first thousand-yard rusher."

"Yeah, I had a lot of carries, though. You yourself have said—"

"Listen to me."

I started to listen.

"Listen!"

"I'm listening, man," I said. "Gotta yell at me…"

"I don't mean listening to the peanut gallery. You're starting to sound like them yourself. 'Oh, but I had a whole bunch of carries…'"

"Come on…"

"Greg, how many carries you finish with, exactly? For the year?"

"Ah… don't know, offhand," I lied.

"A little over 200, according to my calculations."

"That's about right."

"So five yards a carry, then," he said.

"A little less. Nothing to write home about."

"See? That's the champs talking."

"What fucking champs, man?"

"In the stands, at the games. The champs of the peanut gallery."

"You weren't even here, Joe! You were down there in frigging Pepsi-Cola, Florida."

"I don't have to be there to know what goes on," he declared. "Shit… I wasn't at Dealey Plaza either."

"…?"

"And anyway, I *was* there the year before. Right? I heard it for myself."

"Heard. *What.* Joe."

"Why you think I stopped sitting on the home side stands," he asked rhetorically, and supplied his own answer as I heard my teeth beginning to grit, "Because I got sick of having to listen to that shit there. And then in the hallways at school during the week."

"Joe, you're killing me…"

"Remember that time I got suspended my senior year? For that fight with what's-his-name, in the Yellow Cafe? Mr. B. had to break it up?"

"*Joe!*"

"The fucking chimpanzees, Greg. Those moron chimps, up in the stands. And in the halls."

"Oh, 'chimps'..."

"Always weighing in, bending over backwards to make damn sure you get the deficit of the doubt. Explain away each and every next rung on the ladder you reach."

"Yeah," I tried without a great deal of conviction.

"I get that. It's simian nature to want to understand. Dumb apes trying to make sense of what's around them, and the simplest common denominator usually works. They say, 'Hmm, why this guy?'"

"Yuh?"

"'He doesn't *look* the part. Not some great physical specimen, like a Phil Johnson or something.'"

"Right..."

"But they haven't known you all your life, I have. I know you're a natural born running back and you work your ass off, they don't. So they figure–"

"Nepotism."

"Or something, yeah, for lack of a better word. Favoritism... politics..."

"Simplest common denominator.'

"Yes indeedy weedy. The great go-to solution of the masses. I get it. But that doesn't mean I have to sit there and listen to it."

"Chimps." I had to laugh. Then I coughed a haughty sigh. "Well sir, in that case I'm afraid you'll just have to see your way clear to finding some way, somehow, to simply tune those vexing chatterboxes out, now won't you?"

Having none of it, Joe said, "My point is, Colombo put you out there for a reason. And there's nothing wrong with being good for a dirty five every time you get the ball."

"A little bit less."

"There's nothing wrong with a little bit less than five every carry. You know O.J. Simpson, his senior year at USC? His Heisman Trophy year? He averaged less than five yards a carry."

Sometimes when Joe gets on one of these rolls, I think of maybe making a record of it afterwards, preserving select bits of AJD oratory for posterity. "Yeah, I've heard that before," I said.

"It's true. And he turned out alright, right?"

"Yeah, but—"

"If it was good enough for 32 it's good enough for 43."

"I know, but—"

"Fuck that 'but' shit."

"Okay."

"That's all I'm saying. You talk like they just randomly picked your name out of a hat one day. Everyone in the city was out buying up all the candy bars but you got the one with the golden ticket. Hooray! For Greg's a jolly good fellow!"

"No, I just–"

"Greg Dunn earned that spot. And earned the carries. And *you* were the one that got those yards. Yeah yeah yeah, offensive line, yeah yeah yeah – but you were the one out there making all those runs. A thousand yards worth. Nobody else ever did that before until you came along."

"—"

"Whys and wherefores aside, listen: You're the only one to do it, period."

For a minute all I could say was, "Hmn." Then I came up with, "So what am I supposed to do during baseball season now?"

"I don't know. Spring track?"

I felt my head shaking in tacit disagreement.

In another dash of rhetoric (because we both knew that we both knew the answer), he asked, "What was your longest run this year?"

Playing along, I said, "Ah…"

"Shave a tenth or two off your forty-yard dash time with a season of outdoor track and it can't not pay dividends on the field next year. And there's only you and those other two juniors coming back."

As noted priorly in these pages, the *Globe* kept a running tally of eastern Mass. football stats every season. Once a week, it posted updated Scoring, Passing, and Receiving leaders. My brother Joe was a bottom line stat guy if ever there was one. He kicked off each and every morning by reading the two Boston papers front to back, starting with the Box Scores and finishing with the Obituaries. He learned how to play bridge and chess that way, and he never missed the daily crosswords, regularly eschewing superfluous accoutrements like pencils and pens in the process of "doing" a puzzle. ("I'm a purist," he explained to me once with a tolerant nod. "I do it by eye." When asked how the hell he was supposed to tell when a puzzle was finally solved, he tolerated further, "When I get to the last clue.") All in all, this well-informed stat head, who never had much use for books of the text or note-taking kind, was a good guy to have around when questions arose on any number of subjects, or when a hardline opinion was sought. Toward the end of the '78 season, while Matty was battling it out with Giusti and Clivio for the top spot in the Division-1 scoring race, my brother had mentioned to me that the field of scoring leaders in the *Globe* consisted almost entirely of seniors, with very few exceptions, namely 'those other two juniors' to whom he had just alluded in his spring track pitch. (One of my favorite new household tasks, by the way, since Joe enlisted in the Air Force was shipping a week's worth of *Boston Globes* to Pensacola every Monday; a small favor I was only too glad to undertake on behalf of my confidant, trailblazer, and number-one fan.) Cropping up from time to time at the bottom of the Scoring list, among the many also-rans, were the only juniors other than myself: Tom Brennan from Quincy, and Gary Frechette from Newton; both good backs, as I'd seen firsthand when we played against them that year. It was just like Joe to pick up on such a relevant detail, and even more like him to give a shit. It hadn't even occurred to me. All I knew when I turned to the School Sports section was that my buddy Matt Walsh's name was right up there in the hunt. Mine most certainly was not. Since a player's grade in school wasn't one of the provided data points (Name, School, TD, 2PT, 1PT, FG, Tot.Pts.), Joe would have had to perform some due diligence, cross referencing names from the Scoring Leaders roll which came out on Tuesdays, with the relevant game reports from Sunday's paper.

"So get the edge on those two guys, and..." Joe tantalized. "Who knows?" Then, blithely changing gears, "Anyway... Did a set of encyclopedias come to the house?"

"Yeah, they did! Thank you, Joe."

"Oh, good."

"They're really nice, too."

"Good."

"Thank you."

"You're welcome. When'd they get there?"

"Over the weekend. They're great. Dad said they must've cost a bundle."

"I got nothing better to spend my money on down here. Figure you'll get a lot of use out of them. Take them to college. Keep them in your library later."

"We were reading through them last night. I love them, Joe. Thank you."

"Of course," he said. "Is Ma there?"

I said, "She has to work tonight, she's sleeping."

"How's she liking the VA so far?"

"She likes it."

"Any of her nursing school cronies there with her?"

"Don't...think so."

"Oh— I wanted to ask you. The pictures Ma sent me... Were you using bigger shoulder pads this year—"

"Ahhhh... no."

"—on purpose?"

"I don't know, I wore what they gave me."

"Big pads are no big deal for a running back. Unless he's heavily involved in the passing game, which you are."

"Yeah, I guess so. I don't know if I'd call it heavily involved…"

"Well you led the team in receptions."

"No, no," I explained. "Matty—"

"You had more."

"I don't know about that, Joe."

"I do."

"Ahhhh…"

"You had the most your sophomore year too."

"Whuh?"

"Yeah…" he drawled, and I heard the smirk rising in his voice. "You took the lead on the first play of the season and never looked back."

"Heh!"

"So the point is, shoulder pads as large as the ones you've been wearing restrict your reach when you're going for a ball high above your head with both hands."

Joe was absolutely right. In that one particular circumstance, football shoulder pads indeed served to impede vertical reach. So?

I said, "And?"

"As your attorney, I would advise you to wear the smallest pads you can from now on. Quarterback pads if at all possible."

I laughed out loud.

"I'm Dad serious."

"Pssshhh…"

"Is Dad there?"

"Ahhhh…heh! Yes he is."

"Let me talk to him."

"This call's going to cost you an arm and a leg, brother."

"The phone company can go punch a corner."

Little to my surprise, Dad had misgivings over my quitting baseball; not that I blamed him. After all, he knew better than anyone how well I could hit, especially when he had me in the groove. Finally, though, seeing it as a sacrifice in the name of higher football, he acquiesced. In presenting my case, I had made reference to Mike Barry, Mr. Pileski, and Joe's ominous wall writings. (As regards my lingering slumpophobia, I decided to keep mum.)

Now that a life without baseball was out in the open, I started pouring myself body and soul into football prep.

By the way, if I've given anyone the impression that I had my pick of Brockton High varsity sports to play in lieu of baseball, and could do so at a high level when and where I saw fit as the spirit moved me, allow me to enforce curfew on that notion and put it to bed, tuck it in, kiss it goodnight, and turn out the light. For I was not then, nor have I ever been, one of those preternaturally gifted athletes who casually excels hither and yon, regardless of field, course, or court; the football / soccer(ball) / basketball / golf(ball) / baseball / tennis(ball) types. I had my moments, don't get me wrong, but you could count in one scrotum the number of balls I truly knew my way around. Other words: I was a good football player and a pretty good baseball player, that's about it.

Not to mention, the 1979 outdoor track team wasn't exactly hurting for heroes. In fact it was undoubtedly the best squad ever to come out of Brockton, and that's saying something. New England team champs; national-record-setters in the mile relay; it was a privilege to even work out on the same track as those guys. I was but one of the throng of anonymous also-rans, not that it was a problem for me whatsoever. I was there for one reason and one reason only, and although I was allowed to race in very few actual heats that season, those daily workouts at the stadium absolutely did improve my footspeed.

In that spirit of self-central ends and means, I made a point when we traveled for meets against Newton and Quincy to confirm whether my running back rivals, Frechette and Brennan, were moonlighting too. When I was sure they weren't, I scored it as a notch on my side of our imaginary edge ledger, and since I knew for a fact those guys weren't working harder in the weight room than I was, I realistically put myself very much in the hunt for the Division-1 scoring title. Moreover, my personal preseason Player of the Year poll had Yours Truly as the early favorite, assuming of course that it didn't turn out to be our own Chuck Colombo.

I kept that sort of thing to myself, of course, but those dual nemeses, my weight room white whales, were looming larger and larger with every passing day, unwitting bugaboos of my dreams, nocturnal and otherwise. With them in mind, while I was doing my stretching on the track one day before practice, over by the fence in lane 8 at the 100-yard dash starting line, just as a little inside joke to myself, I used the toe spike of my sprinter shoes to scratch out a miniature message in the red Tartan composition track: the current day/month/year, along with the letters PoY. Since it was all the way off to the side, practically underneath the chain link fencing, nobody would ever notice it; but I could give it a wink whenever I was in the area, from that day forward, through the next football season; sort of a personal eye-on-the-prize talisman.

The funny thing is, as I was whisking the last of the little Tartan granules off my handiwork, my old Gilmore/South Jr. High/Boxer Football pal, Mike Cooney, wandered over. Mike's a great guy and a great athlete who left football behind in favor of track, and who would soon be running third leg on our state champion mile relay team whose Massachusetts state record still stands to this day over forty years later. He's a sharp dude, too.

"Player of the Year?"

Caught red-handed getting into myself, all I could do was own it. "Yup."

"Hey, nothing wrong with that," he said, getting down beside me in a hurdler's stretch, lowering his chest to his extended knee. "O.J. says you gotta set goals for yourself. Then you know when you're making progress, or when you might be losing ground."

———

Although Mr. Colombo's Brewster football camp ran for two weeks every summer, I hadn't been back since that first time. However, sensing that the Red-and-Black's upcoming season was going to be a special one, and endeavoring to leave no advantage untaken, a bunch of us signed up. After finishing classes on the last day of school we piled into cars and caravaned to the Cape. Despite rush hour traffic, I remember noticing that the trip to Brewster seemed way shorter than it had on that midnight ride with my parents three years earlier.

A couple days into camp, with groups of backs and receivers being put through their pass pattern paces against rotating units of linebackers and DBs, the coach calling plays barked, "Don't be scared of a little kiss! Kissing's the name of the game! You go over the middle, you're going get kissed. Just strap on your hat, chomp your chew toy, and catch that rock! QB puts it on the laundry, he's doing his job – make the play! He can't catch it for you too!"

The idiomatic barker was none other than central Mass. coaching icon, Dick Corbin, sporting his rock-steady wind-resistant hairdo (which predated Jimmy Johnson's signature coiffure by a good five years), and sporting too a brash audacity of manner that would've taken Barry Switzer aback. Last time I was at camp, Corbin and his Milford High Scarlet Hawks, fresh off their 1975 blowout Super Bowl win, pretty much took over the camp. Whereas there were four or five Brockton guys in residence back then, and clusters of players from one south shore school or another, the entire Milford depth chart was present and accounted for, sixty strong, from seasoned starters and stars to the obligatory passel of wide-eyed overly gung-ho underclassmen. Those guys were rowdy and goofy and good. Of course it goes without saying that if you put Brockton up against any football team around, one game, winner take all, my money's on us – every time, any time; but those Milford boys sauntered through the campgrounds like winning was their property.

This year Dick Corbin was back again and he was his old self, but sans team; which made absolutely no sense until we heard that the illustrious reign of Milford's Richard the Great had recently come to an end when he accepted a position on the Harvard Crimson coaching staff, overseeing the offensive line. I was a little disappointed that the Milford team didn't come too. It would have been weird though, I'm sure, for the players to have the legendary Coach Corbin on site yet standing down as a lame duck, deferring in all decisions and matters to the new guy. I couldn't imagine Armond Colombo in such a position any more than having my father at home but relieved of all standing.

Corbin's bark might have been a bit harsh but he was right about the previous group's receiver reaching way too tentatively for that pass over the middle. The throw was a little high but you got to make some kind of effort.

Like every other camper, I'd been sizing up the rest of the skill position talent all week, and so far only two guys really stood out, other than our own homegrown phenom, Jay McGee.

A junior running back from Nantucket, Beau Almodobar, hung out between practice sessions with us at the Brockton cabin most days. He was a mellow cat, soft spoken, with a handshake as gentle as his demeanor. We all liked him. If he and I had met on the outside, I never would have pegged him for a football player, but with a football in his arms, Almo came alive. He made his way through the line of scrimmage like a scatman sings. The other kid who caught my eye was someone I'd never heard of before named Strachan (per the athletic tape name tag on the front of his helmet) from Burlington, Mass. (This year it was the Burlington Whatevers who'd had the bright idea of getting a head start on the upcoming season by sending the whole show to football camp as a unit.) I never ended up actually meeting Strachan but I found out he was another rising junior. Strong and quick, it was clear he knew what he was doing, though his running style was the diametric opposite of Almo's.

Whereas one was a firefly, dipping, darting, now here and suddenly gone; the other hit the line full bore, slamming with abandon between the tackles.

Standing there sweaty in the Cape Cod sun, I waited with my group to take our turn upon Coach Corbin's next play call. "Oh," he said, noticing the name on my helmet. "So you're Dunn: Leads by example. Tough as nails."

If my trusty carapace of anonymity had to be cracked open, that was a nice way to do it, but in my experience being singled out for praise during football practice never ends well.

He then announced to one and all, "Watch Dunn! Same play! Same play!" Keeping it in our huddle would have suited me fine. "Watch how Dunn runs it. No fear over the middle! Watch this!"

(Seriously...?)

As I lined up flanked off to the right, the whole defensive backfield started cheating in. Had the upcoming play been part of a real game, I might have – in the face of what portended to be an all-out blitz – just broke hot, straight upfield, but with my route so solidly set in stone by Coach Corbin, all I could do was run it as hard as I could, flanker drag.

Fortunately for me it was a good pass. Were I six-nine-and-a-half it would have been perfect, hitting the nook of my right armpit in stride, so all I had to do was elevate about a foot to corral it and brace for the convergence of defenders – in this case, quintuple coverage. Buffeted front, back, and below, I came down at an angle and hit the ground hard on the crux of my lower back.

Coach Corbin called, "First down, Brockton! That's how it's done!"

That was exactly how it's done, my friends, but the next morning I wondered if it had really been worth the doing. Though I was making a priority at breakfast of walking as naturally as can be, Mr. Colombo might have spotted something in the mincing half-steps I was taking. He hailed me to his table in the corner where he was eating with coaches Restic, DeFilippo, and Corbin.

Clenching my teeth I made my gingerly way toward him, lightstepping, almost tiptoeing, like crossing a sticky patch of tar on the street. "Morning, Coach," I gritted. "Coaches."

Dick Corbin said, "There he is."

Hopefully Mr. Colombo wasn't going to ask me to join them. "How you doing, Greg," he said. "How's your back?"

I hadn't said a damn thing to a damn soul about my back.

"Huh? Oh, fine. I mean… little stiff."

It pains me now to write this but, although I felt like the world's biggest prima donna, completely undeserving of Corbin's "tough as nails" portrayal, I ended up sitting out the big scrimmage game on the last day of camp in favor of quieting the sassy nag in my back. I don't recall if I even dressed for the game; I'm going to say no. I do remember Jay squirting free for a couple nifty fifteen- or twenty-yard runs toward the boundary. This season he was going to be just a sophomore, but already we could tell that the kid was a for-real phenom on the field. Strachan had a nice twenty-yarder too, up the middle. I watched from the sideline on one knee, ignoring but taking notice of every teammate's sidelong glances. They reminded me that the enforced alienation which attends any team-sport injury is as real and sudden as the injury itself – to wit, the terrible case of Donny Barlow – and the less conspicuous the physical impairment, the more suspicious perforce your downtime must be.

—

Shortly after the Fourth of July holiday, an Oxford Ruled 3x5 index card serving as a postcard arrived at our house in the mail addressed to me:

  E.B. KEITH FIELD WILL BE

  AVAILABLE AUG. 14 THRU 25

  FROM 6 - 7 P.M. FOR

  CONDITIONING

        acc

In none of my three previous Brockton Football seasons had I received such a note.

"Dad, look what I got today. For captains practice."

My father took it, turning it over a couple times. "No return address," he nodded in approval. The index card's lined side contained the above message scrawled in capital letters. On its reverse, a meter printout rather than physical stamp had been used to assign the .10c postage. It looked fairly obvious to me that two completely different handwriters were involved in the postcard's composition. The name and address had the smooth style and poise of penwomanship the world over, while the rough hewn words of the notification itself looked as masculine as a wood pile. "Colombo had the assembly line going at the kitchen table," Dad sized it up. "The daughter writing out the names and addresses, and sliding it down the line to Chuck or one of them to do the information."

That made as much sense as not, I thought. Delegate each step for maximal efficiency and speed. "Assembly line..."

"Means you're going to be a captain this year."

"Oh, ah... I don't know. They have a vote for captains later."

"How much you want to bet?"

When it comes to Dunn family fortune-telling, I learned a long time ago: Bet against the Austins, senior and/or junior, at your peril. "No, but..."

The details of that makeshift postcard have etched themselves into my memory. I can see them all now, right down to the red ink of the postage printout, partly because they represent such a signal moment in my athletic life, and also due to my having discovered the index card twenty years later in my copy of *The Dead Zone* and used it ever since as my go-to bookmark till this day, during which time it has become the favorite and most visibly worse for wear part of my bedroom bookshelf.

—

I might have made mention of this before but if so it bears repeating that those years I participated in organized sports I was very fortunate to count myself among the happy few who somehow (i.e., pure shit luck) managed to traverse the passing seasons unscathed injurywise, having only to deal with run-of-the-mill discomforts of the nagsome variety.

With tough talented runners all around me every year on the Boxer depth chart, to have missed playing time in any season, for any reason, would likely have cost me my job. I'd certainly seen it up close during sophomore year (where it worked to my benefit of course), as well as junior season right in front of me in the varying cast of fullback assignees. What can I say? I've been on great terms with the Gods of Good Fortune literally since my date of birth; and the old homily is true: It's all well and good to be good, but sometimes just lucky is best.

Post-Cape-Cod-Football and pre-Brockton-Football that year, I treated my achy back with rest when convenient and applications of heat every night after dinner. By the time double sessions rolled around, I was good to go in shoulder pads the smallest yet of my career.

In the morning session of our first day of doubles, Mr. Colombo had me and Jay working together in the starting backfield, running our playbook along with Chuck and a rotation of three or four prospective fullbacks against non-contact "D". Following the midday lunch break, our second session was always devoted to Defense. Since neither Chuck, Jay, nor I played both ways, afternoons saw us running non-contact pass patterns ad infinitum, and just filling in anywhere a warm body was needed. I recall right after lunch on that first day, we were waiting our turn as part of a single file line, facing a similar file of DBs five yards off. Their first man in line would approach ours at a perfunctory getting warmed-up quasi-walk-through kind of clip, put his facemask between the numbers, lay hands on our shoulders or hips, and dance us backward. As human tackling dummies, we'd do a little hop step at impact and backpedal for a yard, tangoing with our tackler, nice and friendly-like.

After a couple times through, it was my turn again. An overenthusiastic guy, who shall remain nameless – a veteran who really should have known better – closed on me like a sophomore transfer trying to make a name for himself. I added a little altitude to my hop in order to absorb the extra impact, and it would have worked fine had he not wrapped me up so tight around the waist, pinning my arms to my sides, and driven straight through me like a varsity wrestler (which he was) on a bulldog take down. Up off my feet with no way to protect myself, I went backwards bent at the waist and was ground into the ground with the full force of his weight and mine coming down hard on that mysteriously delicate point of the tailbone, my good old coccyx.

For this "injury" I take full responsibility. I was guilty of breaking **Football Survival Rule #6: *Always protect yourself in drills, "non-contact" or otherwise. Always.*** It was a rookie mistake, never to be made again, believe me. Never.

The frigging thing was so damn sore for so damn long that season, and had me walking so weirdly, that I'm convinced it had to be the root cause of my first and only ever case of *shin splints*, of all things. (No, they are not a myth!) Every day before practice, every night after dinner, and every game on the sideline, I was reduced to using ice packs to numb the thrumming ache in my shins. It was ridiculous.

However, the funny thing about tender tailbones, and shin splints, and lower back pain too for that matter, is that they are virtually painless – provided you happen to be running your ass off. I don't know if it's got something to do with the adrenaline factor, or what; but as long as you're going full out, hard as you can, you will be for all intents and purposes momentarily immune to the pain. Thus, a player suffering from any of these annoying little ailments could, in the context of a forty-eight-minute high school football game, reasonably expect to enjoy the brief bliss of pain-free play, meted out in four- or five-second intervals on average, a good fifty times over.

Now don't get me wrong, I don't want to sound complaining. A blissful respite is nothing to sneeze at, and I learned long ago, from mentors and peers alike, to take bliss where I find it – and gladly.

By the way, although I've never been one to "take plays off" when the ball wasn't going to me, as soon as I became hip to the whole Full-Speed~Pain-Relief connection I readily identified the self-serving advantage in everyday activities such as the carrying out of play fakes on the gridiron. From a strictly succor-centric perspective, the longer and more frequently I went at it full bore, the better; AND(!) if the extra effort came across as laudable to those who mattered, or even those who didn't, all the better still. Of course, standing around, or walking, or kneeling, or sitting, or ramping up to speed or slowing back down, was still a real pain in the ass.

In school it was where it was worst. Unlike the terrible reign of a toothache, for example, which constantly dominates your very being and all that you survey, the reason such ailments as befell me that summer are said to be "nagging" is that they decide to have at you again just when you're starting to forget about them. Taking your seat in class, tying your shoelace, rising from the lunchroom table to bus your tray, the nag pipes up, "Ay! Member me?"

I'm sorry to admit it but that unfortunate tailbone incident engendered a sometimes unseemly intolerance on my part in the remaining years of my football life (college included) toward teammates at practice whose innocent zeal during half-speed drills would suddenly rankle me down to the last hackle on my back.

———

When the Boston newspapers put out their annual Suburban League previews, our seven returning starters on each side of the ball prompted the *Globe's* School Sports staff to speculate that this looked like the year we could return to the Super Bowl.* While that felt better than a punt to the nuts, their prognosticators two years earlier had sung our similar preseason praises, and everybody knows how that turned out. This time around, it was almost as if they were intentionally trying to jinx us, the way they just proclaimed: "Brockton is awesome."

At our no-pads walk-through on the Friday in advance of our opening game, everyone was in high spirits, including Mr. Colombo.

"Let's go everybody!" he boomed on his way out of the Armory. "Let's go-ohhhhh!"

After practice he reminded us to go to bed early, if possible, and to eat a full breakfast in the morning. "You're going to have a hard time getting to sleep tonight with tomorrow's game on your mind. That's why we told you yesterday: get your rest *the night before the night before.*"

Later, I went to my room right after taking Mr. Colombo's bed check call, and stared in the dark at high hopes on the ceiling until I finally drifted off.

We started the season against feisty Dedham again, at our place this time. A few minutes before opening kickoff I was sitting on the sideline, facing the field, stretching out my back. Jay McGee came over and sat down opposite me, legs wide apart like mine, cleats to cleats, forming something more rhomboid or trapezoid than square, so we could hook hands in the middle for a few stretchy reps of rowing back-and-forth – the start of a new pregame ritual for us.

*[Speculation Citation: see *"Brockton Looks Strong With Another Colombo"*; 04 Sep, 1979, p.36]

In those days, if you won the toss you elected to receive so that's what Dedham did. Their first drive ate up several minutes before stalling, but when they punted to us we muffed it deep in our own territory, leaving us to start from just inside the one yard line. Obviously, that tackle in the endzone for a safety the year before, which ultimately cost us the game, hung huge in my mind like Doom's own shadow. Although it doesn't make actual sense – because one season has absolutely nothing to do with another – all I could think of was redemption; redemption for that weird loss last year, of course, but more specifically for the inexcusable transgressions that I myself committed along the way.

As with my junior year, and sophomore year before that, we launched our opening drive of the season with a play called to me, this one a straight quick hitter over left guard. Sure enough, those peevish first-play Fates had their way again, plugging the dive hole like Lambert, Russell, and Ham. In what was now becoming some kind of ignoble anniversary rite, play number one in game number one going to Dunn produceth none.

On second-and-ten, we tried Jay over the right side behind our fullback, good for a yard, giving us a little bit of wiggle room. (When versatile Sanford McMurtry won the fullback job in training camp, he established himself as a mainstay for the next two years at a position where we hadn't known stability since the days of Rodney Heger, and in so doing he became one of our rare two-way starters which, when you think about it – i.e., beating out every talented Brockton Football competitor at *two* different positions – speaks volumes as to an athlete's abilities. This particular athlete was one of those slow-fast guys. The ease and smoothness of gait when he ran, with no apparent exertion, belied his natural speed, of course. It only registered truly when he blew by you.)

Fortunately, field commander Colombo the Younger orchestrated an efficient 98-yard drive featuring a number of crucial first downs which culminated in yonder endzone. Furtherly fortunate, and just like last year, Dedham's offense posted no more than zero points the whole game; but of vitalest importance, and not the least little bit like the 1978 contest, the visitors' opportunistic defense was also pointless. For our part, I scored two short touchdowns, Jay scored one medium-range. That was all we needed because, heralding the bloom of this new season as surely as the hardy perennials of the field, our niggardly defense shut 'em up and shut 'em down. Call me spoiled – I could hardly dispute you – because by this point I had come to fully expect the safety nets of Milletts and Colletts (et al.) protecting our butts and our leads. Final score on this fine sunny Saturday, Boxers 20, Marauders zip.

> You've doubtless heard by now the lore
> Of Brockton's football team of yore
> Which posted such a high CRIQS* score
> That no one's ever touched it!

Well, football fans, the 1979 team was *that team*. You see, once upon a time, the fabled all-time best mean CRIQS* rating was established by our very own Boxer starting offense, a record-setting mark that has long since transcended the realm of legend on its way to assuming the truly sublime status of *urban legend* and which still ranks as by far the highest score ever posted by a football team that was actually any good. In fact, the categorical anomaly perpetrated by our 1979 offense was so far off the charts that it defied exaggeration. Like Ruth's 60, or his 714 for that matter, to embellish wouldn't occur to you any more than adding plus-one to infinity. Reading about, or hearing tell of, Brockton's unbelievable 4.29 mean rating strained the absolute outer limits of understanding, to the extent that it seemed more like a theoretical abstraction than an actual achievement.

Seriously, though: We had some good players, no doubt about it, but superior talent was never our main selling point that year, and it sure as hell wasn't size.

*[(Class Rank ÷ Class Size) x Intelligence Quotient]

We had grit, we worked hard, we had great attitude, we had talent, but the true key to our offensive success was, as expressed in the foregoing fairy tale, that we happened to be in real life a pretty sharp bunch of guys from top to bottom. The schools at which that starting offensive unit matriculated speaks for itself: Amherst College, Brown, Harvard, Harvard, Hawaii, Holy Cross, Holy Cross, Maine, Worcester Polytechnic Institute; and this is not to mention the two guys called upon to fill in as spot starters that year who went on to pursue their studies at no less than Boston College as well as Boxer Country West, better known as the College of the Holy Cross.

1979 was a good year for me personally, and an excellent season for our team. We picked up where we'd left off the previous year, continuing to steadily climb back toward our rightful place atop the Massachusetts heap.

The funny thing is, whenever I'm reminded of that year's team, it's not necessarily the sparkling statistics (both Offense and D) or the traditional highlights that emerge, but rather a handful of particularly oddball tidbits along the way. When I go from one to another in my mind, they don't even seem related – apart from their all having taken place during that very special season.

For instance, on the second Sunday in September, my dad and I were watching an evening NFL game, Cowboys -vs- 49ers, mainly because former BHS star Ken MacAfee was playing tight end for San Francisco.

I was sitting up straight with my back flat against the hassock, admiring the bright white of my pristine Adidas Countries, bestowed upon me earlier in the day courtesy of Ma and Dad at the little Carvel cake birthday ceremony held in my honor.

"Whoop, see that? That's why I always say," my father alerted me, pointing to the object lesson playing out on television. "Don't hang around the pile." MacAfee was in pain on the field. "He wasn't hanging around, but the guy who fell on his leg wasn't even the one he was blocking." The critical mass of the collision was replayed in slow motion. "See what I mean?"

"Yup."

"Your sneakers look sharp. Those are the ones you wanted, right?"

"Absolutely."

"They any good for going lateral?"

"No," I admitted. "I don't know, I think they might have been originally for jogging."

"I didn't think so. They don't look like side-to-siders."

"I'm just going to use them for wearing around, though. They feel great just to walk in. I love them."

258

One of the weirdly off-putting things in a football season, more so than in other sports, I think, at least based on my own experience – baseball, track, lacrosse – is a potential rainout; "potential" being the operative term. Thinking back now, I'm reminded of a college buddy's words of wisdom with regard to a not entirely dissimilar situation. My jocular buzzmate, Goldie, was a burly Southern California tie-dyed in the wool hippie linebacker who bled Grateful Dead. By the time I first met him at the elegant Pi Eta Speakers Club on the outskirts of Harvard Square, he had already logged miles by the thousands, and burned cerebral nuclei by the millions, following the Dead around the country on tour, "seeking the urgent awareness" as he liked to say. I don't know whose perpetual smirk appeared more… *complicit*, Jerry Garcia's or his. Goldie looked a lot like Pigpen McKernan too, actually (before Pigpen got sick and lost all the weight). Anyway, we were sitting on the steps of the Pi one night, waiting for his guy, and I finally said, "What the hell, man? Where is this dude?"

"Dunner," Goldie explained in his easy west coast drawl, "The only thing fer shure about a drug deal? It's not fer shure."

That sense of indefinite dormancy is sort of what it's like when you're hanging around the locker room on tenterhooks before a game, betwixt and between, waiting for a rainout to be declared. You can't give outlet to your mounting pent-up energy, nor can you very well leave your post. Then eventually, on that line dividing footballs in motion and footballs at rest, like a wobbling spirit bubble resisting level, there comes a point where you start to feel yourself leaning toward the desire for postponement.

Our second matchup that season was indeed postponed until Sunday due to heavy rain. We ended up winning the hard-hitting game against a tough but far less talented North Quincy team at their place, thanks once again to our ruthless defense. Tony Kelly in particular was a one-man battering ram. His sack for a safety in the opening minutes was a masterpiece of old fashioned thugroughing, and it would be all the scoring we'd need that day as he and his brethren banged out another tidy shutout, 16-0. Frankly, our offense was an embarrassment, barely able to yank the chains at all in the face of North Quincy's effective defensive scheme, to wit, the assignment of a surly mid-sized linebacker to the detail of shadowing me on every play. Though conventional, this tactic – brilliant in its simplicity, like many a successful gridiron game plan – neutralized me completely. All I could do was hope that our other Suburban League foes wouldn't come up with the same bright idea. Fortunately, good old Jay ended up icing things for us in the final quarter with a 35-yard TD on one of his patented diagonal bursts toward the boundary.

By no means as competitive as the score might suggest, this one was nevertheless too close for comfort and it stung, believe me; almost as much as film time at the Armory stung the following afternoon.

—

Our next game, versus Brookline, was played at Northeastern University's Parsons Field, again on a Sunday. I can't remember why it wouldn't have been a normal Saturday game. The weather hadn't been a factor, I'm sure of that, and the SAT tests weren't scheduled for another month or so, so it couldn't have been that either. Maybe the NU football team had dibs on the field the day before to play a home game of their own – don't know. All I remember is that the day before our Sunday game it was nice out, sunny, a warm slice of Indian summer. If you're wondering how I can be so sure of such a long lost Saturday's specific weather report, trust me. I am so sure. I was in the backyard that day, our dog Gretchen at my side and the *Globe* spread out on the picnic table, squinting and blinking as the sun's glow bounced so harshly off the pages that it washed the normal greyness of the paper away and blanched the margins bordering the newsprint into an almost unbearable glare.

However, it wasn't Gretchen, glow, nor glare that's made this particular day – September 29th, the year of our Lord 1979, for those calendarily inclined – to stick in my memory for all this time. Rather,

Pope John Paul II's upcoming visit on Monday, marking the first time in history that any sitting Pope had blessed Boston with his presence, dominated the news of the day with items great and small: Governor King's signing into law a bill making Monday October 1st a holiday; US District Judge Mazzone's refusal to call the holiday an unconstitutional advancement of religion; the Pontiff's itemized itinerary, including his precise touch down time at Logan on the Aer Lingus flight from Ireland and the estimated hour of day at which the papal motorcade would be passing such and such landmarks along its route through the streets of Boston (At this piece of minutiae I remember hearing a skeptical hiss from the angelic Now-Wait-a-Minute demon who lives in my ear. He was bristling about too much public information, about Lee Harvey Oswald, snipers, E. Howard Hunt, etc.); construction and sound engineers preparing the unique outdoor altar on the Common where His Holiness planned to celebrate Mass later Monday evening; law enforcement and security details for upwards of a million people gathering downtown; editorials; negative letters to the editor (in response to the travel restrictions along the motorcade route and the unilateral inconvenience imposed on those of the Jewish faith due to this sudden holiday falling on the same day as Yom Kippur that year).

The other front page story, the one that cemented it for me, was of a scenario right out of Hitchcock. A teenager from Jamaica Plain was shot in Charlestown the previous afternoon in broad daylight, minding his own business. If you're from around here, you might be thinking, 'Yeah, so? Since when is that front page newsworthy?' and, sad to say, you'd have a point.

The thing is, this unfortunate young man was minding his own business in the endzone of Charlestown High School's football field, gathered with his Jamaica Plain teammates at halftime of their Friday afternoon game, paying heed to his coach's instruction, when a single gunshot fired from the roof of the nearby Bunker Hill housing project struck him in the neck, felling him where he stood. Paralyzed, Darryl Williams would lead the rest of his life as a quadriplegic.

While the Pope's forthcoming visit was referred to here and there during our Saturday morning walk-through earlier in the day, the Darryl Williams shooting dominated conversation. Prior to any suspect having been apprehended, the preliminary facts (Charlestown's overwhelmingly white population of working class poor; Williams being black) bespoke racial criminal intent as motive. Considering the distance from the rooftop to the field (in excess of 100 yards) it was assumed that the weapon used by the "sniper" must have been a rifle. Boston Mayor Kevin White gave voice to the prevailing assumptions as well as his "gut" reaction on the day of the shooting, denouncing the "ugly, vicious, apparently racially motivated attack." As evidence of the tenor of the times, nobody of any hue cried foul or raised so much as an eyebrow of disagreement.

By the way, among other odd items of interest on that day's front page were a notice to the readers that, due to substantial increases in printing and distribution costs during "these difficult times", newsstand copies of the daily *Globe* would increase to 25 cents beginning October 1st. (Home delivery was remaining a more than reasonable 20 cents per.)

Also on that noteworthy page, albeit below the fold, was a report that a student had been paralyzed during an incident of college party horseplay. While of less importance to Greater Boston than the news of Pope John II or Darryl Williams, and of far less importance to the *Globe's* readership in general than the twenty-five-percent price hike, this item earned a spot on the front page by virtue of its concerning horseplay at a HARVARD college party, pure and simple. (On a strictly personal level, the reported incident's relevance, if not importance, expanded over the next several years, vis-a-vis your humble narrator, by having taken place at the notorious Pi Eta Speakers Club – yes, the same to which I would be closely, although not officially, associated during that period of intellectual ennui better known as College; and yes! – the same in which I was first to meet one Jeff Goldsby, better known as Goldie, whose easygoing wisdom I felt compelled to shoehorn into the preceding vignette.)

After reading through every article on the Williams matter a few more times apiece, I asked my father not to throw away the paper when he was done with it.

"Do you know the area of Charlestown they're talking about, Dad?"

"Sure," he said with a single slow Bogartian nod.

"The projects, the football field? How far it is?"

"I know right where that is. Hundred-fifty yards. If you ever shot a gun, it's not hard from there. Easy with a scope."

"Really?"

"They better make sure the roofs on Boylston Street are clear when the Pope shows up, put it that way."

When it transpired that the weapon in question turned out to be a handgun and not a rifle, my father altered his assessment of execution, if not motive.

"No way that poor kid was the target. You'd have a hard time even hitting the huddle from that distance with a pistol." Shaking his head he concluded, "Their coach is a black guy. They were probably aiming at him."

This was the first time it had ever occurred to me to save a newspaper, but I wanted to keep it for the sake of documentary preservation, and I did, rereading the whole thing through maybe a hundred times over the years, which accounts for the level of detail I am able to provide you now. (I mean, come on – my memory's pretty good, but not this good!)

While I'm aware that we're straying a little far afield here, please indulge me for one last strangely noteworthy item from that historic 9/29/79 edition of the *Globe* before we steer the streetcar back on track...

I wouldn't even mention this theater review were it not by far the nastiest, most insulting attack on a performer – by far! – that I've ever seen in print, the target in this case being Gilda Radner's one woman show at the Colonial Theater. The critic's bile runs so thick that it is impossible for me to see it as anything but the public settling of a personal score. If I'd read this review as a parody in an issue of

National Lampoon, I'm sure I would have laughed rather than cringe. However, the cringes I felt myself undergoing weren't for Radner; they were for the critic. If you're ever in the mood to be flabbergasted, look it up – but caveat lector: It comes across as the impotent whining of a jilted premature ejaculator.

Ahem... NEXT STOP, BROOKLINE!

The following morning just before noon, when the team bus pulled into Parsons Field for our Sunday game versus Brookline, skies were overcast with a little on and off drizzle, temps in the mid-fifties: Not bad.

Once we took the field for warm-ups, I was reminded how well Northeastern's plush artificial turf agreed with our footwear. (Two years earlier when we'd played there, Mr. Colombo had announced "Cleats are betterrrr!" upon my endorsement.) Even in the damp conditions, cutting was sharp and firm. After just a minute or two on the turf, I couldn't wait for the game to start. I felt something I'd only experienced once before in football. For whatever reason, this rare feeling of strength, agility, and speed all at once, the heightened combination of which I would never have again as an athlete, visited me that day.

The stadium at Parsons Field is not a particularly large one. With the inclement weather, and perhaps the day of the week too, the crowd in the stands was sparse; so sparse in fact that when I dropped back on punt return in the first quarter, I clearly heard, "Run it back, Dunna!" I looked over to see teammates from last year's squad, Paul Capachione and Tom Thibeault, standing in the bleachers, a two-man huddle, braving the elements without rain gear but with boisterous whoops and most likely some form of comfort in a bottle. They each raised their fist, "Run it back!" I nodded and returned the salute.

Sure enough, I did run it back 75 yards for a touchdown. Unfortunately, one of my comrades was flagged for some overzealousness or other, thereby nullifying what would have stood as my lone punt return for a TD ever.

There were no hard feelings, of course, but from there this game got weird to watch, and I do mean watch – as in 'from the sidelines.' Although our defense kept forcing Brookline's one-dimensional offense (in the person of their misleadingly named bruiser of a fullback, Allison Jones) into third-and-long situations, the home team kept benefitting from our multiple untimely penalties and/or Jones's shedding of one usually sure-handed Boxer tackler after another en route to crazy sideline-to-sideline circus runs that resulted in first down chain-measurements, each made *barely* by the length of a cut hair. Four different times on the same never-ending drive, I buckled my chinstrap to take the field, but no. As a team, Brookline rated a distant third best of the three we'd faced thus far. Frankly, they sucked! Yet they were dominating time of possession, and they actually took the lead early in the second period, 6-0, putting us in the hole for the first time that season and ending our formidable D's scoreless quarters streak at nine.

Their ensuing squib of a kickoff skidded and slid between our return men like a seeing-eye single, leaving us to start out around our own fifteen-yard line. Having yet to carry the ball one time so far, other than the ill-fated punt return, I was goddamn delighted to hear the first-down call was a straight dive to me. Although still very much atingle with that supersensory high octane horsepower idling under my hood, the frustration of the first period had brought a decidedly all-revved-up-with-no-place-to-go element to it.

As a halfback, there's a certain point in certain runs where your eyes goggle and you say to yourself, "I'm going to fucking break this!" It could be a couple cuts past the line of scrimmage, or bouncing it outside and vying for the pylon, or – believe it or not – it could be the moment you're handed the ball. What can I say? (Told you I was *on* that day.) Before I'd even reached the dive hole, I could tell, clear as———

I tripped over my own lineman's ankle. Could've been our center, could've been our guard. I don't know, I wasn't looking down – until I fell flat on my face.

DAMN IT!

"Same play, Chuck. Same play. Give it to me again, give it to me again."

Two plays later he did run the same play. (Third and long, deep in our own territory, he calls me a straight dive! Chuck's the best.) This time, of course, I would be sure to high-step through the line. **Football Survival Rule #17: *Always high-step through the line. Always.*** There were no ankles in the hole to cross me up the second time, but neither was there much of a gap through which to go.

After trading possessions, our rangy split end Billy Mitchell caught a short scoring pass, sending us into halftime with a 7-6 advantage that felt a hell of a lot like a deficit.

Crowded into the locker room we waited for an obviously irked Mr. Colombo to address us. I was on one knee, shaking off the frustration as he paced. There was a whole other half to play, and I still felt unbeatable. My buddy Rod took a knee beside me.

"Dunna, what the hell's going on out there?"

I exploded, "I'm not getting the fucking ball!"

Everybody in the locker room, be they knelt in thoughtful pause or apace, turned a sidewise eye on me. Admittedly not among my finest moments, it was nonetheless one of those spontaneous blurts of unfiltered candor that you really can't hold against a guy.

My first carry of the second half I took 55 yards for a touchdown, then I scored again on our next possession as the axis of planet Earth began to right itself.

If you asked me, I could have kept on going, tapping into the endless reserves of overdrive all game long, but I ended up contributing just eight rushes on the day, by far my fewest since sophomore year. It was just as well, though, because along with Billy Mitchell's ice-breaking touchdown earlier, the ever steadfast Sanford notched his first of the season, and then Chuck threw the final dart of the game, a bull's eye to Tom Dinopoulos for our talented tight end's very first TD too, as we ran away with this one, 35-6.

The next day, after watching the film of our game (it turns out that the clipping call which nullified my punt return took place a good two yards behind me...), Chuck and I embarked straight from the Armory as part of a caravan of Catholic boys setting out for Tremont

Street in Boston. However, this pilgrimage wasn't undertaken to celebrate Mass on the Common with His Holiness. Our intentions that day were strictly secular in nature, namely getting our asses to the Music Hall for a much anticipated rock & roll show.

Though we suffered gladly the reasonably priced ducats, and the trip to town's rainy but not at all unreasonable longitude, we were by no means true believers at that point, or what you'd call disciples of the relative newcomers, The Cars; but we were all nevertheless psyched to be seeing this hot homegrown band live in concert that night.

We parked at Government Center and headed through the drizzle for the Theater District on foot as evening fell. Despite the damp conditions, I have never again to this day witnessed such an awesome mass of people all congregated in one place.

"The frigging Pope was just right down there," somebody said, indicating the stagelit makeshift altar in the distance. "Big as life."

"At least no one took a shot at him."

"Drizzle must've kept the assassins in their cellars."

Later that night I first learned the difference between a studio band and a live band. The Cars were touring in support of their *Candy-O* album. Songs were performed on stage with the same controlled precision you hear on the records, but unlike other bands we had seen in concert, the Kinks for instance, they never let loose or so much as cracked a smile. Surprisingly absent too was the tongue in cheek playfulness you'd hear in some of their songs (and see later in their videos once MTV broke). On the contrary, the band members stood stock still the entire show, almost as if under pain of penalty. The staid atmosphere of the Music Hall didn't help either. Ushers patrolled the aisles, reprimanding those spirited enough to leap to their feet in festivity.

"Was it me or did that kind of suck," I said after the show on the way out.

"No shit!"

"They don't belong on stage," Chuck seemed to agree. Then, displaying a musical acumen rivaled only by his brother Donny, Jack

Condon, and my brother Joe, he countered our general unison by positing the thentofore unconsidered theory of Studio Band -vs- Live Band.

"Some bands come alive on the open stage, they rip it up, but then the electricity doesn't transmit when they're confined to a little studio. Other groups are craftsmen, at their best tinkering in peace and quiet. They're uncomfortable having to get up there and play the songs live for a different crowd every night. It's not them."

I don't know if Chuck had that one hiding in the holster or not, but I can't help liking it when a theory is presented that hasn't occurred to me and yet seems to make good sense. Studio Band -vs- Live Band: Hmmm...

—

In those days, high school football coverage in the *Herald* and especially the *Globe* was excellent. They took it seriously. After a few games, once the dust of the new season had settled, the Coaches' Poll would start to appear every Friday alongside that week's schedule of games. Friday's paper also carried a feature which nowadays would be unheard of north of the Carolinas, namely "Larry Ames' Games to Watch" wherein the five or six most anticipated matchups from that week's slate would be singled out for prognostication by the *Globe's* School Sports swami. Fortunately, in the enlightenment of thenadays, the dogmatic shadow of our modern Cult of Complaint had nowhere to fall. Unaffected by notions of overweening political incorrectness, or fear of toe treading, Larry Ames was going on public record on a weekly basis specifically predicting the winners and (gulp) losers of each big game, right down to the final score with pithy rationale in the Comment column in 20 characters or less, God bless him.

Then, on the Tuesday following games, in addition to statistical leaders, and standings for all the leagues in Eastern Mass., updated Super Bowl rankings would be posted. Also, an Offensive and Defensive star of the week would be named in each of the four divisions, along with two honorable mentions per star.

Although most of us feigned cursory disinterest in the leaders of Scoring, TD Passes, and TD Receptions, the offensive skill position players among us secretly scoured that feature every Tuesday, our spirits sighing or twinging at each and every rise and slip in rank.

The month of October saw the emergence of one of my arch enemies, Quincy's Tom Brennan, who had broken fast out of the gate to lead all Division-1 scorers. Alas, no Brocktonian was anywhere to be found in the top ten. The closest thing to a homeboy was fellow Cape Cod football camper, Steve Strachan of Burlington, somewhere toward the bottom of the list, but on the list nonetheless. Good for him. If it couldn't be a Boxer, then why the hell not him, right? Heigh-ho, Strachan!

A quick perusal of the leaders in Divisions 2, 3, and 4, showed that none other than soft-spoken will-o'-the-wisp, Beau Almodobar, was tops in all of Eastern Mass., regardless of Division. Just three games into the season, he already had over 50 points to his credit. Go, Almo!

It was kind of funny how my fantasy rivalry with Brennan, and Newton North's Gary Frechette, had cast them in the role of four-flushing backstabbing bogeymen, while all the other scorers across Division-1, unencumbered by curse, jousted as knights on the fields of fair play, with my compliments and blessing. Seeing so many new names on the list from unfamiliar teams like Woburn, Norwood, Walpole, put my own chances into properly measly perspective.

"You don't give a whole half-shit about that anyway," said my father later.

"No," I agreed. (Well, let's be honest... a quarter-shit, maybe.)

Seriously, though: As long as we were winning, it was all right, and our nicely balanced offense had begun hitting its stride, performing at a level more commensurate with that of the D.

It was good to see that the rest of the local football world was starting to take notice, too. During the next several weeks, the Coaches Poll had us jockeying with Woburn between 1st and 2nd place; likewise, we and Woburn were pulling away from the pack in the official ratings race.

Also, WBZ TV sent firebrand sportscaster Jimmy Myers to Eldon B. Keith during the week leading up to our game against Newton. He conducted brief interviews with Jay, Sanford, and me. I thought I came across as confident rather than cocky when I saw myself on the news saying that we had the talent and the depth to beat any team in Division-1.

We handled Newton whose defense wasn't nearly as good as the year before, although, contrary to the game versus Brookline, this was one of those out-of-the-blue unaccountably slow-motion dream games for me where I just couldn't seem to get unstuck all day.

Our next couple games were easy wins over weak teams, 33-0 against Weymouth South (Jay and I scored all 5 touchdowns before being pulled in the third quarter in favor of our subs), and 41-12 over Cambridge Rindge & Latin. For me, the memorable details of that game didn't occur on the field of play, per se, but just a matter of inches off to either sideline. On ours, early in the third period, Mr. Colombo surprised me by asking, with a playful gleam theretofore reserved for the practice field, how many touchdowns I'd scored.

"Two."

"Let's get you another one."

On our next possession, I was driven out of bounds on the Cambridge sideline, tumbling to a grunting stop at the base of the first-down marker. The big guy manning the chain said sorry for not dropping it sooner. With an expression of what looked like real remorse, he loomed above me. The thing that made this moment most memorable was his gigantic maroon windbreaker, so vast it could have billowed on any sharp updraft and carried the guy off – as long as the guy was not in fact the one and only Patrick Ewing himself, basketball phenom of whom Rindge & Latin coach Mike Jarvis had declared during Ewing's sophomore year that he would one day be better than Kareem Abdul-Jabbar, citing his star protégé's superior work ethic. "Kareem doesn't work," Jarvis had charged!

On the last Saturday of October we faced our first real test against Leominster. The defending Central Mass. Super Bowl champs brought an 18-game winning streak to Marciano Stadium. We knew we'd have our hands full trying to contain their dynamic quarterback, Dave Piermerini, whose reputation for game-seizing exploits preceded him; and we were dearly missing our own dynamo, Jay McGee, out with a sprained ankle. As expected, though, a bunch of our guys stepped up in what turned out to be an honest to goodness back-and-forth slugfest, as evidenced by the order of TDs scored: Broc-Broc-Leom-Broc-Leom-Broc-Leom-Broc-Broc-Leom-Leom.

Chuck had two long touchdown passes, one a joy forever to Billy Mitchell; Sanford took off down the middle of the field, slow-fast, for a 50+-yard score; tight end Tom Dinopoulos was a dipsy-doodling dervish on clutch first downs, catching the eye of Holy Cross scouts in attendance, sealing for himself a full athletic scholarship in the process; and Johnny "Hands"* Hancock earned his nickname that day, hauling in a 60-yard TD reception, recovering a fumble, and fielding both of Leominster's onside kicks including one with just a minute left to play. So, despite our failing to convert on *five out of six* points-after-touchdown, be they kick, pass, or rush, I am happy to report that the home team hung on, prevailing 37-32. (It was a good thing our guys thwarted three of their PAT attempts too.)

*[As the original coiner of this apposite moniker, I was its primary proponent. Alas, "Hands"...she never caught on.]

We knew that beating Leominster would put us over the hump, ratingswise. Rather than a full-blown playoff system, the Massachusetts Interscholastic Athletic Association had implemented in 1972 a rating system by which strength of schedule played a major role. In addition to being awarded 10 points for each of your own victories, you would receive 2 additional points for every game your defeated divisional opponent ended up winning that season. So, vanquishing a powerhouse team like Leominster boded well for us.

As for strictly personal memorable moments from Leominster '79, there are but two.

First, a spell of recent rain plus even more recent windy cold temperatures had left the Marciano Stadium turf rock hard, or perhaps it was a different sequence of climate instability causing it. All I know for sure is that the dirt out of bounds felt like cement when the back of my helmet slammed against it at the end of a sideline tackle. My eyes dotted. That collision, the hardest I've ever felt in football, set off a headache, sharp, immediate, and tenacious as George Millett on fourth down or at breakfast.

That day's next suicentric take away, like every other fumble or costly faux pas over the years, has been a burr under my balls ever since. Halfway through the fourth quarter, at around midfield, Chuck called a 38-Jet to me. Bear in mind: unlike many a Boxer running back before me and since, literally 99.2% of my BHS rushing yards were tallied between the tackles. Nevertheless, to keep up appearances, and to keep this secret to ourselves, Chuck would occasionally toss me a token sweep play to run.

Leominster's D-line must have gotten a right proper chewing out over Sanford's 3rd-quarter scoring dash because they collapsed on his belly fake like a Ponzi scheme on Black Tuesday. All I saw when I tucked the ball was our nimble right tackle, Steve Barry, leaning into his sprint around right end, and wide open spaces beyond. I had been fairly contained by the swarming Blue Devils all game long (a student photographer took a picture showing me at the bottom of a pile with no less than six of their guys on top of me), but a running back's break away sensors never rest. On the 38-Jet they sounded the alarm: This one's going all the way, or damn near it, or I'll know the reason why!

Next thing I knew, though, I was all by myself in the clear, flat on my face, mystified and pissed. What happened to my slipshod footing I had no idea. That same student photographer later gave me a black-and-white shot of this puzzling play which captured me a split second before planting my facemask into the turf (the kid's name was Bob McGrath, as I recall – excellent live-action photographer).

A touchdown there would have iced it. Instead, I had to sweat out two Piermarini fourth quarter scoring drives before Johnny Hancock took the game in hand with a minute left. On the plus side, a touchdown scored by your humble narrator from a few yards out early in the final period turned out to be the game-deciding TD, thank you very much. (An *Enterprise* photo of Billy Mitchell hoisting me in the endzone showed my Dad and uncle Kevin on their feet in the background, up high in the visitors stands, making that picture one of my all-time faves.)

A few days later, Chuck's big-game passing performance snagged him *Globe* Star of the Week Honorable Mention. It was nice to see that this year's more evenly balanced passing attack – potent, precise – still resonated with the powers that be, despite the absence of gaudy stats and flashy *uber* wideout Matty Walsh.

—

On Halloween, my younger brothers and sister were out trick-or-treating. Dad and I had been tasked with holding the fort against the unrelenting onslaught of barbarians at the gate while my mom slept before her scheduled night shift at the V.A.

Under his breath Dad mentioned, "Hut-hut," and hit me on a back-shoulder timing pattern, hurling a Namathian* spiral with expert touch before I'd even turned to look.

*[lacelessly wobbling]

"*TRICK OR TREAT!*"

Generic hand-me-down hoboes and bedsheet ghosts predominated, as I recall, but there was no shortage of store bought characters, too.

I answered, "Treat! What do you guys like? We got everything."

They sang out in a candy cacophony.

I said, "Hey, Banana Splits! Tra-la-lah… Lah-lala-lah! "

One of them – Snork, I think it was – said, "You can't give us beer!"

"Very funny. No candy for you." My little joke went over great with the other Splits.

Having dispatched that wave of marauders with a minimal expenditure of sugary ammo, another one came up the lawn right behind them.

"Trick or treat!"

"Treat! Wow, High Plains Drifter."

"I'm a witch!"

"Not you!"

Some Bubble Yum and Razzles into her bag sent the weird sister on her way.

The Drifter said, "I'm a cowboy."

"Exactly." I drew a fistful of chocolate dollars and shot him with them. For Dad's amusement, I sniped under my breath, à la W.C. Fields, "Get out of here kid, you bother me…"

More sweet tooth supplicants masquerading as Kiss, Pink Ladies, princesses, Bat, Spider, and Super men, plus a host of nonspecific monsters, limited greatly my hassock slouching down time. After a while I just stayed standing guard by the door.

Except for chocolate bars, of course, the hot items were Pop Rocks, Bottle Caps, Peanut M&M's, and Smarties. As I recall, Bulls-Eyes were oft requested but very seld delivered. Dad and I were partial to the caramel cream classic ourselves. We ended up splitting the whole bag (60/40 Dad).

Best costume? Hands down, the cute little football player done up in his big brother's equipment. You could have spun the oversized helmet around on his head without requiring the slightest adjustment afterwards to his eyeglasses.

"Hey-hey!" I said. "What team you play for?"

His dad nudged him and the kid proclaimed, "Brockton High!"

"Oh, they're the best."

It was then I noted that the magic-markered numbering on his makeshift sweatshirt jersey was #43. Before I had a chance to compliment the coincidence, he added, "I'm Greg Dunn!"

Once the confectionary transaction with my diminutive doppelganger was complete (I emptied our remaining stash into #43's pillow case), we closed up shop.

"You hear that, Dad?"

My father's never been an I-told-you-so kind of Dad. This moment is about as close as he ever got. "Remember what I said?"

"Yup."

We both knew what we meant.

"Hut," he smiled, throwing a long bomb with the tightly crumpled Bulls-Eyes bag. "Hey, nice catch."

--

Whenever the Quincy Presidents came up on the schedule, we knew we were in for a tough fight whether the score was close or not. They were comprised of scrappy city kids, many of whose families had arrived from nearby Dorchester and South Boston during the recent busing diaspora, and they featured at least a couple outstanding players every year; the same with North Quincy. Combined, the Quincies would have been very hard to kill. Unfortunately for them, though, the vagaries of municipal districting had conspired to keep those two teams ever ununified (unlike the case of the Weymouths, North and South, who had suffered a similar fate by way of a *re*-districting in 1970 which broke perennial powerhouse Weymouth into two far lesser halves). Serves them right, though. I always hate to use the verb hate when it comes to people. *Hatred* is a nasty deep-seated thing that shouldn't be bandied about lightly, so I'll substitute the word "abominate" (the verb form, presumably, of *abominatred*), which means the same thing as hate, of course, but comes across as somehow more theoretical. Anyway, beating either of the Quincy teams was always particularly satisfying to us because we didn't appreciate the tendency they had of expressing at the bottom of certain gang tackle piles their less than egalitarian opinions on race.

After spending all of game day Saturday indoors amid the anticlimactic funk of a monsoon rainout, I remember lolling on the parlor couch that night and watching the weird debut of Ed "Too Tall" Jones' professional boxing career on TV with my father.

The next day, I didn't have a particularly remarkable Quincy game, but our defense held them to one touchdown for a hard fought win. The only thing that really stands out for me was being stopped on fourth-and-goal just before the half. Having reached out with the ball in a futile lurch for the goal line as the play ended, I lay there thus outstretched, lingering for a moment of rueful second guessing. Just then, right on cue, a Quincy player speared me in the ribs with his helmet which evoked a flutter of heaving grunts neither familiar to my ear nor intentional at all. (Dad would later say, "See, that's why I tell you. Never hang around a pile or lay there on the ground. Get right up and get right out.")

"Penalty!" I could hear Mr. Colombo yell from the sideline. "Throw the flag! Penalty!"

The ref shook it off with an innocent shrug that seemed to say: *Really? Do tell!*

The booming reply from Armond Colombo rang out through a near empty Veterans Memorial Stadium with evangelical vehemence, "He's the toughest one on the field! If he's still down, they did something wrong!"*

Later, as we sometimes did to wind down a night out with our buddies, Chuck and I went to my house. With Dad and Ma both working that night, we had the parlor to ourselves. Similarly, our wind-down sober-up might find us quietly slipping into the Colombo house and sneaking "down cellar" to check out some new music Donny had recently hipped Chuck to. As young guys still finding our sea legs, Budweiserwise, it was not uncommon for one or the other of us to catch his companion, be he guest or host, succumbing to a catnap partway through the proceedings.

---

*[Hey – *hey!* Hold on now... Let's not murder the messenger quite yet: Those were Coach Colombo's words, not mine. All I know is I spit out my mouthpiece right then and there and swore on everything I held dear that I'd – mark my words! – even if it took forever, I'd – if it took me 44 years! – I would find some way to somehow squeeze that little footnote into a bit of

dialogue somewhere for all the world to see: a Memoir, perhaps; or fact-based Drama; maybe even a self-published collection of local Vignettes. I don't know, you get the point...]

So, following the Quincy victory festivities, we found ourselves in the family parlor of 134 Deanna Road. I had been telling Chuck about *Cool Hand Luke,* which according to TV Guide was scheduled to run late that night.

I remember groaning to contain the pain of falling into Dad's wing chair.

"Ribs still sore?"

"Arch," I said, adjusting position. "Gnah..."

"My father'll probably get one of those flak jackets for you, like John Hancock wears."

"Ah, that's too bulky."

"Well probably something."

"Nah..."

From the couch, Chuck turned the endtable lamp on but turned it right back off.

"Yeah, it's better off," I agreed.

"You didn't go to that party the other night."

"I was here promoting neighborhood tooth decay."

"Heh! Get a lot of trick-or-treaters?"

"A nonstop shitload."

"What was the best costume?"

I said, "Well, as a matter of fact—"

"Oh, shit! I just remembered. A bunch of us from the party went across the street at midnight to the cemetery. And me and Mark Colombo—"

"How was it?"

"The party? Eh."

"Girls dressed up?"

"Ho-yeah."

"Was 'Q'?"

Chuck gave one long nod of thanks and praise. "French maid."

277

"She look good?"

"Dolly Parton figure," he reminded me, reminding me further, "Cuter than any Jolene."

"Dolly plus Jolene..." I calculated, doing the math.

Chuck multiplied it by a factor of ten: "French maid."

"And–"

"She gets to go through life like that!"

"So–"

"'Did she look good...'" he chided me.

"Heh!"

"She looked fucking delectable."

"Hah!"

"If I'd've had the chance, and thought for one second I'd've gotten away with it, I'd've started delecting her myself, right then and there."

"Good party then."

"The ratio sucked, though; the only thing."

"Ahh..."

"Oh – so we're all wandering around the cemetery, and Mark says, 'Hey, look at this.' On one of the gravestones it says, 'Emmaline–'"

"No!"

"'She lived her life in a song.'"

The song by Hot Chocolate was one of our favorites. I was amazed. "Could it be the same one?"

"Fucking spooky."

In the dark on the couch during *Cool Hand Luke,* Chuck caught himself a half-dozen kittennaps. Maybe I did too, who knows? As the credits rolled, he stood up stretching and stated, "That was a great movie, Dunna. Good call."

—

As the regular season was wrapping up, our blockade defense only seemed to solidify more and more each week, and the offense kept firing on all cylinders, as they say – well, almost all: Jay had had to check out of the Weymouth North game early after tweaking his nagging heavily taped ankle. Everyone except the opposing coaches eagerly awaited his return which, considering his unique dynamism, couldn't come soon enough.

Don't get me wrong. Nobody was calling for my head or anything; I was having a good year by competitive standards, and we were undefeated, but Jay McGee was a special kind of weapon — obviously.

We gave Weymouth North an old-fashioned Brockton beatdown despite his absence, 44-0. Even our QB had a rushing touchdown that game!

There was a good picture in the *Enterprise* the next day of me crossing the goal line after catching a neat wheel route dart from Chuck. To give you an idea of the high level our offense was operating at that season, the original play in the huddle was set to go off on "first sound", yet Chuck apparently had no qualms about calling an audible at the line. Bear in mind, "first sound" meant literally that: Once we had gotten set at the line of scrimmage, the very first sound out of Chuck's mouth (could be a color, could be a number, could be the name of a Stooge) would set us off. The standard Boxer cadence that year was: Color! Number! Hut(s)! (e.g., a play that was set to go off "on two" might be called out by Chuck as, "Blue! 44! Hut! Hut!"). However, if something in the defensive alignment presented an exploitable mismatch, it was at his discretion to call an audible, the signal of which was "Black-Black!". This would alert our guys that the play called in the huddle was being scrapped. If so, a predetermined set of colors meant either a run-play or pass-play, followed by a number which indicated the direction, left or right, and the specific play being called — easy enough. Obviously, though, the particular play Chuck had called in the huddle came with a higher than normal resistance to change, being that it was set to go off at "first sound"; moreover, we had never accounted at practice for such a contingency as an audible being called on a first-sound play. Nevertheless, half-a-hair before everybody was set, Chuck barked "Black-Black!" and believe it or not nobody went offsides, and sure enough his dart throw scored a bull's eye. 'Tis precisely *this* brand of heady play, football fans, that can launch a team on their way to mythical stratospheric CRIQS* score heights.

The best thing to me about that *Enterprise* photo is that my delighted little sister Julie and her best friend are pictured on the home sideline cheering me on my way as I go by. Julie and Lori Epstein's resulting celebrity in the neighborhood put their photogenic faces on multiple Deanna Road fridges that week, and earned all the Dunns Christo's for dinner that night.

My *second* favorite thing about the touchdown picture is that in it I'm sporting my idol Phil Johnson's number 42. On my first carry of that game, my jersey had been torn at the shoulder. I was only too pleased to swap it out. Yes sir, Mr. Referee! I went right to the back-up DB who had masterminded the dreaded Coccyx Affair on day-1 of doubles, and made the switch – as quickly inconspicuously as possible so as not to expose the foam rubber ribcage harness I was now wearing. The last thing I wanted was to suggest to onlookers that I was in any way incapacitated, especially potential scouting Waltham Hawk onlookers. (I was very pleased to see in the newspaper photo that the snug fitting apparatus was all but invisible under my jersey.)

Thus adorned in Johnson's mantle, I channeled the big halfback's superhero strength as much as I could.

*[(Class Rank ÷ Class Size) x Intelligence Quotient]

The only cloud of chagrin darkening the day of my otherwise fortuitous uniform tear was that the *Boston Globe* failed to register at all my points against Weymouth North in the weekly Scoring Leader tally. I figured the unannounced switching of jersey numbers must have been what led to the mix up, but when I would try to explain the discrepancy to friendly well-wishers inquiring as to my latest position on the charts, it sounded like an entirely baseless alibi, even to me. I'd watch friends squinting back suspicion, straining to suspend the kind of pity we normally reserve for sore losers and the petty.

"You're Greg Dunn," Joe took the opportunity to remind me one night on the phone, suggesting that my masquerade as Philly J. had somehow offended the jealous gods of serendipity. "Any success you've ever known has come from you being yourself," he said. "Right? Remember that."

—

Every Eastern Mass. team scheduled to play on Thanksgiving appreciated greatly the additional days of preparation and, more important, recuperation afforded them during the extended break between their penultimate regular season game and their Turkey Day finale.

In our case, the improvement of Jay McGee's ailing ankle ranked high on our holiday wish list.

Before practice one day, I hopped onto a taping table when Jay was just about to hop off the other. Mr. Colombo finished him up, patting the tape job snug as if polishing Mercury's own slippers. "How's that feel?"

Jay nodded, "Good."

"Ready to get back at it?"

"I've *been* ready."

Mr. Colombo gave Jay's foot a congratulatory slap. "Next!"

—

The day before Thanksgiving, during our pre-gameday walk-through at the Stadium, we were doing calisthenics in the endzone when I looked over to see my brothers Rich and Steve coming through the main parking lot entrance. From that distance I wasn't yet able to discern the block letter "B" shaved onto the crown of Rich's head, but backlit by the golden glow of the afternoon's setting sun, Steve's completely bald pate verily gleamed in tribute to his big game excitement and my mother's tonsorial handiwork. It's fair to say that the waterboys Dunn were as pumped as any player.

The next day, five or ten minutes till kickoff, Jay came over and suggested, "Stretch?"

We sat on the sideline grass, legs akimbo, cleats to cleats. Resumption of this pregame routine indicated to me that Jay was ready and raring to go. For games that he was out injured, we hadn't done our stretch. Although the subject had never been brought up for discussion, I interpreted those lapses as reluctance on the part of my young protégé due to the weird sense of exile that accompanies injury in team sports.

It's good to have a semblance of routine on game day.

We grasped hands. Jay was facing the playing field while my view was of the steadily filling home stands. As fans filed past, a number of them nodded to each other, pointing our way, noticing an evidently activated Jay McGee, I presumed. You really couldn't blame the SRO crowd packing Marciano Stadium for sensing they might be on the verge of eye-witnessing a talented understudy's imminent star turn on the big stage.

"How's it feeling," I asked as he very slowly lay backwards.

Jay nodded. When I pulled him up toward me, equally slow and sure, he said, "How's the shins?"

"Good."

Bob McGrath would later give me a nice wallet size black-and-white picture of Jay and me stretching, hands clasped, capturing me at the beginning of my descent, Jay on the rise; one of my all-time favorite photos.

When we were done stretching, my brother Rich came over to apply a stripe of eye-black to each cheek bone for me, and to activate a cold pack so I could numb my shins.

This Thanksgiving game was even more of a defensive struggle than last year's was. To be honest, and fair, the 1979 Waltham Hawks were tough and gutsy as hell. They went for it on 4th down almost every time, a tactic of savvy (i.e., keep our offense sidelined) as much as of machismo.

Our ____ defense (supply the strongest adjective you can and it still won't quite suffice) thwarted their 4th down try from our own

12-yard line in the first quarter, and from our 15-yard line late in the fourth. It was the baddestass defensive performance against a quality team that I'd ever seen.

However, nobody who was there that day – not coaches, not fans, not refs, not our defenders themselves – remembers this game as anything other than the true *DEBUT* of one John Joseph "Jay" McGee.

Waltham took a page from North Quincy's book by dedicating one of their linebackers as a shadow to key on me for the whole game, and as with the North Quincy game, I was thoroughly neutralized.

Nevertheless, I did contribute to the success of what turned out to be my personal favorite play of the season. Early in the second quarter, on third-and-short from just inside our own 40-yard line, a "49 Cross Fire Seal" was called. This was an end-around variation of one of our bread and butter off-tackle running plays that had accounted for a good deal of my rushing yards over the past two seasons. The variation involved an off-tackle-right fake to me followed by a hand off to Jay coming from the right flanker position to sweep around the left end.

Taking my spot at tailback, I stole a couple serious glances at the off-tackle-right hole for the benefit of any sneaky Hawk defenders looking to get a jump on the play. When Chuck took the snap I ran as hard as I possibly could, bent at the fake, slamming off-tackle. Three or four determined Waltham guys met me there, force majeure. Digging and pumping my best did no good. They ground me down under condescending curses and grunts.

Then I heard the crowd. Jay went untouched 61 yards to the endzone.

Unfortunately, a couple possessions later, a partially blocked punt gave the ball to Waltham at our 38-yard line, and they did not fail to capitalize, tying it up, 7-7, with less than a minute to go in the half.

As a rule, I refrain from telling tales out of huddle, but understandably the offensive guys on our kickoff return team were unanimously scalded with remorse for having put our defense in that tenuous 38-yard line predicament. Young Jay was clearly the most out of sorts of anyone. "It's alright," I nodded at him, and at everybody else, "It's alright."

It sure was.

With the ball in his hands, Jay had a gift for immediately recognizing a developing play's fundamental geometry. His best runs bespoke great vision, as well as a brilliantly efficient economy of cuts; then there was the dazzling speed. He ran that kickoff back 80 yards for a touchdown, relieving Waltham's kicker of his jockstrap somewhere around midfield.

The short-lived expansion of Waltham's sails was reminiscent of 1978's *Giudizio di Giusti* momentum swing.

That 14-7 score held up.

The main flaw of the Key-on-one-Guy defensive scheme becomes manifest whenever there exist other guys who are as good as or better than the one being keyed on. Jay and Sanford finished the day with 160 yards rushing between them, and I chipped in with 45 or 50 myself.

In the process of avenging every '78 defeat (thank you!) we had recorded ten straight victories. Mr. Colombo was quoted in the paper as saying ours was "the most unassuming undefeated team I've ever coached." It was good to win the Suburban League championship outright, and it was very good to earn a postseason spot in the Division-1 Super Bowl. Also unexpectedly good was the way news reports would say how Brockton was "returning" to the Super Bowl, as if the absent years were the exception rather than the rule, and this season's crew was merely righting our wayward ship. That felt very very good.

I don't want to sound complaining, but on a slightly less good personal note: When the *Globe* posted their end of season Final Scoring Leaders the next day, they had NOT made a correction to my points total as I'd half-hoped they might. So, as far as the *Boston Globe* and any interested parties in its readership were concerned, "Greg Dunn, Brockton" hadn't so much as notched a single new point since... what? The Quincy game twenty damn days earlier? Well that was that. There it was, right there in black and white for all to see, so it must be true.

—

In the days immediately preceding Brockton's championship matchup with Woburn, I had the idea that it would be fun to wrap up my Boxer football run with a bit of poetic counterbalance, if possible. At some point, preferably while hoisting the trophy for the Division-1 title, I was planning to announce, or yell my head off, as the case might be, "Welcome to Brockton Football!" Armond probably wouldn't recall that moment from double-sessions my freshman year when he bestowed the same winking salutation on me; then again he might, who knows? The other guys would dig it, though, and so would I.

As it happens, on December 1, 1979, at Boston College's Alumni Stadium, we were categorically outplayed by Woburn. For openers, they dominated the all important time-of-possession category. Their passing attack had been cause for great concern, but their star split end was hamstrung with extreme prejudice by our man-to-man master, Dwayne Lopes, who marooned him from start to finish on Lopes Island. However, Woburn deployed a surprisingly effective ground game that day, amassing 285 time-consuming yards. On the defensive side, they managed to hold our usually potent offense in check.

Our lone score came early in the third quarter. Woburn had been moving the ball when Dwayne intercepted a pass inside our 20-yard line. From there we put together the only sustained drive we had all game, capped by a short off-tackle touchdown run that Jay bounced outside. The scoring play featured one of my three or four successful blocks I ever threw during my high school career as I sealed off the defensive end from my left flanker position, helping allow Jay to scoot around behind. (I just never got the hang of it, somehow. To paraphrase Groucho Marx, I was an ardent but ineffectual blocker.)

On such a low-scoring day, it was yet again our resourceful defense, straining to the point of breaking but only just, that kept us in this one. Sanford had an interception deep in our own territory too, an acrobatic one-hand stab like a centerfielder (which he was, come spring) twisting at the wall to rob a home run.

Woburn continued their crucial game of keep away, and they made the big plays down the stretch. Nevertheless, we were actually ahead 7-6 with half a minute to go, and we had their offense 3rd-and-long. Beside me on the sideline, my buddy Rod said, "We did it, Dunna!"

"NO!" I blared. Was he *trying* to jinx it?

Woburn's unlikely second touchdown, about which the less said the better, and successful conversion pass put them back in the lead, 14-7. As both teams were taking the field for the ensuing kickoff, I hurried over to Mr. Colombo, grabbing his arm.

His focus was squarely on the game clock which showed 19 seconds remaining. Although I had been slipping and sliding all over the field that day, getting nowhere fast, I interjected, "I'm going to fucking run this back! Welcome to Brockton Football!"

Something pulsed across his features then, something wry. His eyes flickered and his stiff lips almost cracked a smile. Cheers to Coach Armond Colombo! In the heat of this predicament, he was exhibiting, as far as I could tell, the relish of competitors at their moment of truth. I think what I caught sight of in that face was the very personification of *Sport*.

Then again, maybe he just didn't want to break it to me that Jay was getting the ball.

"Do it, Greg," he told me with a nod. "Nine return. Nine return."

Their squib kick eluded our midrange return men long enough to allow several Woburn defenders ample time to make an immediate gang tackle once we had finally gathered it in. From there it came down to sending to the heavens our desperate *Ave Marias* which, unfortunately, fell futile.

I am loath now to even mention this but, in the spirit of grudging disclosure, everybody at Alumni Stadium that day knew: If any one player could be singled out for blame in the Brockton loss, it had to be the guy in red-and-black wearing number 43.

Let's leave it at that.

—

Whether intentionally or by nature, Mr. Colombo – much like my dad – rarely used two syllables where one would suffice. If pressed, he'd go to a third ("Chicopee", "Leominster"), or once in a while even four ("Championship").

On the bus after the Woburn game he addressed his team. "It's painful," he said. "But we really had a heck of a year." He smiled, a mist of wistfulness in his eye. "And it was fun. More than any other Brockton team I've coached," he said. "You guys... *amused* me. Thank you."

Despite the sour way it ended, 1979 was of course not without its high points. There were tough hard-nosed practices and memorable hardfought games. For me, though, the season's foremost accomplishment was how we helped steer the culture of Brockton Football away from a notion of institutionalized harassment, moving instead toward its diametric opposite. In this regard it was truly a watershed season. The weak were not preyed upon by the strong that year. Underclassmen talented enough to contribute were welcomed into the huddle. If our 1979 team is remembered for nothing else, it should be that we took real strides toward ensuring that shibboleths like bully entitlement would eventually be retired for good at Eldon B. Keith Field.

—

There were times I thought my brothers shared some kind of sixth sense when it came to Dad's bad moods. We'd be lounging around the parlor in the evening, a few on the couch, or laid out on the floor, some bold one of us in Dad's chair maybe (rarely), Ma at the table with her coffee, entertaining Julie, and as soon as my father's headlights leapt across the parlor walls the other guys would disappear down the hall. These Pavlovian exits were never discussed among us, but it eventually became understood that I would be the one to stay behind.

Nor were there any hard feelings. Dad and I have always enjoyed each other's company, so in augmenting my store of fraternal capital, as it were, these sometimes silent (often garrulous) evenings in the parlor, redolent to this day of burnt wood, also served to anneal my already rock solid bond with my father.

However, one night as soon as Dad walked in, he called, "Richard!"

I took my position on the floor in front of the hassock as Rich duly appeared, standing in the hallway, expressing in his demeanor nothing so much as absolute defenseless expectation. "Yes?"

"Yes, what?"

"Yes, Dad."

I kept my eyes trained on Rich's face. If he looked my way, I wanted to communicate him a measure of courage.

Dad waited. When he was sure he had his young son's undivided attention (he did!), he said, "Ma told me you got your report cards today."

My brother nodded, glancing momentarily at me.

"You didn't do better in math, did you?"

Rich shook his head and gave me another quick downcast look.

"But every other class you went up."

Rich nodded a little.

"Give me five."

They slapped hands loudly.

"Good job, Richa. We told you you could do it, right? Now you just have to keep it going. The hardest part's already over."

Ma said from the table, "Give him a couple of bucks, Joe."

—

1980s
(a blur)

For some reason, minutiae of the 1970s stand out for me much more vividly against the background of the past than do those of the 80s. Don't ask me why. But, that being the case, it wouldn't be unreasonable to expect somewhat shorter vignettes for the time being, or at least fewer long ones, to the extent that these tidy little bits of remembrance will float and descend, weightless, from here on out like so many strips of ticker tape fluttering over the glorious parade of our passing years below…

Chuck and I traveled together that winter on several college recruiting trips. We both liked the campuses and overall vibes at Bowdoin College and Colby College, and each of those football coaches seemed to genuinely like us, but when former Milford High head coach and current Harvard offensive line coach, Dick Corbin, reached out to us we were only too glad to shunt every other inquiry to the backup pile.

While touring Harvard's athletic facilities during our visit, we were shown the indoor track where members of the varsity football team were being timed in the ten-yard dash, of all things.

"Want to give it a try," the timekeeper said.

I was in street clothes, not warmed up or anything, but what the hell? I was game.

After what seemed an immeasurably short eruption of thrust, it was over.

"How'd I do?"

"1.66."

"Is that good?"

"So far it's tie for fastest."

In the coaches office, waiting to see Joe Restic, we talked with Coach Corbin and Coach Leo Fanning. With matter of fact candor, they explained, "It's looking good for Chuck. Greg, you're in the picture but it's borderline. I mean, stranger things have happened. Look at our Olympic Hockey team. But you're riding that borderline."

That made sense. Chuck's GPA and class rank were better than mine. I remember after our first semester freshman year, my class rank and Chuck's were identical, a dead heat. I'm not going to print the exact number here because, believe me, you wouldn't believe me. Since then, Chuck had pulled ahead, and I'm pretty sure he was taking a senior Science and/or Math course, which I most certainly was not, having opted instead for Piano-1 and some other non-trigonometric elective. Apparently certain colleges noticed that shit, even if our guidance counselors didn't.

One of the coaches at a desk in the corner overheard us. He said, "Come April 15th, if the mailman brings you one of those, ahh... thin envelopes, it's not necessarily goodnight Irene. There's more than one way to skin a cat."

"That's right," agreed Dick Corbin. "You don't get in this time around? Do a PG year at one of the preps. You go to a Choate, an Exeter? Andover? Do good there, and you're golden."

This was all news to me. "Really?"

Corbin lit up like a coach on 4th-and-short. "In like Flynn, Dunny."

Our hosts for the weekend were freshman players on the team who were also roommates; wiry quarterback Jack Riordan from Abington and fullback Mike Ernst of Clinton, a smiling soft-spoken fireplug. They took us to their dorm in Harvard Yard where we all got to know each other over endless games of cards and beer. I made a point of inquiring about the prep school post graduate thing. It turned out that Jack and Mike knew all about it, both of them having gone the PG route themselves, playing together in the same backfield at Phillips Exeter the year before.

"Really?"

To be honest, I kind of hated the idea. To watch all my friends go off to college while I stayed behind, spinning my wheels for another year of high school, would fairly suck. I knew Harvard was a long shot, but if they decided not to take me it wasn't a death sentence or anything. Good old Colby College and the bustling city of Waterville, Maine, would suit me just fine. Also, William & Mary,

the only scholarship school showing any real interest, had me ship them some of my game films, so there was still a chance they'd be an option too.
—

The middle of April brought my buddy Chuck great news from Cambridge, and it delivered to my door the dreaded "thin envelope" with 02138 postmark. Ah, well...

It was going to be weird for both of us next football season running plays without one another for the first time in a long time.

Fortunately, along with one terse Dear Gregory letter, I also received congratulatory documentation, along with hefty onboarding packets, from Colby, Bowdoin, and William & Mary. So, theoretically at least, I had my pick of three pretty damn good schools.

Realistically, though, Bowdoin wasn't even in the running. Their head coach – who by all accounts was a well-respected high quality dude – struck me as kind of backwoods odd, and he several times during our initial meeting reaffirmed his dedication to the toss-sweep, a partiality that served to estrange us all the more, if anything. "It's a good play," he'd say with solemnity. "It's a hard play... It's a *fun* play."

To which I say: "Orhno... e-NOW-a... SHE-yoh."* Which means, "This guy – this is not my kind of guy."

I hadn't heard anything from the Williamsburg coaches in weeks, and there was no mention of scholarships or grants in their acceptance paperwork, so all signs were pointing to the White Mules of Colby College. I'd been keeping in regular contact with their head coach, Tom Kopp, expressing my interest in joining his team. I mailed him a note that day informing him of my intention to enroll at Colby. I can't quite name what it was about that particular school that made it feel so attractive to me.

*[Phonetic, supposedly from the Korean, per F. Costanza.]

The wintry tucked-away campus, the comfortable level of football (NESCAC, Division III), the conversational coach and the general impression he gave of being genuinely interested in *me,* the fact that a BHS hero of mine, Art Sullivan, whom I had met for the first time on my recruiting visit, spoke so well of his time there, all conspired to make the fit right.

"Hear anything from William & Mary," my dad asked.

I told him, "No, just the admissions."

Coach Kopp called the house a couple days later. He sounded thrilled, like we were embarking together on a noble and noteworthy mission. "I see great things ahead, Greg."

"Oh—"

"Great things for you. Great things for Colby."

———

Later in the week I received a call from Phillips Academy, the prep school in Andover, Mass. It's always a nice boost to your confidence, not to mention ego, whenever a recruiter expresses interest. I thanked the coach for the call, but explained that I had already committed to Colby, and we wished each other well.

My mother said, "Who was that you were talking to?"

"Coach from Andover. The prep school."

"A little late to the dance, aren't they?"

"Must be trolling for guys who didn't get in where they wanted to."

"Horse sense," Ma nodded, appreciating a good work ethic when she saw one. "Shopping for last minute bargains."

"Well, this shop's closed."

She lit a cigarette. "Ever consider prep school? Andover's one of the best. Even I've heard of them."

"Your boy's fixing to be a White Mule, Momma! Shooooot... Don't need no stinkin' prep school."

My mother took a puzzlingly slow drag. A car beeped out front.

"That would be Chuck, Mum. We're off to parts unknown."

"Thought you were going to the movies."

"We are."
"What are you going to see?"
"No idea!"

—

Little did I know my dad would come home from work and another trolling coach would call. Littler still, the two of them would hit it off, and Lilliputianest of all I would have an *interview* at fucking *Exeter* on *Friday!*

"But Dad–"
"We're just going to drive up to see what they have to say."
"I already told Coach Kopp for cry–"
"It won't hurt to hear them out."
"He put a big announcement in the school paper…"
"It's alright, I'll talk to him."
"The Colby Echo…"
"Next time he calls, give me the phone."
"Ah, man…"

—

Later in the month, lounging with my father in the parlor, he said, "Staying in tonight? No movie?"

"Nah," I stretched against the hassock.

"Chuck busy?"

"Oh," I said. "He and some of the guys are in Florida for April vacation."

"Yuh? How come you didn't go?"

"Nah…"

"You should've said something."

Honestly, I hadn't the slightest desire to spend a hammered week of sweating among the Fort Lauderdale sleaze throngs. "No, Dad, I'm fine. I don't need that shit…"

"Alright. Long as you're sure."

"Absolutely."

—

In mid May, as senior year was wrapping up, the *Sunday Globe* published its annual spring recruiting update, a full two-page spread "Where the Best Schoolboy Athletes are Going to College." Almost a thousand football, basketball, and hockey players were listed along with their corresponding collegiate destinations. Among my Boxer teammates, Chuck (Harvard) made the list, John Millett and Tom Dinopoulos (Holy Cross), Glenn Reagan (BC), Tom O'Brien (Norwich), John Hancock's older brother, Mike (Springfield).

As if the word "Undecided" next to my name wasn't insult enough, I felt myself clench in a full body cringe when I saw smack-dab in the middle of the 500+ football player names, the lone football player photo, depicting me awkwardly flat-footed in our game against Waltham. The corkscrew dagger caption read, "Brockton's Greg Dunn is still up for grabs."

I could have spit rocks.

A few days later, the running backs coach at William & Mary surprised me with a call to offer a full scholarship. I figured one of the recruits ahead of me on the depth chart must have changed his mind at the last minute and gone elsewhere, which accounted for this eleventh hour offer. I hadn't heard word one from these guys in over a month.

"Wow," I said. "Thank you very much, Coach. But I've already committed to Phillips Exeter Academy in New Hampshire."

"The preparatory?" He couldn't believe it.

"Yeah..."

"I'm talking about a free education, guy! At a Division-1 program."

The Williamsburg campus was absolutely beautiful, and the school was a great school. If he had called five or six weeks earlier I might have accepted, but I'd be damned if I was going to go through the same thing I did with Coach Kopp again.

"I appreciate that, Coach, but I've made the commitment, in writing."

"Is your daddy at home?"

"He's not, but–."

"You ain't got Ivy League marks, Dunn."

That was the exact same thing Kopp had said. "My father insists on Exeter."

"Boy, this offer ain't going be here tomorrow."

He hung up before I finished saying, "I understand."

—

On graduation day, my family had a little party for me at the house, toward the end of which was heard Chuck's arrival out front, heralded by eleven staccato beeps of his brother Pete's Celica: One, two! One, two, three! One, two, three, four! Let's go!

The evening sun was still fairly high in the sky. As I was getting in the car, my father called out from our front door, "Gregga!"

We saw him walking down the lawn toward us holding by their necks a couple 12-ounce bottles of Miller High Life in one hand. He gave us each a congratulatory beer. "Here you go. Be careful tonight. And have a good time."

"Will do," we said. "Yup. We're just going to hit a couple parties."

"Congratulations, guys."

Once we were on our way, I apologized, "Sorry about sticking you with driving."

"No problem," Chuck said. "But yeah – thought you were rolling out grandpa's Pinto for our special night."

"I was! Then there was this whole big thing. My father was saying how it's bad for multiple people to drive a manual transmission because everybody has a different feel for the clutch, so–"

"He's right."

"What?"

"That's true."

I said, "You guys are in cahoots!"

Chuck spit a laugh. "No, but–"

"I know a cahoot when I see one."

"It's just that—"

"Yeah yeah yeah."

"If the friction point is—"

"Cahoot!"

Later, on our way home for the night, I was driving for some reason. Chuck said, "You were going to tell me about the William & Mary thing."

"Yeah, I was going to. Until this whole cahoot business…"

Chuck chuckled, "Cahoot…" Then he said, "Dunna?"

"Chucka?"

"What say we do our best to completely avoid all the lawns on the way, okay?"

"If you insist. But more importantly, is the Playmate of the Year issue out at your store yet? That beautiful blonde girl sitting on the grass?"

"Yessuh."

"Tits till Tuesday?"

"Oh, yuh."

"Let me know the next time you're working, I'll stop by."

"Tomorrow night, seven to close."

"I'll stop by."

"So you said your dad got mad when you turned down the full ride?"

"Not mad – fucking *pissed*."

"I thought he was dead set on Exeter."

"Me too! He was!"

"So…"

"He is."

"…you *are* going to prep school."

"Don't rub it in."

"So you are *not* quote-unquote undecided."

"Very humorous, Charles."

Chuck said, "Free ride, though… I kind of see his point being pissed."

"The two of you are in cafuckinghoots!"

In my experience, suburban teenagers are generally in favor of hosting little overnight gatherings when their parents are away. Although my mother and father were hardly ever the out-of-town-for-the-weekend type, several of my friends' parents were. Some of the best times I had growing up were spent at the homes of Donny Barlow and his sister Laura, Mike and MaryEllen Barry, and Chuck and his several siblings.

With Mr. and Mrs. Colombo on the Cape for a week with their youngest, Tommy, in tow, Chuck invited a few close friends over for cocktails and hors d'oeuvres.

At this particular soirée, Dan Colombo's BHS baseball buddy, Bob Tanzi, and I were at one point immersed in a *tête-à-tête* drinking game involving as penalty – or was it reward? – the consumption of Blue Nun sparkling wine served from one of my Converse turf shoes.*

Later, at the height of the night's festivities, I remember Chuck and I spent some time down cellar taking turns lying with our head between the speakers with the live version of Dylan's "It's Alright Ma (I'm Only Bleeding)" ringing out. Chuck had chosen a line from that song to go with his yearbook picture.

By this time a seasoned veteran of such events, I had no intention of trying to make it through the entire night unslept. I came-to in the morning on the living room sofa with a crashing champagne headache.

*[Hearing Out His Say: Recently, at a Brockton Hall of Fame ceremony honoring Bob Tanzi and Jay McGee, among others, I reminded him of our dippy contest at the Colombos and how it seemed somehow effete that night, in the middle of such a raucous throng, that we had chosen athletic footwear from which to spill the wine. "*We* didn't," Tanzi gainsaid. "*You* did." I corrected him, "We did!" "You did!" "We, brother!" This playful ping-pong went on until all that was left to do was laugh it off and simply disagree to agree.]

At the kitchen table, several of the older guys were quietly recovering.

I shambled in. "Keep it down in here, will you? People trying to sleep for Christ sake. Chuck around?"

"They went out to breakfast."

The mere sound of breakfast in my ear was enough to swamp me for the time being. I heard myself say, "Uhhh…"

Splashing cool water on my face at the kitchen sink did little by way of encouragement. I was about to get right back on the firm sofa when a car was heard pulling into the driveway.

Jeff McDermott said, "I hope they brought coffee."

"Shit! It's Armond and Betty!"

Like bad actors in a Feydeau farce, everybody in the kitchen bolted for the nearest door, leaving me standing there with the faucet in my hand. They all bunched up in the front foyer, these athletes of yore, peeking through the window, piling against one another until the Colombos made a clear commitment to using the breezeway side entrance. That was everybody's cue to scatter to the cars out front, which they did with the quiet agility of scooting cats.

I daresay Coach Colombo was genuinely pleased when he found, to his surprise, me of all people standing there in his kitchen.

"Hi, Greg!"

"Hi Mr. Colombo," I greeted him. "Mrs. Colombo."

She sniffed at the air and sneered. "Where's Chuckie? What'd he throw a party here last night?"

"Party? Oh, no, no. Naw…"

"No?"

"He's out to Dunkin' Donuts. Or somewhere." I started rinsing under the running water pieces of cutlery that were in the sink. "But no, I wouldn't call it a party," I pooh-poohed. "Few of the guys stopped by for a while, that's all. How you doing, Tom?"

Young Tommy Colombo, ever wise beyond his years, took in my little tap dance with a wry semi-smile, not unlike one I'd seen his dad flash from time to time over the years. "Hi, Dunnah."

My old coach chided me. "Greg, you have to use hot water and soap!"

"I'm rinsing them first! Sheesh."

—

The Dunn family is hardly a superstitious bunch. Having never set much store by omens or auspices, we govern ourselves by the fairly secular belief that obstacles are for overcoming, and luck is pretty much what you make it. However, perceived patterns do inevitably take shape along the way, and trends will sometimes seem to generate their own self-sustaining inertia.

"Remember," Dad has said at the hassock, "A lot of first impressions last forever. So whenever you make one, make sure you make it a good one." True words. "You can't avoid it. This is Brockton, you're a Dunn. It's a reflection on you, and it's a reflection on all of us."

We still recount to one another how Dad, culling from his phrenic storehouse of sports trivia (an encyclopedic cataloguing talent which we all inherited, albeit to varying degrees), would say that during the wane of Dimaggio's career, the great center fielder knew he had maybe one good throw per game in his painfully thrown-out right shoulder. "He always made sure to let that one good one fly, he said, to show everybody – his teammates, the opposing players – that he was still Joe Dimaggio and was not to be fucked with; and, more importantly, 'Because there might be someone at the game today who's never seen me play before.'"

As we all know, beginning on a good note has eased the handling of many an otherwise trying endeavor enough for it to be seen through to its successful conclusion. Likewise, starting out on the wrong foot usually precipitates subsequent shortfalls, if not outright failure. As J. Robert Oppenheimer, not to mention A. Joseph Dunn, often emphasized, "One thing leads to another!"

So on the drive with Dad up to Exeter, New Hampshire, in the last days of an August panting-dog swelter, I was focused on thinking cool thoughts and projecting positivity about this "PG" year I was embarking on.

"How's your back?"

I nodded. "It's alright."

"Ma give you the muscle relaxers?"

"Yut."

"Those aren't for during the day, though, she said. Just at night. They'll help you sleep."

"Okay."

"And you probably want to put your mattress on the floor too."

"Oh, okay."

"Better for you."

I remember saying, "What if they stick me with a roommate?" It really didn't matter to me, I was just trying to be funny.

"The hell with that. What do you give a shit what some roommate thinks? Tell him you're afraid of heights."

"No, I know," I laughed.

As we slowly drove through campus toward the Field House, Dad assured me, "You're going to love this," daring to further stretch the already strained limits of positive thinking vis-à-vis the Exonian experience and its manifold charms.

"I know."

He said, "There's the coaches. Stretch your back out a little as soon as we get out. Don't want to go hobbling up to them your first day here."

Having come from a football program like Brockton's, it wouldn't have been fair to Exeter for me to try to compare the two – because there was really no comparison. Phillips Exeter Academy's athletic facilities were first rate, I'll leave that at that.

—

It turns out that the Academy was going to be celebrating its bicentennial that year with dozens of "Exeter200" events scheduled from early fall right through to graduation day next spring. As if that heaping scoop of SPECIAL wasn't enough, coincidentally our annual finale with archrival Andover would mark the 100th football game between the two teams.

Being founded while our newborn nation was still learning to walk, both schools' lineages include direct contact early on with a number of founding fathers of the Revolution. For sheer cobblestone cred, you could scarcely do better in this country than these two paragons of academe, courtesy of the Phillips family's largesse. (John Phillips helped fund nephew Samuel's Andover academy in 1778 before securing the charter for his Exeter school three years later.)

As for the 1980 PG football season itself, I suppose it could have opened to better reviews. Things started out normally enough with our first two days as a team being spent sweating together wearing our white helmets and academy-issued grey t-shirts and crimson* shorts on the practice fields and outdoor track, doing conditioning (timed sprints, agility drills, timed quarter-, half-, and full-mile runs, position drills) or helmetless in the weight room and field house for strength tests and position meetings. Other than that, we studied our playbooks, sat for meals, and slept. Typical of any organized pre-season period of captivity, our itineraries allowed no time for much else.

On the morning of our third day together, we were all in the field house waiting our turn in line at the equipment manager's cage to receive practice gear and pads. Our head coach stood at the front of the line, chatting with each passing player. When I reached the counter, he smiled at me, "Morning, Dunn. Feeling alright?"

"Feel great, Coach."

"Oh," he said. "Because your gait looks a little rusty."

*[Lions Rampant Note: It went without saying that the primary color of Exeter's Big Red, aka, Lions (technically "Lions Rampant") athletic teams was intentionally modeled after the Harvard Crimson's, whereas our arch rival, the Big Blue of Andover, followed the uniform design of the Yale Eli. The understanding, of course, was that Phillips Academy in Andover, Massachusetts, was a well known grooming ground for students who would later matriculate at Yale, while Phillips Exeter Academy served as a similar pipeline from New Hampshire to Harvard. Apocryphal or not, this tidbit of lore was apparently so well ingrained that no self-respecting scholar from either academy ever mentioned it: They just *knew* it.]

I said, "Huh?" (Was this guy trying to break my balls? And what's with the goofy punning? He suddenly looked like the coach I'd seen in every low budget movie that ever had a dimwit blowhard coach in it.) "Ah... just a little back ache. It's nothing."

He kept smiling but now he had an I'm-onto-you-fella gleam in his eye, like he'd caught me red handed at the club mixer without an invitation. "They say most back pain is psychosomatic, you know," he informed me.

"Really?" Just then the harried but good-natured equipment manager guessed my waist size correctly at a glance. "Right on the money," I told him.

Coach said, "It's probably just in your head."

With a nod of dutiful resignation, I quipped, "But if it was in my head it'd be a headache."

His gotcha gleam went cloudy as a cataract, while his smile weirdly remained. "No, I'm serious."

"So am I, Coach."

The equipment manager plunked a pre-folded pile of gear on the counter and topped it off with a pair of brand spanking new shoulder pads. I said, "Ah, do you have a smaller size shoulder pad? Smallest one you got, if possible. Other than quarterback's." Having seen it all over the years, he didn't blink but I noticed a quizzical smirk as he started away to fulfill my unusual request. "Smaller, ay?" he said over his shoulder. "Coming right up." When he returned, smirk intact, with a musty well-worn yellowed harness-like contraption, I said, "Ah – thank you. Perfect."

He nodded. "You're not from around here, are you?"

Taking my bundle of equipment in my arms, I winked at the coach, "Just acts up sometimes on its own," I assured him. "Ain't nuttin' to do wit m' headbone, suh."

The morning of our first full practice the following day, I went in early and checked the trainer's room to claim first dibs on the ankle taping table. Our head coach was the only one in there. Sitting at the desk, he looked up from some paperwork.

"Dunn," he stated with the implied ellipsis of interrogation.

"Ankle taping?"

He asked me why.

I gave the little joke a little smile, but his accusatory frown soured it. Apparently he was in earnest. I said, "Why tape? For the supp–"

"Your ankles acting up too, now?"

—

Needless to say, the problem of my ailing lower back was not rooted in my mind, and for this new football season the discomfort was screaming for dear life, by far the severest I had yet experienced. My mattress on the bedroom floor didn't seem to help, nor did Ma's muscle relaxers. As usual, on the field it was at its worst during the speeding up from a standing start and, especially, the slowing down to a walk.

I didn't do myself any favors that first day of doubles when, after the morning session, the metal tips on my cleats proved a poor match for the smooth stone flooring and stairs in the locker room. I skidded down the last few steps on my ass in front of all my new teammates. Luckily, at least my tailbone came through it unscathed, which was more than I could say for my pride.

It was really rather easy getting along with the other guys on the team, whether they were "four-year boys" or postgraduates like myself, and I guess it was only natural that the PGs tended to gravitate first toward their fellow newcomers rather than seeking entrée at the door of established cliques.

I must say, I was impressed with the talent level of PG players the coaches had brought in. Tim Hickey was a good back whose name I immediately recognized from when I had been keeping tabs on Division-1 scoring leaders. He'd bagged a couple of Star of the Week awards too last year playing for Melrose.

Another excellent halfback was Mark Harrington from Chelmsford, nickname "Dirt". Along with me and Hickey (fullback), we formed the Exeter backfield that season behind Johnston, Rhode Island's Bob Radoccia, a slick natural-born passer who commanded the huddle with a confidence completely devoid of affect or juvenile bravado. Apart from his gridiron imperturbability, he was a cool admirably atypical cat, very much his own dude, his own drum. He was an unapologetic Disco fanatic, for instance. Waiting in the huddle for everyone to assemble, he might bide his time tapping out little dance steps in his immaculate white cleats, rolling his shoulders, singing "Strawberry Letter 23" to himself, sporting white knee socks and a white turtleneck beneath his pads. The rest of us wouldn't have been caught dead in such a get up, but that was Radoche.*

I caught two of his touchdown passes that season before he broke his wrist in a game and was out for the rest of the year. He was, and still is, one of my favorite people at Exeter. We got a kick out of each other.

That winter, he and I were playing backgammon in Dirt's dorm room, talking about our football season and how his injury had somehow ended up estranging him from the team despite his continuing to come to every practice.

"I've seen that before," I told him. "One of our captains. He blew his knee out in double sessions. And next thing you know, we started losing touch with him. Right before our eyes."

"I felt invisible like in a bad dream and you can't get through to anybody and you can't do shit about it."

"That weird pack animal dynamic – pack animal mentality. Little by little, day by day, he was becoming less and less one of us."

"That's why I stopped going to practice, only games."

"And seeing it with my own eyes, I hated it. I hated it then, and I hated seeing it with you. Guys I know to be good guys. Guys I like. Guys who like *you*. Shunning an injured member of the herd. They talked to you different. Looked at you different. I could see it. Sometimes they wouldn't look at you at all…"

With no rancor in his voice whatsoever, he said, "You too, Radoche."

*[RADOCCIA MINUTIA: Not only did everybody call him Radoche, but he called everybody else Radoche too.]
—

One day during a practice at Eldon B. Keith when Chuck and I were sophomores on the team, we came up with a sort of game, or exercise, you might call it, or time-kill drill. Forgive my not being more precise, but neither of us ever got around to classifying the activity so specifically, or even assigning it a working title for strictly referential purposes. The fact is, we never so much as exchanged word one on the subject.

About halfway through each practice, once Mr. Colombo had finished putting the starting offense through its paces for the day, our first team defense would take the field and we'd repair to the sideline for a few minutes of downtime. On one such day early in the season, I happened to casually catch Chuck's eye about ten yards down the sideline from me. At practice, unless he was actually on the field of play, in the huddle or under center, Chuck had a football in his hands. When we noticed each other, he did the natural thing and threw me a pass, shoulder high, which I caught one-handed and threw back to him in the same motion, spiralish, head high. With his right hand, Chuck caught the pass and held it there for a moment, demonstrating to one and all that the completion met minimum quality standards (i.e., clean catch, no bobble, tight grip, no slippage) before passing it back again to the same shoulder high target area of maximum convenience and catchability.

It went without question and without saying that this new activity of ours was a cooperative effort, not a competitive one. We were on the same side. No score was ever kept, nor records ever set. The goal was purely Facilitate Another Catch.

After that first time sophomore year, Chuck and I did this religiously during every padded practice of 1977, '78, and '79. I'm a great proponent of such time-passing exercises. They're fun in the moment, Zen-centric, and they hone by cumulative degrees a useful applicable skill. I specifically attribute both of my single(right)handed receptions in games (screen passes, 1 soph. year & 1 jr. year) to our little diversion, as well as any number of tricky two-handed grabs I made along the way.

It's always kind of nice, too, to have some form of quiet routine in your daily life, to decompress, even if only for a few minutes.

On my first morning of double sessions at Exeter, I almost tried to start one up with Dirt, but at the end of the day I was glad I hadn't. Playing Chuck's and my game with a different partner gave me a weirdly sneaky feeling, and I hardly even knew this guy, anyway.

—

We opened the season with a hard fought loss at Worcester Academy. Of course, as protocol dictated in those days, our team's first offensive play went to me. By now, having resigned myself to the initial-play-of-the-season outright futility which had apparently been predetermined as my fated lot, I complied, just to get it over with, by immediately fumbling the ball away to the Worcester Academy defense. If I didn't know me better, I might have suspected that this guy – this *Dunn* character – had some kind of deep-seated syndrome or phobia, like chronic opening night jitters or something. But of course nothing could have been further from the truth…

Our next game was a nice home win against Tabor Academy, 47-22. I rushed for 3 TDs and a 2-point conversion, Dirt scored twice, Radoccia threw for one touchdown (to Dirt) and ran for another, but the best thing about this game happened during the week leading up to it, while we were watching Tabor's scout film.

"This is our game two years ago," coach Fraser said, hitting the lights as the film started ticking through the projector. "'78 was a *team*."

'78 was indeed a team, and John Fraser was indeed a coach. He wasn't technically ship's captain, he was first mate, but that was in name only because our titular head coach could have passed for Alan Hale III – but rather than the Skipper's affable good intent, our guy's bemused smiley demeanor was laced with wholly unfounded streaks of condescension. It was Fraser keeping our ship run tight.

"Watch this," he told us. "Watch Mike Ernst."

I blurted, "Hey! I know that guy."

The film showed Exeter in punt formation at midfield. My future Harvard recruiting host was one of the two up-backs positioned as a blocker in a two-point stance one yard behind the offensive linemen. Instead of long-snapping the ball to the punter, the Exeter center tried to send a short snap directly to Ernst but it went way above his head. He had to leap straight up, stretching as high as he could to one-hand the ball. He tucked it as he landed and broke through the line before the defense knew what happened. With only the Tabor deep man to contend with, Mike Ernst executed a flawless Last-Man-Planting maneuver. Every running back's dad taught him this one: When it's just you and one other guy, you run right at him. This throws all the advantage in your favor. If he commits toward you, you got him; just cut to daylight and you'll leave him in the dust. If he plants his heels, you got him; cut hard one way or the other. If he follows, immediately cut back across his body and you're home free while he's left tangled up in his jock. If he *doesn't* follow, you just keep on trucking and blow right by him. (My father added by way of editorial, "It's so basic – just run right at him – that a lot of guys overthink it and start that shake and bake shit.") Mike Ernst made a full on bee-line for the badly miscast punt returner. About fifteen yards from his prey, he angled 45 degrees to the right, setting the trap, reminiscent of Jay McGee against Waltham. The Tabor defender, God bless him, started after Mike who immediately cut back, surgically relieving the guy of his athletic supporter.

"You know Mike Ernst," Coach Fraser asked as we watched him cross the goal line in rich cinematic black-and-white at ¾ speed.

"Yep."

"A *player*."

———

If the football atmosphere at Exeter left something to be desired vis-a-vis Brockton's, that divide was not nearly as vast as the canyon of culture shock separating the Prep School overall experience from that of Public School.

It started with little cosmetic differences, like mandatory jackets and ties for boys at all meals, classes, and assemblies during the week – which, honestly, I kind of liked – and although the lifting of the dress code on Saturdays was a generally celebrated liberty among the perennial students, we PGs scarcely noticed or cared, being much too disturbed by the very idea of *Saturday classes!* We were all accustomed back home to encountering minimal distraction, mind and body, on game days.

Not all of the differences struck so sourly. For one thing, there was history around every corner – actual American history. The namesakes of every edifice, playing field, academic program, and even reading room, rang a bell to one degree or another. You'd pick up peculiar tidbits of Exeter trivia here and there, so oddly specific that they could hardly be mere apocrypha, like how the Academy had the most alumni in the College Football Hall of Fame of any high school.

Every day on our way to practice, we smacked the Amos Alonzo Stagg memorial stone. When I was reminded that the author of *A Separate Peace* was an alum, I swore I knew which tree on the river bank Phineas had fallen from.

Come to find, the school had given rise to a flourishing literary tradition. Two of the biggest books of the era were penned by Exonians: Peter Benchley '57 (*Jaws*) and John Irving '61 (*The World According to Garp*). Later in the semester I would be introduced to the work of James Agee, '28, whose line by line prose is nearer to poetry than any other novelist's, and although I'd had little more than a passing interest in the Literati of the times, I was certainly familiar with the names George Plimpton and Gore Vidal, and I'd even heard of Salinger's talented nymphet, Joyce Maynard – Academy alumni all. (Bringing myself up to speed on Ms. Maynard's work, I learned that she had not only won the same annual nationwide scholastic writing award that such luminaries as Bernard Malamud, Truman Capote, Sylvia Plath, John Updike, Donald Barthelme, and Joyce Carol Oates had all managed to win once in their own time, but she won it no less than five times between 1966 - 1971.)

At one of our biweekly assemblies that year, the featured speaker was indeed Gore Vidal '43. He mentioned his new novel, *Creation*, and then immediately opened the floor to questions, garnering a standing ovation when he answered an inquiry about his reasons for deciding against college.

"After graduating from here I didn't need it."

The subjects of our assemblies ranged from the ridiculous to the sublime: a faculty talent show one week; a lecture the next on human rights by Elie Wiesel.

It soon became clear to me that Phillips Exeter Academy was really quite something.

The main and most daunting adjustment, in my opinion, involved dealing with the overwhelming increase of homeworkload. Similar to the way our past Loves pale once we're floored by the real thing, I'd had no idea homework could be like this. Comparatively, handling my Public school "workload" was as challenging as controlling the depth of my bath water, whereas Prep school meant retarding the flow of an ocean tide using sandcastle pails and shovels.

The teachers of my four classes routinely meted out homework assignments requiring 1.5 to 2 hours of reading and/or study per class per night – in other words, a bit too much. I found this by turns unreasonable, unfair, and finally unmanageable. None of them seemed to understand or care that I had other classes in addition to theirs. I dealt with it the only way I knew how, by cutting corners wherever possible, which usually meant skimming through sections of the required reading in European History and in 20th Century Literature.

After a few weeks of this, it struck me: Not only did the teachers realize they were overloading us but, rather than the supercilious martinets I had taken them for, they were most likely working in tandem for the long-term benefit of their charges. By having too much assigned work for the time allotted, we were being taught perforce to prioritize tasks and to juggle and manage multiple difficult problems at once; in short, Exeter was more concerned with

preparing us for the greater rigors of collegiate study than with any short term information regurgitation.
—

To keep myself abreast of Brockton's progress, I made it a point of picking up a *Globe* every Sunday; Tuesdays too, to track my old teammates' individual rankings for Scoring, TD Passes and Receptions.

By mid-October, the Boxers in general and in particular couldn't have been faring any better. The team was undefeated, Jay was the Division-1 Scoring Leader, Johnny Hancock led in TD Receptions, and QB John Asack (Chuck's backup the previous 2 seasons) led TD Passes. [Future Perfect: All three would finish the season atop their respective categories.]

Meanwhile, north of the border, during a late season practice in the week leading up to our ultimate grudge match against Andover, while working on our goal line offense, I was genuinely startled and, to be honest, somewhat taken aback, to hear one of the coaches scream, "Dunn!"

"Yuh?"

"Are you afraid to stick your nose in there and take a hit?"

"Whuh?"

It was Coach Wharf, our team's obligatory young firebrand line coach. "These guys are working their ass off out here. Look at them! Fighting in the mud every down to gouge a hole out for you to hit! The least you can do is hit the damn thing."

"The hole was closing, so—"

"Nope, nope, you just gave up on it. This is football. You gotta take a hit once in a while whether you like it or not."

Alright, they got me. If this was a practical joke, they got me.

"Run it again! Same play!"

"Hold it, hold it—"

"Same play!"

"Yeah, but hold on. I bail on a hole when there's nothing there. When it's the right thing to do."

"Same again!"

Saliva was welling in my mouthpiece. "Screw it," I spluttered, tagging his shoulder with a spray of spittle. "Sorry–" I interrupted myself, swiping my muddy palm on his jacket. Again, "Sorry–" Then, "You want me to bang straight into the first guy I see? Like I got something to prove? Let's do it. No problem."

"I want to see you take on a tackler for a change!"

For a fucking change? I practically shouted, "No problem!"

On the next play, if I had made a cut – or just leaned a little – this way or that, I'd have had a good shot at breaking the goal line, but I zeroed in on the noseguard's numbers. He gave a snarling growling inch and I dug hard for more but that inch was taken right back as I was piled over by a bunch of tacklers for no gain.

Coach Wharf was yelling, "At a way, Dunn! See? That's the way to bring the fight to them!"

"Words of a 1-and-4 coach," I grumbled on my way back to the huddle (not one of my finer moments, granted), setting a few members of our O-line a-chuckle.*

"What's that, Dunn?"

"... I'nt say nothin," I muttered.

"Got something on your mind?"

I bit into my mouthpiece. I sighed to cool and collect myself. I said, "Who was it said, 'Run to daylight?'"

"Gayle Sayers [incorrect] said that."

I gave a diplomatic shrug.

"You're not Gayle Sayers," Wharf reminded everyone unnecessarily.

Another more emphatic shrug preceded a nodding and apparently too loud utterance (for Wharf heard it): "And you're not George Halas."

The blinding glare that shot through his eyes could have been taken a few different ways, I guess. I took it to mean it was fortunate for me that there was only one game left in the season. Otherwise, our little contretemps might have developed into a depth-chart-shuffling feud.**

*[Record in Fact: Technically our record at the time was 1 win, 4 close losses, and 1 very close tie. The fact that our entire season would span but seven games – we were done for the year on October 25th – gives as clear an indication of where Sports stood in the eyes of the New England Preparatory School Athletic Council (NEPSAC) as one could expect, which is to say it was undoubtedly valued (Exeter required all students to participate in a sport in each of the fall, winter, and spring seasons, be it Varsity, JV, Freshman or Club), but it was held in proper perspective. Athletics were important, absolutely, but not *too* important.]

**[Feuder's Note: Evidently I had made a bigger deal out of this quarrel than did young Coach Wharf. (Maybe he'd been trying to make some kind of example out of me to light a fire under our asses before the big game – don't know; we never discussed it further.) He and I ended up on good terms, though, no hard feelings, getting a kick out of each other whenever we happened to cross paths on campus from the end of the football season on.]
—

The morning of our 100th game against Andover started out completely overcast, as expected, with a fearsome forecast on the way. As of yet no precipitation had formed but the tumid atmosphere felt like it was definitely going to burst to the high heavens sooner than later. A few students on their way to breakfast already had umbrellas with them. Otherwise, it was just like any other Saturday morning at the Academy, i.e., casual dress code with a half-day of classes through which I was determined to cruise on autopilot, under the radar, expending the utleast amount of energy possible until it was time to go get ready for the big game.

Latin class ended on time without turbulence, so my auto-pilot flight plan was still right on schedule. The next class was Math, taught by lacrosse coach and all around good guy, Mr. Bergofsky. A former athlete himself (standout midfielder on the national powerhouse Johns Hopkins lacrosse team in the early '70s), I think he sympathized with the football players in his class that day. We did a quick review of last night's homework (a 10-step computer problem) and then rather than keep us for the entire hour he said each of us could leave early but only after writing his own new program that would run successfully on the big computer in the back of the room, using the homework program as an example. With that, Mr. Bergofsky wished us luck against Andover and bade us adieu, leaving us to our own devices as we happily set to work.

Dirt was first to the computer and the first one out the door, with forty minutes to spare.

Radoccia was right behind him. He had gotten his cast off the week before but there was no chance of him playing in the game. At the door he said, "You good, Radoche?"

"This fucking thing…" I mumbled. "Yeah, I'm alright."

"You sure?"

"Get out of here."

A few minutes later, Tim Hickey got his program to run.

One by one our other classmates took their leave until only Walt Donovan and I remained. A tough tight end from Medford, Walt's a major dude. We took turns at the computer for twenty minutes straight, faltering one after the other again and again like a couple of failures.

"FUCK!"

Nothing's more brain-drainingly aggravating than technology you can't make work.

"What time is it, Walt?"

"Time to get to the stadium."

"No shit!"

Walt said, "You know the main problem with computers? They only do what you tell them to do – not what you want them to do."

"What time you got?"

"It's rare situations like this," he said sheepishly. "Very rare… That I might not mind being a left-brain guy for one day."

"Fuck those guys."

"10:55, Mr. Dunn."

"Jesus! And kickoff's at 1 today?"

Walt cried, "Bingo! Got it!"

"It ran?"

"Under the wire, baby!"

I sang. "Walterrrr!"

"Let's go kick some Andover ass."

"I got to get mine to run first."

The befuddlement on Walt's face was genuine. Had he missed something? Was I pulling his leg? He said, "You coming?"

"I'll be right there."

"It's eleven o'clock. Class dismissed, go in peace."

"Get out of here."

"Alright then…" Walt said. "BYEF."

I kept at it alone in the classroom for another fifteen futile minutes until my brain hurt too much to continue. I finally spewed, "Fuck this!"

I would deal with Mr. Bergofsky's wrath on Monday.

—

If you ever wanted to see thousands of onlookers evacuate jam-packed bleachers in a drenched and orderly fashion, the second quarter of Exeter and Andover's 100th football game was the time and place to be.

The few remaining hardy fans, members of my own family among them, were treated to an understandably low-scoring slogfest which was lost, 14-6. My personal highlights, such as they were, included withstanding a clock-cleaning halfback option pass in a failed attempt to hit Walt for a sneaky score at the end of the first half; a 55-yard kickoff return to open the second half; a short 4th quarter touchdown run (which the *Globe* attributed with unexpected formality to, ahem… Gregory Dunn).

On the way to the locker room at halftime, a hunched sopping Exeter fan said, "Dunn: Colombo says hi."

In one of his hilarious letters, Chuck had foretold of such a verbatim message. The messenger was one of his freshman roommates at Harvard, the brilliant John Moore, former Academy four-year boy. As trying as the first half of football had been (a mere thirteen offensive plays run for us, most of which in the face of typhoon winds; being laid flat with the wind knocked out of me on

317

the option pass to Walt; zero points scored), I couldn't help cracking a smile at Moore.

―

The following Tuesday when I opened the *Globe* School Sports section at my dorm room desk to check on the status of my Boxer brethren, I was surprised and quite well pleased at the headline "Jay McGee ranks with Brockton's best" which ran beneath a large photo of him scoring one of his long touchdowns against Waltham last Thanksgiving. The article opened, "At Brockton, they breed running backs like the Baltimore Orioles breed pitchers." That was a compliment at the time, believe me, and an audacious one at that.

I heard myself say "Wow" out loud.

The reporter certainly had an excellent eye for talent: John "Jay" McGee would go on to win the 1980 scoring title *by ten touchdowns*. He would win it the following year too, shattering in the process just about every BHS rushing record there was.

In the interview, good old Jay was gallant enough to make a point of mentioning my name. It made my day reading, "I gained experience on the varsity and Greg Dunn would tell me what to be aware of. He helped me a lot."

When I said "Wow" again, my roommate came up behind me to peek over my shoulder.

"Somebody you know?"

"Former teammate of mine," I told him. (I didn't want to say, "Yep, ahem... Got m'name in the paper!")

It was funny, a couple weeks later, at my desk with the sports section again. Among the small college rundowns was a picture of a Tufts running back hurdling a Bates defender about whom the caption was none too flattering. The would-be tackler, unfortunately mentioned by name, "got nothing but air" when he reached for the runner "who jumped over him and picked up 11 yards." The funny part was that the acrobatic Tufts running back was none other than the scourge of BHS Thanksgivings past, John Giusti.

My roommate heard me say, "Hah! Wow."

Looking over my shoulder, he said, "You know that guy, too?"

"Yes!"

The funny thing is, I felt like I really did know him, what with the profound connection he'd made to Brockton's collective psyche a couple seasons ago.

———

Home for Christmas break that year, I took up my old spot in the parlor with Dad, leaning back against the hassock.

He said, "You working on applications?"

"Oh, no."

"Been typing away for a while in there."

"It's a story. I was typing it up."

"School?"

I shook my head, trying not to seem like I was being intentionally vague or cavalier, "No…"

"What, like a short story? That you wrote?"

I was nodding. I wanted to tell my father all about it, about unexpected inspiration, about a new world of dreams and goals that I still didn't even understand, but somehow everything I had to say came out in a nearly mute, "Yeah…"

Hear, hear! Cheers right now to A.J. Dunn, Sr. In our house, the subject of one of us creating any kind of piece of writing had never once come up in conversation. Dad rolled with it without so much as a blink or bend of brow. "Yuh? What's it about?"

Now I had the opposite problem. It was impossible to explain what I was going for in just a few tidy sound bites, so I replied with the title of the piece, "A Game of Chess."

Then my father said those magic words. "Can I read it?"

The next night when he came home from work, he had with him a pristine hardcover journal, the front cover of which had inlaid gold print 'BFD.'

"We use these at the firehouse to log the alarm calls that come in."

"Oh, wow." I riffled through the three hundred college ruled pages. "Thank you, Dad. This is great."

"You fill that one up, I'll get you another one."

So, not to put too fine a nib on the quill, but that year at Exeter was, among everything else, where my romance with writing first began to flower.

—

After football had wrapped up, I was perfectly fine with kicking back for a while, fulfilling my winter sport requirement with house basketball, or club squash, but somehow Dirt talked me into running indoor track with him. He said, "Frase is coach. It'll be fun." Other than that, I can't for the life of me remember a single "pro" that might have offset any of the self-evident "con" entries on the ledger, but there we were in our first meet of the season versus Andover, neck-and-neck, digging hard to edge each other out for a distant 2nd place in the 300, clearly outclassed by Andover's guy, when Dirt pulled a hamstring. We didn't know it then, but he wouldn't be ready to run another race for the rest of the season.

I scored my share of points that year but I was basically an also-ran. Our team was actually pretty good. There wasn't the depth of talent like that great Brockton team my junior year, but we had a couple bona fide stars. Our distance runner, Sean Lawlor, was undefeated in league meets, and ranked throughout New England. Brian Donahue at the shot put was even nationally ranked. He broke the existing track record at every meet we competed in that year.

Like I say, I earned my share of points, so don't be dismayed if you're touring the field house some day and you notice that the 1980-81 Indoor Track Team photo does not bear my likeness. Dirt, if you can believe it, was informed that since he had failed to score the requisite amount of points to earn himself a varsity letter in Track, his presence at the team photo would therefore not be abided.

Well, sir!

In light of such ill treatment, my loyalty knows no bounds. For wasn't it my friend Dirt himself who had convinced me to go out for

Track in the first place? Flush with righteous indignation, solidarity, and perhaps a touch of postprandial drowsiness, I carried out a near Parksian display of civil disobedience by boycotting (i.e., napping through) the photo session.

—

Recruiting visits that winter were somehow far less fraught than before. Maybe it was naive of me, but I kind of felt like Harvard was in the bag, goofy as that sounds. I was Honor Roll my first semester at the Academy, though, and Coach Corbin had stated pretty clearly that if I did thus then they'd do thus and Dunny'd be *in* like the proverbial *Flynn*.

I had applied to a few schools, but I was only really serious about Amherst College and Harvard.

Walt and I drove through the Berkshires in a blizzard to visit Amherst. We had to stop multiple times to scrape the ice off his wipers and headlights, and to reassure ourselves as to our precise location vis-a-vis the ravines. We arrived at Amherst just after 10pm.

On the other hand, my visit to Harvard was a ball, hosted by one Armond C. Colombo, Jr. We sang our heads off to "Sympathy for the Devil" at an outdoor party in Harvard Yard that night like it was the Barlows' house, circa March, 1979.

Earlier that day, the coaches office was just like it was the year before. Dick Corbin was there, along with Coach Leo Fanning. Even the coach in the corner was there.

"We don't have to go through the whole shebang again," Coach Corbin said. "You already know what's what. Is Chuck here yet? Where's Chuck?"

"Dunny," the coach in the corner said. "Flutie's here this weekend too."

"Oh." I was familiar with the name; Natick quarterback.

Corbin asked, "Who's his host?"

"Steve Ernst," Coach Fanning said.

"Dunny, keep an eye on this guy. Got to show him a good time."

I laughed at his joke, but the coach wasn't kidding. He said, "I'm serious. I think we're close with him."

Although a part of me wanted to say, "Hey, I'm being recruited too, you know!" it was comforting that they regarded me as part of the crew already.

Corbin said, "We are close. This kid's the real deal, Dunny. We need him. I'm talking Ivy League championship a couple years down the road."

"I'll see what I can do!"

———

Come spring, the thought of playing baseball for Exeter was amusing for a few days but Mr. Bergofsky surprised me and Dirt after class by suggesting we go out for the lacrosse team.

I said, "I've never played."

"Me either."

"Both of you guys are athletes," the coach said. "Better still, you're both running backs. Running backs are naturals for lacrosse."

"Jim Brown," I said.

"That's right."

It turned out that Dirt and I picked up the new sport pretty fast. By our season opener, we were the starting defensemen, compensating for our lack of game experience with a rough-and-tumble style and sheer tenacity.

When vaunted Pinkerton Academy came to town, I was assigned to cover their star attackman who had scored seven goals last game. He was quick on his feet, constantly in motion, but I was right there with him and I held him scoreless through the first period. The guy's stick work was super slick, though. The one goal he did score came when I figured out that he liked driving to his right, so I committed hard in front of the net and he just went lefty and scored a no-look behind-the-neck layup like Larry Bird.

I missed a few games with a cracked clavicle, but luckily I was able to return before the full-fledged herd shunning kicked in.

During the Choate game, while serving time in the penalty box for a flagrant foul, I heard a voice from up in the bleachers behind me, "Gregga!"

It's always so damn nice to look in the crowd and see your dad at your game. I had no idea he was driving up from Massachusetts, and I had absolutely no idea he was driving up from Massachusetts with the one and only Jay McGee in tow. It made me wish I'd familiarized myself better with the rules of lacrosse before I laid out that unsuspecting Choate midfielder earlier. He had just passed the ball when I cleaned his fucking clock, much to the vociferous disapproval of his teammates and the refs alike. Come to find out, it is only permissible to body check an opposing player if the player is within five feet of a ball *that is on the ground*. Although when I met up with my father and Jay later, the first thing Jay said was, "Nice hit."

"I got him good," I agreed.

"You're number forty-three in lacrosse too?"

"Of course."

Jay smiled, "Were you in football?"

"Of course!"

"Right!"

I said, "Dad, Mum didn't come?"

"Ma's working on the financial aid packet for Harvard before the deadline. She wanted to come."

"Mr. Colombo said she can call him if she has any questions on it."

"She did. The very first question, she said, 'How much should we put for expected family contribution?' Colombo said, 'Zero! You expect to contribute nothing!'"

The next time I saw my dad was at our graduation ceremony on June 5th – a *scorcher*. We who would graduate were arranged outside in rigid rows of folding chairs, sweltering alphabetically, trying to think cool thoughts. I heard Glynnis Dunn, seated to my immediate left, groan under her breath as the endless succession of arcane graduation awards, scholarships, prizes, medals, and cups somehow continued on and on and on and on again and again and on again. I recognized none of the names of the four-year boys and girls being so honored. Glynnis counted out in a whisper "Forty" when yet another special award was announced, her forehead and cheeks flushed not unfetchingly with pin points of perspiration. The only graduation award holding even the least little bit of interest for me was the as yet unbestowed Yale Cup, presented to the student who best combines athletic proficiency with good academic standing, or some such; in other words, the scholar athlete award. My money was on Lawlor or Donahue, although there were dozens of standout athletes to choose from competing in the range of sports at Exeter: hockey, tennis, baseball, swimming & diving, soccer, basketball, gymnastics, lacrosse, wrestling, golf, track & field, softball, field hockey, etc., etc.

As if reading my mind, Principal Kurtz recited, "...athletic proficiency combined with good standing..."

I was trying to remember any other sports we had at the Academy. Fencing? Skiing?

Glynnis Dunn elbowed me, "Hey, that's you!"

Wow, she was right. I went up to the podium, shook hands with the Principal, accepted a fine looking spittoon-sized silver cup, and carried it back to my seat where Glynnis tested its heft while I read the card that came with it:

YALE CUP

5 June 1981

Gregory,

Congratulations!
Please keep this cup nearby, and return it to Mr. Thurneyssen or me before you leave. Your name is engraved on the cup, but it must remain here at Exeter.

David Dimmock
Prize Committee

—

I want to make one thing perfectly clear: Dick Corbin is my kind of guy:

a.) He gives it to you straight.

b.) When it comes to promises, he takes the old old old old world position that a man who makes a promise runs a debt.

c.) He honors his debts like a gentleman: In full, on time, no fuss.

It had been just a few words and a handshake the previous year in the coaches office when he diagrammed for me the surefire, albeit circuitous and easier said than done, path to Harvard's hallowed halls. I kept my end of the bargain, graduating with honors from the Academy, so he kept his; enough said.

—

The first week of September, my father dropped me and my footlocker off in bustling Harvard Yard on the front terrace of my dorm, Matthews Hall.

"Alright, I'm going to hit the road. You all set?"

I said, "Yup."

"So this is the famous Harvard Yard? It's nice in here – the trees."

"Dad," I said, going in for a hug. "Thank you, and Ma, so much."

"We love you, kid."

"I love you."

"Don't let any assholes around here try to buffalo you."

"No, no," I assured him.

"You got in through the front door just like everybody else. They got nothing on you."

"Oh, I know."

"Here, take a couple bucks for your pocket."

Upstairs my two roommates and their parents were milling around the fairly spacious common area. They had waited for me to show up to sort out the issue of which guy would get the single bedroom, and which two would spend the first semester bunking together in the double.

Greg Kouvelas, a Merrillville, Indiana, quarterback and David Stampfli from rural San Diego looked like nice enough guys. The quarterback's dad suggested, "Shall we draw lots? What can we use...?"

Lots struck me as a tad formal, not to mention unfriendly. "Oh, no need," I said. "Everybody got a coin?"

The Stampflis weren't carrying change so Kouvelas handed David one of his coins.

"Okay, everybody flip."

Mrs. Kouvelas said, "But how do—?"

"Odd man gets the single. Tails."

David Stampfli said, "Heads."

"So I can't possibly win," Kouvelas laughed. "How about two out of three?"

Stampfli and I shook him off.

"But how—?"

"Heads."

I gave a modest shrug while the parents nodded at the whole process suspiciously.

Putting my stuff away in the single, I heard a knock at our door and, "Hello-ooo! Greg Dunn in here?"

"Chook!"

"Welcome to Harvard Yard, brother."

"Thanks. And a happy birthday to you."

"Hah! Oh, yeah, it's your mother's birthday too, right?"

Chuck had been on campus with the varsity team for a couple weeks already. In those days, Ivy League freshmen weren't eligible to play varsity football, so my first day of Freshman practice was still yet to come.

After I introduced him to my roommates, he asked me, "So how was it?"

"How was what?"

"The farewell."

"I mean, it's not like I was going off to Vietnam," I said. "Home's what, 28 miles away?"

"I know, but still – it didn't get a little emotional?"
"Oh, yuh, of course. A little…"
"Your Mum?"
"No, me!"

—

Entering that first year of college, I was still very much undecided as to a field of concentration. The default choice in those days, and by far the most popular among football players, was Economics. So if pressed, it's the field I would have gone with, that is until we received our first papers back in Expository Writing, a required freshman course. Our first assignment was intended to provide our section leader (local poet William Corbett) with an idea of where everybody stood, writingwise. In lieu of grading this first round of papers, Corbett returned them with a brief handwritten comment at the end. I had to reread mine a couple times before it sunk in: "I'm lost and it's somewhat repulsive. Not to be lost but to be here at all." [The palliative 'somewhat' inserted after the fact via editorial caret.]

That was the moment I knew: English was the major for me.

—

The freshman members of the Holy Cross junior varsity came to play our freshman team early that season at our place. I think we did pretty well, considering they were a scholarship school. It was a close low-scoring game. For their part, the Crusaders' attack was limited to pounding the rock between the tackles with its powerful tailback, none other than your friend and mine, Sanford McMurtry. He must have had forty carries that day if he had a-one; very impressive.

—

Meanwhile, back in Brockton, Jay continued to dominate. For the second year in a row he led Division-1 in scoring, and for the third year in a row he led the Boxers to the Super Bowl.

On the night before the big game, Chuck and I were pounding some beers in his dorm room with a few friends. Toward the end of the night, as he or I were sometimes inclined to do, Chuck sat himself down on the couch amid the music and festivity and promptly dozed off.

One of his roommates thought it might be funny to reward his early retirement with a friendly shaving cream crown, or some other prankish adornments.

"Naw, no no," I said.

"What do you mean, No?"

"Not happening, fellas."

"Really?"

"Nobody's treating him like a jerk."

"Who made you—?"

"It's not happening."

Don't get me wrong, I'm no kind of fighter but I never went in for that fratboy crap.

"It's just a goof."

"Everybody's going to leave him alone. Unless you want a broken beer bottle up your ass."

"Come on, Dunna…"

I crashed on the couch that night after Chuck had gone to bed and I'd made quite sure I would be the last one closing my eyes.

The next day in the *Globe*, there was a big close-up of Jay posing in a button-down shirt, with the article headline, "Oh, Jay…" presumably in reference to the great running back of the day, O.J. Simpson. Chuck's brothers, Donny and Danny, drove in and we all went over to The Heights in Chestnut Hill for the Division-1 Super Bowl. I bumped into my Dad and Uncle Kevin in the crowd before the game.

Kevin said, "That's all you're wearing, t-shirt and dungaree jacket? It's supposed to snow."

"Nah'm good."

Jay scored a 45-yard touchdown run on the third play of the game. Watching from the sideline when he took off, I was suddenly overcome and I chased him all the way into the endzone, clapping him on the back so hard that he almost went down. Unfortunately, the snow came indeed, and the good guys lost this one.

By next football season, the fall of 1982, our old pal, Johnny Hancock, was a sophomore on the Brown University team. When Brown traveled to Cambridge for our game, he and I had planned for him to stay over at my dorm afterwards for a night of fun in and around Harvard Square. Although I had a JV game scheduled the next day at Holy Cross, what could I do? My old buddy John was in town and it also happened to be Halloween, a guaranteed good time at any college campus. The stars had aligned too well for us not to make the most of it.

After our game (neither of us got in), we started things off with a visit to Chuck's dorm where we drank cans of Schlitz for a couple hours and listened to one of Chuck's King Crimson albums. John and I then ventured out into the festive evening together on foot, stopping by the Pi Eta once and Whitney's multiple times. Soon, what started as a promising college night turned out to be a long strange trip indeed, about which the less said the better...

Back at my dorm, I think I thought I dozed for a while, or I dreamed I slept, but next thing I knew the sun was up and so was I, dragging my jangled ass across the river to meet the team bus.

On the all too brief ride to Worcester, a bed of little damp clam shells sprouted on the back of my neck and on my forehead, clinging there like leaky carbuncles the whole way.

This was one of those otherworldly slow motion experiences (not the good kind of slow motion) where just being awake felt absurd. It would have been taxing enough to even attend a football game in my condition (all that air all over you; all the requirements; *other people*), let alone play in it. I recalled an old and oft ignored Hangover Note: Hangovers and sports don't mix.

The sky above Fitton Field that day was overcast and vivid, nauseously vivid. Looking up into the massive home side stands, I remembered having watched Pete Colombo from up there a few years earlier (I still have the ticket stub) as he led the Holy Cross offense, completing passes to Phil Johnson in the process, on this very field. Ronnie Perry, Jr., had sat a couple rows down from me. People came up to introduce themselves to him throughout the game.

I waded through the miasma of our pre-game warm ups using someone else's legs. I was thinking maybe if I was lucky, and if everything worked out just right, I'd be injured somehow during jumping jacks.

Holy Cross was a big, talented, scholarship team. Our work was cut out for us.

No one in the empty stadium was more surprised than I was when on our first possession I took a Chuck Colombo screen pass fifty-something yards for a touchdown which would put us up 6-0 were it not for a nullifying clipping call.

From there our offense was pretty well bottled up, hardly venturing beyond the Holy Cross forty. Other than floating my way through that dreamlike fraudulent touchdown, the highlight of the game for me was a second-half punt return of about ten, eleven yards; or, more specifically, the double-crossing espionage which led up to it.

On our punt return team, I was the lone deep man. Rather than joining the other ten guys in the huddle, where the direction of our punt return play would be shared in secret, the powers that be had long since determined that it was most expedient and beneficial to our cause to have the punt returner immediately take his place downfield where he could presumably settle himself on tenterhooks until the huddle broke and one of his teammates signaled him with the call. Since the use of flags and flares to communicate the signal might come across as a tad theatrical, and since electronic arrows were at that time logistically unfeasible (it was 1982), the signalman – a player elected by the coaches for his sober judgment and trustworthiness, or entirely by chance – would turn from the huddle and deliver the verdict to his distant teammate by banging a fist in centurion guard salute against the chest plate of his shoulder pads. The fiendish brilliance of that particular code (hey, this was Harvard after all) lay in its simplicity. With the signaler facing me, a punch to his heart signaled Punt Return Right, whereas striking the other side of his chest would signal – wait for it! – a Punt Return *Left*. (What'd I tell you? Brilliant.)

Holy Cross had only punted a few times in the first half but, having a somewhat cynical side when it comes to coincidences, I suspected that the several consecutive punt return ass-kickings I had thus far undergone might have been the result of those crafty Crusaders having somehow deciphered our elaborate coding system. At halftime I requested a sidebar with Gerry Leone, our punt return team's honorable centurion guard.

"Would you object to mixing up the return signal a little?"

Gerry shook his head, smiling. "Couldn't hurt."

"No shit."

"How come," he squinted. "You think they're onto us?"

Recalling the old Dunn family sock-pull-in-the-huddle trick, I suggested that if and when Holy Cross was to punt again, Gerry should send a signal straight from the huddle. With his back still to me, he should pull up his right sock for a Right Return, or his left sock for a Left Return. Then, when he turned to face me – and this is where our cunning little stratagem took on Sitting Bull / Crazy Horse proportions – Gerry should signal me in the usual chest thumping way to indicate the *opposite* direction! (See? Huh? Yuh?)

So, later in the game when our defensive coaches eventually yelled, "Punt return! Punt return!" I hurried out to take my position, snickering to myself. Backpedaling to somewhere around the fifteen-yard line, I focused on Leone in the huddle. Sure enough, he casually tugged at his right sock. A moment later the huddle clapped and broke and Gerry gave the opposite decoy signal for all to see.

Coach McCarthy shouted, "No! No!"

McCarthy was a good guy, a local guy. During our first day of double sessions that season, he had seen my name on the front of my helmet and asked if I was any relation to Jimmy Dunn.

"He's my uncle."

"Oh, yuh? We played in the park league together," he told me. "Tell him I was asking for him."

"I will."

"Your uncle was really something," McCarthy said, nodding to make sure I understood the gravity of his compliment. He cracked a smile, "Hot shit, too. We called him 'Dunzo.' That's what we knew him by." I watched the coach assessing his first impression of me, comparing me side by side in his mind with the memory of Uncle Jim, and clearly finding me wanting. "Yeah, hell of an athlete, your uncle," he concluded. "Hell of an athlete. And they say his kid brother was even better than he was."

Now, somewhere around the fifteen yard line, trying my best to blend into the Fitton Field scenery, making a point of not looking Coach McCarthy's way, I patted the air, nodding as nonchalantly as I could to let him know the situation was firmly in hand. I didn't think there was any reason for Holy Cross to have tied his outburst to the phony return signal, so all was well.

"Dunzo, no!"

Jesus Christ…

"Dunzo! Dunzo! It's Return–!"

I screamed, "I *GOT* IT!"

When all was said and done, we had fought fiercely but our side ended up on the short end of this defensive struggle, which is to say that for most of the day we found ourselves on the defensive; and every down was a struggle.

As the tingly cloudful afternoon came mercifully to an end, the final score felt for me somehow fitting, spiced with the arsenic of just desserts. O' Fair Harvard had managed to tally zero legal touchdowns to go along with a field goal in every quarter other than the last three, while we managed to hold the Cross to barely fifty-seven points.

—

I ended up playing in a few varsity games that sophomore season at garbage time, tallying a few carries of which nothing notable came. Truth be told, the football fire had been dying out for some time and it showed in my preparation (barely minimal) as well as my performance (hardly special). Toward the end of the season I wasn't even going to daily Position Meetings anymore. When Greek- and Chinese-to-me formations would be called at practice, I'd drift over to Chuck as the huddle broke so he could direct me in our shorthand where to go and what to do.

In our final game of the season, Harvard's 99th versus Yale (for what it's worth, if I held on for just one more season, I'd be able to say I played in the 100th Exeter-Andover game and the 100th Harvard-Yale game too), I was granted yet another unobstructed view of "the writing on the wall." By the 4th quarter of a game we were winning handily, reserves were being called in to replace the starters. I was standing beside running backs coach, Larry Glueck, when he called out, literally right over my head, the name of a plucky junior halfback who had only one arm. Then later, when Yale was lining up for an onside kick, the same kid was put out there for onside kick return. A flabbergasted Yale coach was screaming, "Kick it to the guy with one arm!"

—

Mike Ernst and I eventually, seemingly inevitably, became good friends at Harvard. One night that winter we were hanging out in Chuck's dorm room playing cribbage at his coffee table and drinking his beers with the oldies on the stereo when who should come walking in but Chuck!

"Fellas," he said, ushering his lovely girlfriend in.

We both stood up. Alicia frowned at our unnecessary formality, ordering us at ease by chopping the air with a dismissive salute. "Hi guys," she said, continuing straight to Chuck's bedroom. "Bye guys."

"Night, Aleash."

Alicia was the coolest of the cool so I assumed her slamming of the bedroom door was unintentional, or at least not intended for us.

Smiling innocently, I inquired of Chuck, "Back so soon? Thought you guys were going out."

"We stopped by the Pi and ended up just hanging there."

"Worthwhile goings on?"

"Mixed doubles beer pong tourney."

"Really? How'd you guys do?"

"I believe all beer pong objectives were achieved."

"Nudity?"

"Except for that."

"Want one of your beers," offered Mikey. "There's a couple more in there."

"A couple? When we left there was a whole case – ye blokes."

"We were trying to finish them off before you got back. Thought we had more time."

From the other side of the door we heard, "Chuck…?"

He winked on his way to join her. "Duty calls."

"Sorry, Charles," I apologized. "We've been drinking as fast as we can."

"Oh, Dunna," Chuck said. "Hockey game Tuesday night. Want to work it?"

"Goddamn right."

We watched him soundlessly open the bedroom door and saw his shaking head disappear into the darkness as the door slowly closed behind him.

Chuck ran the concession stand at Harvard hockey games and basketball games, so he hooked me and a couple other guys up with this nice little gig. It was fun and it put a few bucks in our pockets. Harvard had a great hockey program, so the Bright arena was usually packed. Sometimes my old BHS Health teacher, Mr. Ronkin, came to games. I didn't know which player he might have been there to see, but whenever I spotted Mr. Ronkin in line I made a point of being the one to take his order, and sent him off for free with a wink and a nod. Bob Neumeier from Channel Four also showed his surprisingly florid face at the concession stand between periods sometimes. He rated the wink and nod discount too.*

Mikey and I stayed put, playing our cards and drinking at a much more sober pace now that time was no longer an issue.

After a while we started hearing the unmistakably erotic strains of low feminine moaning.

"Fifteen-two, fifteen-four, pair-six," Mikey said, shrugging his eyebrows at me.

In the tacit sign language of accomplices everywhere, I nodded and delivered a mute shrug in return. Then I counted out my hand, "Double run for eight."

The moans continued in a regular pattern, with intervals of tantalizing silence serving as precursor to more mounting exhortations.

On our side of the door, we sang along as The Monotones espoused "The Book of Love" and we sang "Remember Then" with The Earls. When "Double Shot (of My Baby's Love)" ended, Mikey had to admit with a complimentary cock of the head, "Go, Chuck."

Once things had finally died down, we heard Alicia put a gavel to the proceedings with an exhausted, "Oh... man... *whew*..."

Another couple songs played and then Chuck quietly emerged to hit the bathroom.

"Trips for six," I vamped, scoring my crib. "Right jack..."

With an apologetic sigh, he said, "Sorry."

"No, no – hey..."

"She's embarrassed."

"Nonsense." "Nah, come on..."

Chuck winced. "So you did hear her? Throwing up?"

*[Brush with Greatness: My one brush with true pro sports greatness came when I crossed paths with Bobby Orr in the subterranean tunnel beneath the Bright hockey rink before a game. (Actually, this was our second meeting, Dad, Joe, and I having lined up to meet him and shaky Mike Walton at the southside K-Mart when we first moved to Brockton. I recall after greeting them being struck by how huge the hands of both Bruins were, and it was this brief encounter that prompted me to ask my Little League coach if I could change jersey numbers for my second season on King's from Yaz's 8 to Walton's 11.) I was carrying a 50-ounce bag of pre-popped popcorn from the storage closet for use at that night's concessions when I saw Orr walking toward me in the narrow corridor. As we passed, I nodded, "Bobby." To which The One And Only replied, "How you doing, guy?" Please don't get me

wrong. I do NOT mean to suggest that Mr. Orr recognized me from our K-Mart encounter.]

―

Due as much to my own insistence as Harvard's suggestion, I took the next year off from school, but that didn't mean I wasn't keeping current with the College social events, and how the team was doing.

I met Dan Colombo and Jeff McDermott at The Bow & Arrow in Harvard Square for a few dollar drafts and 10-cent hot dogs before the 1983 season opener against Columbia. We drank and ate to our hearts' content until we heard Bob Gamere on the radio behind the bar announcing the Crimson's starting offense.

"At quarterback, senior from Brockton, Mass., Chuck Colombo..."

We scooted to the Stadium (at Harvard, everything's "the" uppercase Something, so obviously foremost that there could hardly be another) and took seats on the sunny visitor's side.

We watched Harvard move the ball at will. Chuck was having a very good game, en route to completing ten passes to his talented split end alone, former Woburn star and current roommate, John O'Brien. (Columbia should've had Dwayne Lopes covering him.)

"Too bad Armond's not here to see this," I said. "Who's Brockton got today?"

"New Bedford. Tommy's probably lighting it up."

Then, unless I was mistaken, I noticed that one of the assistants on the Columbia sideline was none other than my great Exeter coach, John Fraser.

"Frase!" I yelled. "Frase!"

When he turned, I jumped to my feet, waving urgently for a fair catch.

Recognizing me, my old coach shook his head. Oh, the *disappointment* on his face...

―

At our house that Thanksgiving, we were all enjoying the culinary treats of the season, as usual – all, that is, except my brother Rich who, instead of munching on Ma's hors d'oeuvres, was crunching and spitting ice chips. Such was the cross borne by high school wrestlers of the era.

When it came time for our family to sit at the table, Rich took his leave, dressed in sweats and vinyl, to jog the roads of Southfield rather than suffer all the succulent aromas of our holiday feasting in vain.

My brother's perseverance, and exceptional prowess of course, paid off as he won the state championship and New England championship that year (he's still the last BHS New England champ) and he became the first Boxer ever to go undefeated all four years of dual meets.

After dinner, Joe, long since home from the Air Force, ducked out somewhere. With the NFL on TV, I migrated from the hassock to the couch to the land of nod.

Later that night, dozing to the record player in our old bedroom, I was ripped from the clutches of Gardening at Night REM sleep – not so much awakened as aghast – by a creepy tapping at the window. For some reason, Joe had decided he would rather enter the house unannounced, via shushed infenestration.

I said, "What's going on?"

"Who's home?"

"Everybody. What's up?"

"Nothing," Joe said. "Nothing. Here, I wanted you to have this for your trip." He pulled a squashed wad of bills out of his pants pocket.

"Five hundred bucks," I said. "Where'd you get this?"

Quietly kicking off his mud-caked sneakers and peeling off his dirty clothes, Joe told me.

"I figured that'd set you up for a while over there."

"Jesus, Joe."

The storied fogs of London didn't seem half as portentous to me as the unprecedented cloud of underachievement which hung like a bronchial cough in the air at 134 Deanna Road, so I had booked my flight, traveling light, to Jolly Old England on PEOPLExpress.

"What day you leaving?"

"30th."

"You going stand-by? I'll drive you to the airport."

"No, I got a reservation on People's"

"Oh, $169 bucks one way, right?"

"Yup."

"I should be going with you."

I said, "I'd love it."

"I got shit to do, though," Joe thought out loud. "But this dough'll set you up over there for a while at least. It's about a buck-and-a-half per Brit pound right now. Has been forever."

On the morning of November 30th, Joe rolled out of bed all ready to go.

"All set?"

"We got a few minutes," I said, nodding at the TV: "Sam."

In typical Joe fashion, he understood instantly and doubled down with a declaration of Josephian unequivocality. "Samantha Stevens is the sexiest woman in Sitcom."

"All I know is, the final season she was on a bra boycott."

"Ahahhh..." he approved. "Is this a Serena?"

"Heh. No."

My father came in the parlor. "You got everything?"

"Yup." I shouldered my gym bag full of t-shirts, socks, underwear, and thumped my BFD journal (volume II).

"Let me make you some sandwiches for the plane."

At Logan Airport, we were early yet. Joe sat with me for a while as I started nervously eating my way through the day's meatloaf sandwich rations.

I chomped, "Want one?"

"Yeah, give me one of those before they're all gone," Joe said. "I should be going with you. Keep an eye on you."

"Meet me there," I chewed. "That sounds great."

"Nah, I got too much shit to do."

When it came time for me to be processed, I gave my big brother a hug.

"Any words of wisdom?"

Joe said without a pause, and I quote, "Travel in the guise of an American doo-wop singer."

—

I made the best of my time overseas: saw Paris, saw Madrid; worked for four-and-a-half months as a busboy at The Royal Academy of Arts in London; spent 40 days in Morocco. When I came home, I returned to Harvard for another semester, but enough was enough. I guess I never really got the point of college.

Fortunately, a few weeks later I fell ass-backwards into one of the best jobs I ever had in my life, working the door at a Harvard Square dive bar called the Piccadilly Filly. On busy nights, characters of every stripe piled in to join the roar. When it was slow, you might find me passing the entire night at the door in relaxed conversation with the owners or one or another of the Filly habitués.

One such slow night, manning my post, I was chatting with one of the locals. I don't remember the guy's name, but he was a friendly townie ("From *east* Cambridge," he would make a point of specifying); Irish kid, liked to talk and was good at it. He always showed up with a smiling greeting, "What's the buzz?"

To which I'd reply, "You got me!"

"Well if you find out, make sure you let me in on it."

He sported a blonde crew cut. I remember he had a dark-haired crew cut brother who was on the waiting list for the cops. I'll think of his name...

So he says, "Hey, I heard you went to Phillips Exeter?"

"For a PG year, yeah. You a fellow Exonian?"

"Begorrah! Do I look like I went to Phillips Exeter?"

"Sure. I mean... shit. I don't know."

"So where the hell'd you go to college, Mr. Exonian?"

I looked around, assuming it had been common knowledge all along. "I went here."

"Harvard?"

"Yeah."

"No. Really?"

"Thought you knew that."

"How would I have known that?"

"I don't know. How would you know I went to Exeter?"

"Grape vine scuttlebut."

"Heh!"

"And no offense, but you don't strike me as your typical Harvard guy. I mean, I knew you were from Brockton, you told me that…"

I didn't know what to say, so I just said, "I don't know."

"But Harvard, that's… You must've made really good marks in high school then. Right? Great marks. Great class rank. SATs and everything."

"Grades were pretty good, not great. I struggled in math the last few years."

"I had pretty good grades in high school too, bro, come on. Because I remember when I mentioned 'Ivy League' to my guidance counselor–"

"Where'd you go to high school?"

"Rindge & Latin."

I nodded.

"This guidance guy was a nut – what you might call 'refreshingly candid.' The second I said the words 'Ivy League', he pointed to a U.S. map on the wall behind his desk and presented his so-called 'guidance' like this: 'There's a shitload of high schools in the United States; let's say 20,000, and that's being conservative, every single one of which has a senior class valedictorian who you better bet your ass is applying to an Ivy League college; let's say Harvard. So that means there's 20,000 frantic applicants swimming ahead of you from the get-go, and based on your current GPA, no offense intended, they're probably many a nautical mile downstream by now; and they're all vying hard for one of the precious 1,500 or so places in Harvard's next incoming freshman class.

"'Ergo, the cruelly impartial Ratio of Reality dictates that a good 18,000-plus of those valedictorians – all ranked first in their entire graduating class, remember, literally the best and brightest – are going to receive in the form of a single quote unquote thin envelope the most brutal instantly karmic **Introduction to Life - 101** since the Banishment. And just like Adam and Eve, they'll be crying "God damn it!" and wondering how the hell everything could've possibly gone so wrong so fast.'"

Steve's flair for regalia (*Steve!* That was the kid's name. And his younger brother was…? Bobby! Right. Cambridge PD waiting list. Steve and Bobby.) was a credit to his rhetorical heritage. I couldn't have interrupted if I'd wanted to.

"Then my guidance counselor leans back and sighs. He says, 'Now is the point in the oration where I usually sit back in pause to allow my keynote to sink in. Because if you are a graduating senior whose academic rank is only somewhere in the top ten or fifteen percent of your high school class, and you can somehow face the juggernaut *daunt* of this wholly untenable situation and still say, "You know what? Fuck it. I'm applying anyway," then, first of all, hats off to you: you're going to go far; probably don't even need college. And second of all, you sure as hell better be some kind of string instrument prodigy, or a string theory prodigy – a virtuoso *something!* Otherwise, really: what's the point of applying? How're you going to possibly survive that mind-bogglingly titanic tidal wave of competition when you're already sunken 20,000 leagues under the sea?'"

"Heh! Well… What the hell can you say to that?"

"You say what I said: 'Thank you, sir.' That man saved me all kinds of time and stress, anxiety and trouble."

"Right."

Steve pulled a cigarette from his pack and tucked it behind his ear. "So…?"

"So how'd I come to find myself at an Ivy League school?"

He nodded. "Yeah, man."

"Through the proficient transportation of an elliptic inflatable orb," I told him. "Pure and simple."

"Okay, that's better! *There's* the Harvard in you. Rearing its nerdy head."

I apologized for the gaff, "Forgive me."

"But seriously," he mulled. "That's it? You could lug a football?"

"Pretty much."

"But for Brockton, though. So you must have been some kind of high school phenom or something…"

"No," I said. "Not really."

"To even be playing for them."

"I was decent."

"Well, bruddah," Steve concluded, "It doesn't add up. I'm going to smoke a butt."

I said, "I'll be here," wishing I'd had a guidance counselor at my school who so casually employed harmless profanity and threw around terms like "juggernaut daunt."

—

The year I landed that plum job (technically, my girlfriend landed it for me) was also the year I landed my first apartment (technically, Chuck landed it for me) (and him) (we were roommates). As one might expect, since leaving school the atmosphere at home was, let us say, uneasy. Just when I felt like I was getting on everyone's nerves, and no one's so much as my own, good old Chuck came to the rescue.

Our so-called "apartment" on North Beacon Street in Brighton was more specious than spacious. A friend, Vince Martelli, drolly referred to it as our "compartment", whose features and dimensions he deemed "extremely adequate." When my mother asked Mr. Colombo, after he'd picked us up to go to a Sox game, how our new place was, he smiled, "Ah – small."

Who cared, though? It was our place and we loved hanging out there. Chuck was going to law school downtown, a fifteen minute drive in his beat up punch Buggy, and my Harvard Square place of work, former site of the Joan Baezish coffee house, The Idler, was just a 2.5 mile fairweather foot trek, or bike or cab or hitchhike ride.

We had friends over most every week for Monday Night Football, but otherwise it was usually just the two of us, plus our skinny black kitten, Phineas, with music constantly on the box, and V66 or a ballgame on TV.

Speaking of ballgames, the time period during which Chuck and I resided in Brighton, i.e., September 1985 - September 1986, was one of the all-time golden epochs in Boston professional sports history. The Patriots went to the Super Bowl, the Celtics won the NBA Championship, and the Red Sox would go to the World Series, back-to-back-to-back.

Much more importantly, though, my trusty roommate and I were alert enough to capitalize on the good times rolling out of Foxboro, Boston Garden, and Fenway Park.

Fortunately, neither Chuck nor I had ever been badly bitten by the bug carrying a gambler strain of addiction. Like most of our friends, though, when a big fight or game came up we would as likely as not want to get a little action in; otherwise, we could pretty much take it or leave it. That being said, we'd been through enough sporting ups and downs to recognize a hot streak when we saw one.

The Patriots surprised everyone that fall – they surprised themselves – by going 11-5 through the regular season and sweeping through the playoffs. The key, though, from our standpoint was that they went *15-5 against the spread!* (No, we did NOT bet them to cover in the Super Bowl against that badass Bears team. See? We weren't *degenerate* gamblers.)

Next on the agenda, we were treated to watching Larry lead one of the best teams in the history of history to the NBA title, posting 67 regular season wins as cool as you please. In the playoffs, they strolled past Chicago, Atlanta, Milwaukee, and Houston like they were walking onto a yacht. Bird won league MVP and our Celts *paid,* hand over fist.

I will say this, handicapping is SO much less stressful when your horse keeps winning. By the time 1986's Red Sox season started, the 160 North Beacon Street Think Tank & Consortium was rolling on and ready to prove to its stockholders that nothing's a fluke, and dreams do come true.

Sox ace Roger Clemens started the year *14-0!* Are you frigging kidding me? (For that matter, he finished the year 7-0.)

Whereas during the fall we were still fairly conservative with our bets, not entirely sold on the Patriots' sudden emergence, pooling our spare cash at week's end to ensure some token action, the Celtics run had us quadrupling the wager, risking bill money and winning; octupling.

Now with our Texas thoroughbred putting the team on his back like the son of Secretariat, we actually debated toward the end of one month – when every astral body seemed aligned – of venturing the entirety of our rent check on a Clemens start against Seattle.

With the self-kidding confidence of winning streakers everywhere, Chuck proposed, "It's going to be cold at Fenway tonight. Roger on the mound. Shall we?"

Never one to be outdone when it came to sheer delusionality, I said, "We'd be fools not to!"

Clemens went the distance that night, striking out 20 Mariners. He clinched the Consortium Most Valuable Player long before notching that year's official American League MVP and Cy Young awards.

We were raking it in with such great ease that at one point my girlfriend said, "How do I get in on some of this free money?"

In addition to our wave of riches, rolling in with pulse regularity, baseball season carried with it a new responsibility for Chuck, that of coaching the Brockton Spartan AC Legion baseball team.

In due course he invited me along to assist, throwing batting practice, coaching third, and such. Unlike my brother Joe, who would go on to coach youth football and baseball for decades in Brockton, and who would take over the reins of this same Legion team a few years hence, it had never occurred to me to coach kids. Then again, this wasn't really coaching – more like helping out; and these weren't really kids in need of coaching, anyway. At sixteen, seventeen, eighteen, they were for the most part experienced ball players already, and talented, too. Led by Tom Colombo, Peter Hughes, Howie Rosen, and Greg McMurtry, this group could have gone all the way but for an unturned double-play here, a stranded few baserunners there.

It did me good again to take part in the camaraderie of a gelling sports team. I have good memories of packing Chuck's VW Bug with bats and balls, helmets and bases, and driving to practice at Edgar's and to games.

Once while I was throwing BP, Peter Hughes said, "Dunna, ever hit one out of here?"

"I was fifteen. Colt League. Grand slam in a game off Joe Pomerleau, right over the 330 sign. I'll tell you all about it some time."

"You just did," Peter smiled, "Didn't you?"

"Oh, no, there's more alright."

Before each game, as a last bit of ritualized pre-bout routine, Tommy and I would play a couple sets of one-on-one ping-pong in foul territory. I'd serve a low pop-up lob by softly bunting the baseball to him ten or fifteen feet away, which he would in kind bunt back to me, and so on, our objective to establish as extended a pop-up volley as possible.

One day, in praise of my green uniform hose, Tom said, "Dunna, I like your socks. How do you keep them low like that?"

"I don't go for the high stirrups."

"Me either."

"I can do yours for you if you want. We'll stop by the house before the Duxbury game."

The evening of the game, on our way from Brighton to Duxbury, Chuck and I detoured to the Colombo home on Southland Terrace in the Campello section of Brockton.

"Alright, where's those stirrups at," I said to Tom. "And a needle and thread."

I spent ten minutes in the den darning Tommy's socks and chatting with a clearly amused Mr. Colombo.

At the game, we got out to a first inning lead. With a runner on second base, Mark Flanders singled to right. From the third base coach's box I directed our baserunner in no uncertain terms to forge homeward by pointing the way with an outstretched arm and finger.

Mr. Colombo discreetly beckoned me the moment the runner crossed the plate. I hustled over to where he was sitting in the small stand of bleachers behind the visitors bench. He had that twinkling gleam in his eye I always loved, the one he had when I tried to bluff my way through a Z-Out pattern in practice that time; or at the Carrier Dome in 1988 where the Boxers traveled as the #1 ranked team in the country [Not a misprint.] [I say, NOT A MISPRINT!] to defeat a strong Rome, New York, team to open the season, after which I called down from the stands, "Coach! Coach!" Then, "Armond!" When he looked over, I shouted, "It's going to be a good year!" There was the twinkle. "I think so, Gregga! I think so!"; or in later years at Raynham, when he called over from his quiniela crew's table by the window to me and my teenage step-son, Al, "You guys hit again?!"

It was that gleeful gleam, the one shared by some of his sons, I saw again in Duxbury.

"When you want to wave someone in," he said, and lowered his voice, "Or stop him at third. You got to get his attention. Demonstrative. Don't just stand in the box, come way down the line. Windmill him home. Or stop him in his tracks with both hands, and yelling."

Of course. "Thank you!"

—

Chuck, Phineas and I moved from Brighton to a normal-sized second floor apartment in Revere, adding one more roommate in the process, Dan Colombo. After a year of that, it was time for me and Chuck to go our amicable separate ways. One slow night at the door of the Piccadilly Filly we held our album draft to split the CDs we'd accumulated together, with Filly co-owner Frank Castagno as witness. (I won the toss, choosing Eno's *Taking Tiger Mountain by Strategy* with the first overall pick.) Chuck having shown up that night already a little worse for wear, I daresay I got the A-side of our collection, with which Phineas and I absconded to our new, not to mention much closer to work, digs in Allston shortly thereafter.

"By the way, Frank," I said. "I appreciate your standing all my buddies to beers on the house the other night."

"Don't mention it, bruddah."

"I didn't know there was going to be so many."

Frank said, "You kidding? I love it when the Brockton boys show up. That way I know no random townies are going to be starting any trouble in here."

"Heh! I hear you. But that was a lot of beer."

"Not really. What did your boys go through? A keg at most? Bud kegs cost me $25 apiece. $25 bucks for a fight-free night? Come on, bruddah. I'll take that every time."

—

INTER

The immediately pre- and post-millennial
and all of us with the weight of adulthood,
yet divergent from our main thrust here,
and respect between the covers of a singu-

MEZZO

years that followed, descending on one
comprise a story full unto themselves,
and so shall be given their just attention
larly discrete volume of forgotten lore.

Despite having lived through the Brockton Football renaissance myself, witnessing it up close and personal, if you will, I have nevertheless been utterly nonplussed on occasion to be reminded again of just how far reaching is the extent of our Boxer reputation.

After rooming with Chuck those two post-collegiate years,* and residing thereafter for various intervals in Allston, Belmont, and Waltham (of all places), I found myself temporarily "between situations" and holing up once again, tail tucked tight, at the ancestral castle in Southfield.

Reading about the Red Sox' highly touted draft pick, I mentioned to my dad, "Wow, this guy the Sox got coming up – says here he's the number one prospect."

"Vaughn?"

"Yeah."

"Steve met him the other day."

"Really?"

"Playing pool somewhere."

"Playing pool…"

It turned out that my brother had indeed been playing pool at Antonio's in downtown Brockton when a guy put quarters up for next game. As it came time for him to play, the guy introduced himself as Mo.

Steve said, "Yuh, I know who you are. I'm Steve Dunn, good to meet you."

"Any relation to Greg Dunn?"

*[Just Desserts: It is our selfish human nature to regard each blessing, once granted, as an inalienable right, and this seems most true with those blessings that we've done the least ourselves to bring about: a child's gift of weekly allowance, for example, or a young man's full head of hair. The mere thought of losing these things, once bestowed, constitutes in our narrow minds nothing less than personal effrontery. "Better to have loved and lost than never to have loved at all" is bullshit! Such was the bitter sense of victimization – indeed persecution – that plagued me and Chuck once those high flying golden geese of Boston's superb pro sports flock came flap, flap, flapping back to Earth.]

350

Evidently the Red Sox' prize pick had an aunt who lived in Brockton with whom he came to visit regularly from Connecticut as a youngster, and she had taken him to some of our football games.

"See? Goes to show you," my father said. "When you're out in the world, you never know who's noticing you, especially kids. So, act right."

A couple weeks later, I was acting right if you ask me, albeit indoors, out of the public eye, reveling in a rare bit of Dunn house solitude when I heard a vehicle pull up out front.

I reacted the way I do today when I hear my Android go off. "Ah, fuck…"

This bullet-headed brother in an 8-ball jacket was trucking right up across the middle of our lawn as if he ruled the neighborhood, with the wide-striding swagger of *Training Day* Denzel.

Sussing out the situation, I spoke through the screendoor, "Rich and Steve aren't here right now. You want to leave a message, I'll tell them you came by."

"You don't recognize me, huh?"

"Ah…"

"I'm Mo Vaughn."

"Oh!"

"Yo, I used to check you out!"

He became a regular visitor thereafter, calling ahead to make sure there wasn't a crowd of friends over, which as often as not there was.

"Hello?"

"Hey, Greg, it's Mo. What's going on over there?"

"Nothing. Watching a basketball game."

"Who's around?"

"Oh, just me."

"Alright cool, I'm going to come over."

"Yuh."

"I'll pick up some chicken and beer."

One such night when he came over, we were laughing at that silly *Dinosaurs* sitcom when I said, "Oh – congratulations! I saw you get your first dinger in Baltimore."

"Thank you."

"You hit the shit out of that ball. Nearly left the whole stadium."

"With a wooden bat, yo!"

—

A more recent testimony to the reach of Brockton Football's shadow came at Gillette Stadium in 2021. My brother Steve and I, courtesy of Jeff Katz Productions, were in attendance to welcome Tom Brady back to Foxboro for his first game there since his undignified cutting loose by the New England Patriots.

That night I was sporting my red BHS coach's jacket, erstwhile gameday garment of the great Coach himself (and the same one pictured on the back cover of the book you're holding), passed down to me by Mrs. Colombo as a tribute to the depth of warm regard we had shared for each other. With "Brockton" emblazoned across the back, a silhouetted helmet and "Boxers" on the left breast, "Head Coach" on the right, and "Mr. Colombo" on the sleeve, I could not have been more honorably adorned.

The beer vendor we approached said, "You coach for Brockton?"

"Oh, no. Family friend. It was a gift."

Then, having just taken our seats among the 60,000 other fans, the guy in the seat right next to mine said, "Excuse me. Are you really Armond Colombo?"

—

When I stop and think about it, I'm reminded again that the actual number of conversations I've had with Mr. Colombo over the years are more or less countable, as are, practically, the very words exchanged. By virtue of their being so few, they stand out all the more, like each unique coin in that collection I keep shoeboxed in my bottom drawer.

- During a summer party at the Colombos' home celebrating the wedding of Danny and his new wife Lori, circa 1992, I was espousing to Tommy my theory that the Coen brothers had no fucking idea how the story was going to end when they began writing *Barton Fink*.

    Having heard Mrs. Colombo cough a sneeze, I blessed her "Salute!" and kept on, much to Tommy's entertainment.

    Mr. Colombo suddenly scolded his wife, "Betty!"

    "What?"

    With a gleam, "Greg said, 'Salute!'"

    "Oh, thank you, Greg!"

    I gave the Coach a nod for his friendly intervention and said, "Prego. Where were we, Tom?"

    "Things were all balled up at the head office."

    "Ah, yes…"

    Long after dark, when the last of the partygoers were getting on their merry way, with Mrs. Colombo tidying everyone toward the door, a hardy few of us were despairing the lack and unavailability at such a late hour of alcohol.

    Dan Bennett, a close college friend of Lori's and mine, said, "I might have a couple beers at the hotel, but that's about it."

    "Basta!" I kicked the keg. "There's plenty left right here. Let's just take it to the hotel. We'll be out of the Colombos' hair, and set all night for beer."

    Utterings of praise ensued ("Capital suggestion!" "Hear, hear!") until Signora Colombo gainsaid, derailing the party train, "You can't take the keg. We have to return it tomorrow by noon to get our deposit or they'll charge us another day."

    "No problem. We'll have it back, first thing," I assured her. "Dan, what time's checkout?"

    Bennett said, "Ten."

    "We'll have it right back here at 10:15, all the lighter, too, for its emptiness."

"No…"

Mr. Colombo again intervened on my behalf, "Betty! Greg says it'll be here, it'll be here."

His sticking up for me made our night, one of the most hilarious, story-filled of my life.

The next morning in the driveway, battered but unbowed, as they say, bearing the promised keg home from battle like the Grail, I heard Mr. Colombo's voice from inside the house, "See! Here's Greg with the keg right now. Right on time!"

- In 2007, my buddy Harvey was inducted into the BHS Sports Hall of Fame. A quarterback, he'd been a sophomore when I was a senior.

    At the induction dinner I was seated at the same table with the Colombos and my old coach, Dave Fouracre, among others. As salad was being served, I inquired as to the family's well-being, Mrs Fouracre, their boys, Brendan and Blake.

    "Funny," I joked. "Freshman year I had a crush on Mrs. Fouracre. When she'd sit in the dugout during games—"

    "Alright, Greg…" Mr. Colombo surprised me by tactfully advising.

    I hadn't been blathering drunkenly or anything, but 'a word to the wise' being sufficient, I wisely shut up and turned my attention to dressing my garden salad.

- 2013 brought us together again at the Shaw's Center in Brockton for another Hall of Fame induction class, this one including none other than Armond C. Colombo, Jr.

    Mingling during the cocktail hour, Coach Colombo mingled over toward me at the bar.

    "Mr. Colombo!"

    "Hi, Greg."

    "Congratulations. Good for Chuck."

    "Thank you." He said, "Hey, nice jacket. Camel hair."

"Hand-me-down from my dad. Sent it to me from Arizona."

He touched my lapel, appreciating the feeling of it sliding between his first two fingers. I asked how retired life had been treating him.

"Greg, if you've got something you enjoy doing – don't ever give it up."

I said, "Hmmm. Alright, what are you drinking?"

"No, no, put your money away."

"Naw, no, no! What're you drinking?"

"What are *you* drinking?"

- On our way to the Booster Club's annual fundraiser Hungry Man Dinner in 2016, Chuck and I got hung up in traffic at the bridge heading into Boston. By the time we arrived at Thorny Lea, the line for the buffet had already gone through once, and everybody at every crowded table was digging into their food. Chuck and I headed straight for the buffet but as we passed the coaches' table, Mr. Colombo called with a wounded tone of voice, "Chu-uck!"

We went over to him. He said, "Everybody in here came over to say hi except you guys."

I planted a big smackeroo on him. "Yeah, they might've said hi but I bet I'm the only one who kissed you!"

After dinner toward the end of the raffle, Tom McCann, serving as MC, announced that there were just four uncalled numbers left. "Can the four finalists holding numbers that haven't been called yet please stand up?"

Mike Von George and I stood up along with one of the younger guys I didn't know and one of the group at the Archbishop Williams table. Those same white haired gents from Archie's, whose playing days under Coach Colombo predated his taking the helm at Brockton High, attended the dinner every year, testament to the lasting impact he had on his players.

McCann said, "OK, four finalists. Last man standing wins the grand prize. Second to last, second prize. Third to last, third." He paused for dramatic effect. "Fourth place is you're fired. Here we go. Ooooooooh, sorry Dunna. Forty-three! Forty-three is out!"

When it was over and done, Mr. Colombo said in my ear, "Never let them know you're a finalist."

—

Austin J. Dunn, Jr. has always been what you might call a man of the people, by which I mean he never had a problem breaking bread with the lepers.

One evening for a Legion game at Edgar's in the early '90s, after having taken over as skipper of the Spartan AC baseball team, Joe was sitting on the bench watching his starters warm up between innings. The usual crowd of parents, friends, coaches and players from other various leagues around the city, the odd photo-op seeking politicians, filled the stands.

Almost as soon as the home plate umpire announced, "Play ball!" he called for time. Out in dead center field, a scruffy looking fellow emerged from the tennis courts, apparently intent on making a shortcut of the ball field on his shambling road to nowhere, exhibiting an admirable disregard for the restrictive bonds of etiquette.

My brother said, "Aw, shit…"

"What," asked the player sitting beside him.

"I know this guy."

Joe's acquaintance meandered on toward the infield, making a point of finally stepping on second base.

"I better get him."

When Joe stood up the guy stopped cold. "Joe!" He stamped and slapped his leg. "Joe! I got some good shit!"

My brother ushered him off the field and the game resumed.

When it was over, Spartan AC had won. Joe collected the bases, and was wrangling bats and balls into bags when team founder,

356

Larry Reynolds, said, "Joe, you shouldn't be doing that. The players made the mess, they're the ones who ought to be picking it up."

"Nah, they're just seventeen-, eighteen-year-old kids. At that age, all they should have to worry about is playing."

"Joe, when I was eighteen I was lying with my rifle on a muddy hillside in Korea. Chinese soldiers were coming over the hill to kill us. I was shooting them as fast as I could load. So don't tell me these guys can't pick up after themselves."

"You know what, Larry? You're right," Joe admitted. Then he yelled, "Hey! Where you think you're going? Pick this equipment up! The hell you think this is?"

—

The last time I was to see Armond Colombo face to face was at the Brockton - Natick football game, Friday September 14, 2018. Chuck picked me up outside my job in Haverhill, MA, where I'd been living for the past fifteen years with my wife, Nita, and we drove together to the game. Mr. Colombo and his old coaching comrade Gene Marrow were driving in together from Brockton. Chuck told me our Harvard football buddy, and buddy in general, Bruno Perdoni, was going to try to make it to the game, too. Bruno, a football and wrestling all-scholastic in the old days, Harvard nose guard, was a former Natick coach who still lived in town with his wife, the incomparable Maria Perdoni.

Chuck and I made very good time on the drive, enabling us upon arrival at Natick High to take in the stadium surroundings and observe the teams warming up, cheerleaders bounding and kicking themselves limber, bands taking position in the stands.

"Those are what AC/DC were singing about, Charles," I joked.

All the while we were exposed to booming thumping hip-hop of the vulgarest misogyny over the public address system. Not once were our ears shielded by a blessed bleep.

I said, "You believe they allow this crap? I thought Natick was supposed to be civilized. Home of Jonathan Richman."

"It's 2018, Dunna."

"I don't care if it's 2525. Heaven help us."

After warmups, we had a chance to talk with Peter Colombo on the field. He had taken over the head coaching duties when his dad retired in 2003 as the winningest high school football coach in Massachusetts history.

I said, "You guys ready, Pete?"

He nodded. "We're going jet-sweep first play."

Chuck and I went to the visitors' stands, donning sunglasses as the eye of evening sun began to set its gaze on the Brockton fans.

On our first possession, a Boxers halfback took the jet-sweep 50 yards for a touchdown. From the Brockton sideline Pete Colombo pointed up to us with a decisive nod. We won 22-20, blocking a punt in the endzone for a safety with seconds remaining.

Mr. Colombo and Mr. Marrow never did end up making it to the game that evening.

Chuck and I went back to the Perdonis' for a very pleasant night of catching up, and reminiscing, and enjoying again the everlasting bonhomie of old friends.

One of us made mention of Mike Ernst who had been stricken with Amyotrophic Lateral Sclerosis.

"1 in 50,000 people come down with ALS," Bruno lamented. "And Mikey fucking gets it. And they're still not sure what causes it."

I said, "No, they know. They just haven't been able to prove it out 100% definitively yet. They will."

Maria said, "I hope they do in time to rescue him. Before the Mike everybody knows is totally lost in there."

"Well, it's a completely physical disease, right? Mikey's mind's still Mikey," said Chuck.

Bruno and I both said, "That sucks."

"When I first heard about Mikey," I added, "I did some independent research. Since 1979 there've been about 65,000 NFL players, thirteen of whom have come down with ALS. That's 1 out of every 5,000. In the general population it's 1 out of every 50,000.

That's all I need to hear. NFL players are ten times more likely. And that's not even taking into account college football, or high school."

Chuck said, "If that was me, I'd probably commit suicide."

Knowing Chuck the way I do, I told him, "No you wouldn't."

—

Forty-four days later, the great Coach Armond Colombo was gone, having died at home unexpectedly.

At the wake I was shaking hands with his family.

"My father loved you," Tom was good enough to look me in the eye and say.

"I loved him, too."

"No–" he nodded. "He LOVED you."

Cheers and thanks to Tom Colombo for his generosity of spirit.

—

The last time I was to see my brother Joe face to face, we were on the patio outside his cozy little pad in Florida. He didn't mind when I would affectionately refer to his sparse cluttered place as Joe's Garage.

"All lives end in a tie anyway," he argued non-sequiturially. "But where the hell's our Frederick Douglass Day? King's good. He did good work. But he's head, shoulders, knees and toes below Douglass."

"Heh!" I applauded with a chuckle his use of bathos.

"And half the black kids in this country never heard of him."

"Oh, I don't–"

"Mention the name Frederick Douglass and they're probably thinking: Huh? Lincoln-Douglas debates? NBA draft?"

"Now that might be a little–"

"Know what? Screw 'probably.' *Definitely*. And what am I saying? Half the whites never heard of him either. And he's a real-life American hero."

"No, hey – great man."

359

"*Great.*"

"Yeah, but MLK—"

"Who used to cheat on his wife…"

Patience rather than any of its antonyms sighed out of me as I said, "Come on, don't you think Stephen Douglas ever–"

"*Frederick* Douglass!"

"Frederick," I apologized. "Frederick."

Joe narrowed his sights to see whether I was putting him on.

I said, "And you don't think he ever pulled a fast one on his wife?"

"No way."

"Traveling all around the wor–"

"No way!"

"Alright," I shrugged. "Okay."

"Come on, never happened. And without Douglass there *is* no King. So where's our Douglass Day? That's all I'm saying. What are we waiting for?"

"Ahhm…"

"And I know racism's the fashionable problem to trumpet out there right now, but all races end in a tie anyway. The bigger problem is straight-up ignorance. Blissful and otherwise."

A veil of delicate gossamer clouds hung high in the darkening Bradenton, Florida, sky.

The impetus of our conversation that evening had been the subject of Ty Cobb's overt prejudice. Joe circled back toward it, to an extent, but sometimes, like the gauzy clouds above, it can be hard to keep my brother's wispy strands of relevance in sight.

"Those guys were pieces of shit," he went on. "Cobb obviously, Dimaggio not as obviously."

"Dimaggio?"

"When Mantle first came up, Dimaggio should have taken him under his wing, showed him the ropes. But instead he completely snubs him. Refuses to even acknowledge the guy. Never says one word to him the whole time. Like the seniors on the team did to you your sophomore year."

I said, "Oh, they talked to me alright."

"Yeah but I mean they should've been taking you in with open arms, providing guidance. Not dealing you a hard turn at every turn."

"Yeah…"

"I knew those dudes. We graduated together. They were a bunch of slouches. That's why Armond ended up starting you and Chuck that year, and then Owen. Not because he thought you guys were the best at your positions – necessarily; but because he was shitcanning those weak suck seniors. He'd rather bite the bullet, wash his hands of them, and start from scratch. (Maybe a bit harsh, I admit, but that's my brother Joe. He believes what he believes, straight down the line. Very rarely do any shades of gray enter into it.) And the Coach was absolutely right! That controversial move paid dividends many times over. You guys went on to spearhead that great Super Bowl era that followed."

I'd never really looked at it that way, but I was in a good mood and would have just as soon not spent any more of our time on that 1977 season of unpleasantness.

Joe sensed it, I think. "Yeah," he concluded. "Screw them all to hell. At least you fought back, though."

"Took your advice."

"Yeah," he smiled. "One of the few times."

I had to smile too. "You were always on my mind, Joe."

Nodding to himself, he said, "Three or four different guys from that team have mentioned it to me over the years. Made a point of mentioning it. 'Your brother fought back!'"

"Really…"

"But people down here are old fashioned," he said, following the gossamer strand. "So you'll still hear those outdated alpha-mid epithets in conversation once in a while, but there's no hatred behind them. Blacks and whites get along fine here. Down here it's more live and let live. Way more than where we're from."

"Alpha what…?"

"Middle of the alphabet. You know: kike, limey, mick, nigger," Joe explained. "Oriental."

"Ah!"

"And down here everybody understands, black, white, or brown: If you want to level the playing field, you don't do it by making one side higher than the other."

"Right…" To shift gears I mentioned, "Check it out, Joe. Hazy half-moon tonight."

"Stellar," he nodded, tipping his head back.

The moon's darker depressions lent it depth and perspective here and there.

"Looks like the ear of Marley's ghost," he said.

"The left ear!"

"Yup. Bastard's always listening in."

"On who, us?"

"Of course," Joe coughed. "Us. And all those quiet constellations, too, out there trying to mind their own business."

"OK," I said, removing the roach from between his fingers, "I think we've had enough weed."

Once inside, Joe took his usual spot at the end of the couch, settling back, crossing one leg over the other. I sat in the recliner and started testing its rockability.

"That chair doesn't recline," he said, tossing me the remote. He cleared his throat a couple times. "I felt bad for not making it to that event last year," he told me, referring to a reunion of sorts for the Brockton Football team.

"Nah…"

"No, I should've made it up there no matter what."

"You were there in spirit, I knew that. A bunch of guys were asking for you, too. Donny, Peter. Mike Shelby. Umbo."

"Because I was always your number one fan, you know."

"Come on, I know that."

"From day one."

"Never been a moment's doubt, Joe."

Flipping through TV channels for another change of subject, I said, "You see that game Diana Taurasi had the other night?"

"What team's she on?"

"Ah…"

"Exactly."

"You heard about it, though?"

Joe nodded. "Absolutely not."

"Yeah. She–"

"Do I really care if a bunch of mules decide to get together and race at Churchill Downs?"

"I…"

"No matter how you slice it, it's mules. Who gives a shit who the fastest mule is?"

"Oh… kay…"

I continued flipping channels until I heard myself tell the TV, "Ah, screw you." Then I said, "I'm sick of these people, Joe. Comedians, athletes, everybody, all talking about how old they're getting. What the hell's that got to do with the price of beer? How about trying to shut up about it once in a while, huh?"

"I think about it all the time now."

"No…"

"I do."

"Wow. I never do."

"Well," he explained. "We are getting up there, GMD."

"I know, but–"

"Look at all the greats throughout history who we're already much older than."

"Yeah, but–"

"You got Julius Caesar. You got Alexander…"

"Aha – speaking of the greats!"

"Alexander the Great died in just his thirty-third year of life."

"Whoa. Did not know that. In battle?"

"Illness."

"Jesus."

Joe scored me a point for my unintentional contribution with a finger and a nod. He said, "That's right. Greatest of the greats: Man from Galilee."

"Thirty-three…"

"And Joe Strummer. Gone at fifty."

"You called me that night," I murmured. "Remember?"

"Yesterday..." he confirmed.

We both nodded for a quiet moment.

Resuming the litany, he said, "Then there's Lou Gehrig, no offense. Babe Ruth, early fifties. Roberto Clemente."

"I saw a dude wearing a Clemente t-shirt the other day as a matter of fact."

Joe nodded and went on. "We got Bob Ross..."

"Bob Ross... the ah..."

"That PBS painter guy? With the Jew 'fro?"

"Right, right! The 'happy little cloud' guy. He's dead?"

"Cancer, early fifties."

"I saw a dude with a Bob Ross shirt the other day too."

"You see any Buddy Holly shirts?"

"Ah..."

"Gram Parsons? Keith Moon?"

"Nope."

"Then we got Shakespeare, early fifties. Mozart. Hank Williams, Hendrix."

"Yup."

"Harry Agganis... Brian Piccolo..."

"Sing it!"

Joe awarded me one index-fingered point, for spontaneity I guess. Then, impersonating the somberly halting speech of Billy Dee Williams *cum* Gayle Sayers, he said, "I love, Brian Piccolo."

"Hah!"

"Then we have, sadly, Vivien Leigh, fifty-three."

"Mmmm."

Haltingly somber, Joe said, "I love, Vivien Leigh."

"Hell yeah!" I was more than glad to admit. "The girl was Scarlett O'Hara *and Blanche Dubois.*"

"There's something about her."

I knew just what he meant. "There's something about Vivien Leigh the same way there's something about women."

It was Nita, when we were dating, who had introduced me relatively late in life to the thoroughly beguiling Miss Leigh in *Gone with the Wind.*

Joe said, "Nita turned me on to Vivien Leigh when I was staying with you guys that time at your place in Haverhill."

I felt my head nodding. Right off the bat, Nita and Joe have gotten along like lifelong partners in crime. It's always been a source of delight for me.

He went on, "There's James Dean, of course. Marilyn. Monty Clift."

"The Right Profile!"

"Yup. And Frank Zappa, prostate cancer, early fifties; Poor poor pitiful Poe. Jack Kerouac."

I chimed in, "Stephen Crane."

"Yup, Stephen Crane. And we can't forget your boy, Keats…"

"No we cannot."

He cocked his head. "What's so funny?"

"You've been boning up on your Wikipedia, I see."

"I have never run a single search in my lifetime on that communist farrago."

"Farrago! AJD. Word of the day."

"I thought it apt," Joe agreed with feigned smugness. "Am I even saying it right?"

"Yes sir."

"I've only ever come across it in print."

"And you've never looked up the pronunciation?"

"Nah."

"Heh!"

"But so… then there's Sylvia Plath, Anne Sexton. Fellow Bostonians."

"Anne Sexton? Wow. Deep cut."

"Anne Sexton's buried in Jamaica Plain," he said. "And Sylvia Plath *lived* right off the Jamaica *Way.*"

"Don't tell me. Don't tell me: Where she tragically died!"

"No…" Joe tolerated. "She just lived there for a short time as a kid."

"Ah."

"Then we have our Rocky, of course…"

"Hear, hear."

"All the Brontës."

"Hold it right there. The Brontë sisters and Sylvia Plath?"

Joe cracked wry, "A little something for the critics."

"Alright, are we through?"

"Nah I'm kidding. Took an online course through the college last year."

"Oh, okay. Women in Literature?"

"Nineteenth century English and American lit."

"Aha, an aristocrat!" I joked. "But…?"

Joe mimicked me, "…But?"

"Sylvia Plath?"

"Poet. She wrote The Bell–"

"I'm familiar with Sylvia fucking Plath, Joe. But what's she got to do with nineteenth century lit, is my point?"

"Valid point," he admitted. "I picked her up on my own along the way. You know how that goes. You start out on one path, and all of a sudden, somehow, it leads you down one totally different."

"And one way or another your path led to Plath?" I allowed for a short applause break. "I see. So… what books – if any – were on the actual syllabus?"

"Charles Dickens, Mark Twain. Jane Austen, the Brontës. And, by the way, fuck you Greg…"

"Valid point."

"… George Eliot. A collection of Poe. *The Picture of Dorian Gray*. Some Sherlock Holmes."

"Oscar Wilde? This class sounds kickass."

"Wasn't bad."

"And some hefty volumes, too. Nary a *Jonathan Livingston Seagull* in the lot."

"It took two trimesters, fall and winter."

"Ah." (That made more sense.)

"I know how much you've always enjoyed it," Joe elaborated. "Just wanted to see what I've been missing."

"Alright then— go! Who was the best Brontë?"

"Charlotte paved the way," answered Joe without a blink. "Very key. Without her, who knows?"

"But…"

"But… *Jane Eyre* goes on way too long."

"Agreed! And Emily writes much more musically."

Joe laughed. "You could say that."

"I just did."

"*I* wouldn't say it," he smirked. "But *you* could."

"And I like how she doesn't try to wrap every last little thing up in a nice neat bow at the end. It's just: ["Died young, by the way" Joe snuck in there.] Here's a bunch of weird shit that went down during a period of time at a place called Wuthering Heights, for what it's worth, love it or leave it!"

"Kind of like your stuff."

Fucking Joe…

"But I'll take any Brontë any day over Plain Jane Austen… who, by the way…"

"Uhhh…" I guessed… "Expired… prematurely?"

Joe graded me correct with a nod.

"What do they charge for a course like that?"

"Short money. It was Pass/fail. Some good stuff, though."

"And your verdict? Drum roll…"

"*Middlemarch,* hands down."

"You don't say," I said.

"By far the best of the bunch."

"Better than Twain? Dickens?"

"Based on what we read, yeah. But overall… that period… a little dry for me. I'm thinking of going modern American next."

"Aha! Bully."

Joe's roommate, Todd – scruffy, kindhearted – came in the house just then, interrupting my brother's dissertation. I stood up to shake his hand as we nodded our recognition.

"You guys remember each other."

"Oh yuh. We met last time he was here with his buddy."

"Yup," I said.

"Your buddy from Clearwater."

"That's right."

Todd stammered, "Sorry about your– about the... Joe told me you got the–"

"Don't cry for him, Argentina," quipped my brother. "He still gets to go through life as Greg Dunn, that hasn't changed, so..."

"You look good!" Todd blurted.

"You too," I said. "It's good to see you."

Todd pulled a copy of *The Unknown Soldier Reloads* from the wire magazine caddy beside the recliner. "You wrote this book."

"Yeah." I was pleased to see that the pages appeared to be well thumbed.

"That's very cool."

"Oh, thanks," I said. "Appreciate it."

"I never met a real author before."

"He's the paperback writer you've heard tell about," joked Joe.

"It took me years to write," I sangsaid. "Will you take a look?"

"Sh–" Todd stammered. "Sure." Either he failed to catch the humor or he chose to disregard it. "Years..." he said to himself seriously, weighing the book in his hand and the idea in his mind. "Yeah, I mean... well, yeah. I can sure see that. Because, writing something so... heavy. And with the real small print and everything. Must have definitely tooken..."

Impatient to a fault, Joe came galloping in on a snorting non-sequitur to rescue his roommate. "Speaking of nonsense! I've always had a couple bones to pick with that song."

"Oh?" Experience told me that Joe's bones usually had some food for thought on them.

"First of all, the guy says he based his book on a novel? By some 'man named Lear'? That right there's bull. Who bases their own novel on someone else's novel? Unless it's a companion piece to a great work or something, like the Dracula story from crazy Renfield's point of view, or the one they used for that Julia Roberts Jekyll & Hyde spin-off. Otherwise, come on! This is your own personal creation. It took you years to write! And you're basing it on a novel by some other guy? Give me a break."

Todd was shaking his head and I was nodding mine, both of us aligned with Joe on his initial point. My brother was on a little roll. That must have been some good weed he had.

"And secondly," he went on, "You worked for years on this thousand-page book, and right out of the gate you're offering to 'change it round' for some publisher you haven't even met yet? Come on, governor. Show some bloody bottle!"

I had to laugh. Todd was smiling too.

"And if I ever come to cross paths with McCartney, I'm going to tell him, 'With all due respect, Sir Paul, the lyric should have been "It's based on the story *of* a man named Lear. Not 'by' a man named Lear. 'Of' a man named Lear." That way at least we'll know what the hell you're talking about. Instead of basing it on some untitled unknown piece of pop pulp.'" Joe's glinting eye showed he was probably one-third kidding. "But I gotta say," he told us, "Rhyming '*Lear*' with 'want to *be a*' is top shelf."

"Agreed!"

"That right there's some Cole Porter shit," he concluded, adding, "Although, having an actual ending to it would be an improvement."

"You don't care much for those fade-out endings do you AJD," I pretended to want to know, for the purposes of exposition and for the benefit of the uninitiated. In truth I was well aware. Joe and I had been over and over this little bias of his, ultimately coming to the realization that we would simply have to disagree to agree.

"It's weak writing," Joe answered me. "Too weak. You know that. Rare exceptions notwithstanding…"

Judicious Joe had some time ago granted, albeit grudgingly, that there did exist certain tunes, but only certain ones, mind you ("Those one-off anthem songs – 'Na Na Hey Hey', 'Rock & Roll Part 2', 'Hey Jude' – basically any anthem with 'Hey' in the chorus."), for which the fade-out did seem better suited. "But all the others? Bring your damn song to a proper stop, man. It's not that hard. Send it home on its own two feet."

"So what's it about, anyway, your book," Todd inquired, keeping his eye on the ball. "In a nutshell. Joe's not telling."

My brother the pedant intoned, "If you want to know what the book is about, all you have to do is to read some of it." Seeing his roommate's vaguely wounded expression, Joe relented, "It's about character." Then for clarification purposes, he added, "You know *Hawaii Five-0; The Rockford Files*." The dawn of recognition, if not comprehension, was rising in Todd's features. "Both great shows," Joe explained. "But *Rockford*'s better. It's more concerned with strong characters and dialogue than just plain plot. Same with Greg's book."

With that, Joe excused himself to the bathroom. It was about as pithy and spot-on a critique as I could've asked for; typical Joe. He had never voiced an opinion on the subject one way or the other, but that didn't mean he'd never given it any thought – and, to be fair, I'd never asked him about it.

Todd returned the book to the magazine caddy and winked. "Five-O's theme song's better, though."

"Oh, sure."

"Rockford's's pretty good too, though."

I had to admit, "Rockford's *is* good."

He nodded toward the magazine caddy and asked me, in a sort of *sotto* voice, "What's it really about?"

"Love and betrayal," I said. "It's about love and betrayal. Like every other story."

"Any good?"

"It has its moments."

"Yuh?"

"It's beautiful in parts," my brother said, rejoining us.

370

"Read me something beautiful," Todd teased before seeing Joe's eyes level on him. "If you don't mind."

"Ah…"

Joe interposed again, "If you're interested in the thing just open it up and read."

"Yuh, but–"

"Greg doesn't want to talk about something that speaks for itself."

"Yuh, no," Todd equivocated, backpedaling toward the hall. "Well, good seeing you again. I'm going to lay down for a while, Joe."

"Good seeing you too, Todd."

Joe coughed into his elbow. "So. Where was I? Before we were so rudely interrupted?"

On the sly I said, "So what's the deal with this dude, AJD?"

"Todd? Nothing. Guy who overeats, who overdrinks. He overeverythings everything. Like us, so what?"

"No…" I said.

If the two of them weren't living under the same roof, I wouldn't possibly be able to imagine them ever hanging out.

Joe saw what I meant. "Oh – well you might not think it by looking at him, but as you once said to me in the breakroom at Nelly Watty, talking about Lyons: you said 'that boy's handy as cash!'"

"Talking about Todd?"

"Carpentry, floor covering, roofing, dry wall–"

"Wow."

"I know. So where were we?"

"Arm… The… ill-fated young of yore."

"Right. Young being the operative term. Or at least young-er."

"Yeah," I sneered uncertainly, "But these guys you're mentioning… For one thing, I do not have the consumption. And I don't plan on commiting suicide any time soon, or being assassinated. Or O.D.-ing. Or going down in–"

"Oh – Len Bias!"

"Awww…"

"Reggie Lewis."

371

"Come on…"

"And Steve Prefontaine. Remember Prefontaine?"

Sure I did. "Go, Pre!"

"And hey, Roy Orbison died, 1988, after playing a gig. Couple days later. Up in bed. After his dinner. Roy the Boy…"

Joe's eyebrows rose patiently as he allowed the seeds of a pregnant pause to slowly gestate while he waited like an expectant father till I eventually delivered, "… Early fifties!"

"Bingo. Then of course, Pete Maravich…"

"Alright, alright. Sheesh… I just don't ever think about it."

"Well you should," my brother told me. "Our line's not known for longevity, is it?"

"Spirited bursts, right?"

"Hey," he brightened. "It's what we're about. And that's not necessarily a bad thing. It could be a blessing. I mean, the poor Colombo boys, and Beth – they're only two-thirds of their way through this thing. I feel for them sometimes. There's a lot more struggle for them yet…"

Remembering something I'd read once, I came up with, "I believe it was one of the Greeks who said, 'The greatest boon—'"

"Sophocles. 'To never have been born may be the greatest boon of all.'"

"…Right…"

The shelves of Joe's little bookcase at the end of the couch were sparsely occupied, mostly with bric-a-brac and photos in pocket-sized frames; not a Greek tragedy or nineteenth century classic in sight. The only two actual books were on the uppermost shelf, set neatly off to the left, lying flat, one on top of the other: Bibles.

Yet again, Joe, the sage, read my mind. He said, "Once a book is finished, I get rid of it. What use is it to me anymore, except maybe to level out this couch? Otherwise I'd be overrun with them, like some hoarder. Or like Umbo's place at the Whittier. Who needs it?"

"Well, you've always traveled light, AJD. Never been any doubt about that."

"If it won't fit through the window in one hasty trip…"

"You just chuck them, though? I can't—"

"Or drop them off at the Sally."

"But what happens if you ever want to read them again?"

"Again?" Joe was shaking his head at me, as he sometimes did. "That's why your boy Franklin came up with the lending library, right?"

"I don't know, bro. I just…"

"Anyway – spirited bursts: embrace it. Just remember though, none of our brood better be surprised when we catch right up to Audrey and Ma, cause it ain't going to be very much longer."

"And Gram…"

"Yup. And Gram."

"And that's providing we even make the cut."

Joe dismissed the thought with a reassuring scoff. "Judgment Day's pass/fail. You're fine."

"But what the hell," I said. "It's not like this whole thing's a complete and utter struggle, right? There's joy to be had. There's love. There's laughter."

"Slaves had joy, love, and laughter, too."

"All I'm saying is…" I clapped my hands and opened my palms to indicate as a case in point the convivial experience we were sharing right then in his living room. "Let's enjoy it while it lasts."

Joe threw his own palms out as far apart from one another as possible, indicating the larger experience. "Greg, that is exactly what I'm doing. All day every day."

—

The night before Thanksgiving, 2021, I was at Tinrays with John Berksza when owner and proprietor Joe Murray called me to the phone. He'd been talking to BHS Coach Peter Colombo.

Peter told me how sorry he was about my brother Joe who had died the month before at his home in Florida, sitting on the couch, asleep with a book on his lap. During our conversation, I told him, "Joe was behind the 8-ball from the very beginning, Pete. He never caught a break his whole life. Meanwhile, they were falling out of the sky for me." Starting to feel myself choke up, I knew I would have to end the call soon. "And he never once begrudged me that…"

"–He *loved* you."

"That's right!" I blurted. "That's right." Overwhelmed, I said, "I gotta go, Pete. Good luck tomorrow. See you after the game."

Cheers and great thanks to Peter Colombo for that; for giving me something I'll forever keep.

—

To me my brother Joe always came across as larger than life, an aura he somehow projected despite all the while living as small as you possibly can.

—-

This is the End

REFERENTIAL ACKNOWLEDGMENTS:

Countless times during this writing I turned to newspaper reports of the day to ascertain details and to corroborate specifics that lurked in my memory's hazier corners. Thanks go to the *Brockton Enterprise*, the *Boston Herald*, and the *Boston Globe* archives, without which I couldn't have confidently included a great number of relevant historical facts.

LAST WORD:

If there's any truth to the adage "Only the good die young" then I've still got quite a ways to go yet, but I'll be sure to catch up with all of you Boxer brethren (and sistren too, for that matter) later on at the Great Reunion. Save me a seat at the bar.

Made in the USA
Columbia, SC
27 April 2025